A WARREN BENNIS BOOK

This collection of books is devoted exclusively to new and exemplary contributions to management thought and practice. The books in this series are addressed to thoughtful leaders, executives, and managers of all organizations who are struggling with and committed to responsible change. My hope and goal is to spark new intellectual capital by sharing ideas positioned at an angle to conventional thought—in short, to publish books that disturb the present in the service of a better future.

BOOKS IN THE WARREN BENNIS SIGNATURE SERIES

The Art of
Waking People Up

Kenneth Cloke
Joan Goldsmith

The Art
of Waking
People Up

Cultivating Awareness and
Authenticity at Work

JOSSEY-BASS
A Wiley Imprint
www.josseybass.com

Published by Jossey-Bass
A Wiley Imprint
989 Market Street, San Francisco, CA 94103-1741   www.josseybass.com

Jossey-Bass books and products are available through most bookstores. To contact Jossey-
Bass directly call our Customer Care Department within the U.S. at 800-956-7739 or outside the U.S. at 317-572-3986, or fax to 317-572-4002.

Jossey-Bass also publishes its books in a variety of electronic formats. Some content that
appears in print may not be available in electronic books.

Credits appear on page 305

Library of Congress Cataloging-in-Publication Data

Cloke, Ken, date.
    The art of waking people up : cultivating awareness and authenticity at work /
by Kenneth Cloke and Joan Goldsmith.
        p. cm.
    "A Warren Bennis book."
    Includes index.
    ISBN 0-7879-6380-1 (alk. paper)
    1. Mentoring in business. 2. Incentives in industry. 3. Organizational behavior.
I. Goldsmith, Joan. II. Title.
HF5385 .C54 2003
658.3'124—dc21   2002015466

Printed in the United States of America
FIRST EDITION
HB Printing   10 9 8 7 6 5 4 3 2 1

BOOKS BY KENNETH CLOKE AND JOAN GOLDSMITH

Thank God It's Monday: 14 Values We Need to Humanize the Way We Work, Irwin/McGraw Hill, 1997

Resolving Conflict at Work: A Complete Guide for Everyone on the Job, Jossey-Bass/Wiley, 2000

Resolving Personal and Organizational Conflicts: Stories of Transformation and Forgiveness, Jossey-Bass/Wiley, 2000

The End of Management and the Rise of Organizational Democracy, Jossey-Bass/Wiley, January 2002

BOOKS BY WARREN BENNIS AND JOAN GOLDSMITH

Learning to Lead: A Workbook on Becoming a Leader, Addison Wesley, 1997

BOOKS BY KENNETH CLOKE

Mediating Dangerously: The Frontiers of Conflict Resolution, Jossey-Bass/Wiley, 2001

Mediation, Revenge and the Magic of Forgiveness, Center for Dispute Resolution, Santa Monica, California, 1996

To our mothers, Shirley and Miriam, who encouraged us to wake up, be authentic, and express our values through our work.

Contents

Part Three: Techniques: Encouraging Turnaround Experiences

Part Four: Relationships: Sustaining Organizational Awareness and Authenticity

Foreword

About twenty years ago I wrote an article titled, with the poignance of a flower child, "Where Have All the Leaders Gone?" What I wonder about today is, Where will the leaders come from? Not too long ago, I did some pro bono consulting for an outstanding research center with a gazillion Nobel laureates on staff. Over the past few years they've had a lot of difficulty attracting and then holding on to leadership. The problem seemed simple yet intractable. Anybody who was good enough to pass the rigorous scientific criteria of the search committee didn't want the job. They wanted to do science. Having served on dozens of search committees for academic deans and presidents, I know the same problem presents itself in many other forums. There is a genuine dearth of people who are accomplished in their disciplines and want to take on leadership and are competent at it. So every other year the aforementioned research institute, after a long, drawn-out process, hired some reluctant soul who, after a year or so, found out he really wanted to go back to his lab, and the search started all over again. Ad nauseam.

Recruiting and sustaining the most talented people possible is the first task of anyone who hopes to create a successful organization and deliver on its promise. The people who can achieve something truly unprecedented have more than enormous talent and intelligence. They have original minds. They see things differently. They can spot the gaps in what we know. They have a knack for discovering interesting, important problems as well as skill in solving them. They want to do the next thing, not the last one. They see connections. Often they have specialized skills, combined with broad interests and multiple frames of reference. They tend to be deep generalists, not narrow specialists. They are not so immersed in one discipline that they can't see solutions in another. They are problem solvers before they are managers. They can no more stop looking for new relationships and better ways of doing things than they can stop breathing. They have the tenacity that is so important in accomplishing anything of value. And they are aware of what they are doing and bring an authenticity to the process.

Now what's interesting about all this is that more and more of our workers are, to use Peter Drucker's thirty-eight-year-old phrase, "knowledge workers." And today I should add that more and more are "investor workers," bringing their own profitable ideas into their companies. But where will leaders come from to run these new organizations, lead this emerging workforce, and deliver a viable new economy? What about the social contract between employers and employees, that hallowed implicit contract that usually offered some form of loyalty and responsibility to both parties? Roughly 25 percent of the U.S. workforce has been dumped since 1985 and even at present, when the unemployment rate is low, about 6 percent, you can figure on a half to three-quarters of a million employees in flux every year.

An interesting bit of data is that in 1998, about 750,000 workers were laid off or quit or retired, and of those, 92 percent found jobs that either paid more or were equal to what they had been getting. A recent survey reported in the *Wall Street Journal* revealed that four out of ten employees were less than three years in their job, only a third of the workforce works in an old-fashioned nine to five job, and the quit rate this year is 14.5 percent. Ten years ago it was about 3 percent. I figure that the chum of the workforce at any given time is between 20 and 25 percent; that is, the number of workers who are temporarily out of work or looking for new opportunities is roughly that figure. So what about the social contract, which in our "Temporary Society," in our "Free Agency Society," seems to be: "We're not interested in employing you for a lifetime. . . . That's not the way we're thinking about this. It's a good opportunity for both of us that is probably finite"? Is it all going to be many finite trips?

In light of this constant flux, organizations going for longevity need to discover continued sources of learning, growth, and revitalization. But how do we reach the next generation? Do we continue to do what we have been doing, with just a little bit more? Why fix what ain't broken? The discrepancy between the promise of available talent and delivery on their potential raises questions we need to consider. Are we providing learning experiences that will build the cognitive, emotional, interpersonal, and leadership competencies that are required for sustained success in the "new economy"? Is there space in our clogged work lives for the philosophy, the metaphysics, the critical thinking of the enterprise? Are we giving our employees a passion for continual learning, a refined, discerning ear for the moral and ethical consequences of their actions, and an understanding of the purpose of work and human organizations?

It is an intense journey to achieve a positive sense of ourselves and to know our abilities and our limitations. We can get there by understanding what it takes for us to learn about ourselves: learning to solicit and integrate feedback from others, continually keeping ourselves open to new experiences and information, and having the ability to hear our own voice and see our own actions.

Is this a tall order for today's organizations and their leaders? Not when we examine what's at stake. As we face revelations of corruption and fraud in our workplaces; as we totter on the brink of economic instability, and swing from disillusion and cynicism to outrage and despair, the times call for us to wake up, call forth integrity, and have the courage to champion the dramatic changes we require.

Cloke and Goldsmith have created a blueprint for organizational revitalization, renewal, and regeneration. The direct, explicit, accessible strategies they prescribe will transform work environments into living, vital learning opportunities that challenge leaders on every level, from CEO's and middle managers to team members and line workers, to apply their wisdom to the systems, structures, and day-to-day interactions of organizational life and better themselves, their experience of work, and their collaborative endeavors.

November 2002   WARREN BENNIS
                                   Distinguished Professor of
                                   Business Administration
                                   University of Southern California

Preface

> *I have often thought that the best way to define a
> man's character would be to seek out the particular
> mental or moral attitude in which, when it came upon
> him, he felt himself most deeply and intensively active
> and alive. At such moments, there is a voice inside
> which speaks and says, "This is the real me."*
>
> *William James*

Being "deeply and intensely active and alive" is not only, as philosopher William James describes, the best way of defining our characters, it is how we *create* them. Our characters, along with our attitudes, ideas, emotions, bodies, and spirits, are molded not simply by the events we experience but also by the *ways* we experience them. As a result, the more awake we are, the more we define and create ourselves as aware and authentic human beings.

Why, then, do millions of employees arrive at work every day and immediately slip into a hypnotic, semicomatose state? Why do they become spectators and passive observers of their own work lives? Why do they show up only in order to receive a paycheck and begin their "real" lives only when work is over? By failing to be deeply and intensely alive, employees lose their passion and love of what they do. They become cautious and frightened of losing jobs they secretly loathe, or do not care about, or have given up on, or barely tolerate. They grumble and complain, yet feel trapped and unable either to improve their working conditions or leave and find better ones. They become miserable and depressed and engage in pointless conflicts, destructive gossip, and petty personal rivalries. They feel put upon, harassed, overworked, and underpaid. As a result, they slowly die somewhere deep inside. Ultimately, they stop caring and simply wait for weekends, holidays, sick leave, retirement, and death.

Why do so many employees become inactive, inauthentic, apathetic, and unclear about who they are at work? Why is it so easy to get lost in passivity, anesthetized surrender, lethargy, cynicism, apathy, and doubt? What in our workplaces induces this hibernation of the soul? Why do so many people remain in this state for most of their working lives? What can be done to wake them up and cultivate their awareness and authenticity at work?

Ask yourself: What percentage of *my* working life and that of my coworkers is spent being "deeply and intensely active and alive"? What percentage is spent on autopilot, operating in a fog or haze? How often am I fully awake and using all my potential and how often am I sleepwalking or doing only what is minimally required? What percentage of my working day is spent fully in the present and how much is spent recalling the past or fantasizing about the future? On a scale of 1 to 10, with 10 being highest, how committed am I to making a difference? How much of *myself* do I bring to my work, and how much of me is playing a role or hiding behind a mask? Even if I bring 90 percent of myself to work, what would happen to me, my coworkers, and my work if I were able to bring that extra 10 percent?

If we never face these questions, we may fail to realize that what we produce at work are not simply products and services but the processes, relationships, and social and organizational environments in and by which they are created. Most important, we create *ourselves* by the things we do, the ways we do them, the people with whom we do them, the environments in which we do them, and the attitudes we bring to doing them. The best way to become an aware, authentic person is to practice being awake and alive eight hours a day every day at work.

It is therefore a matter of personal and not merely organizational importance that we decide to wake up, choose who we want to be, and practice being that person every moment of every working day. Our characters and personal lives depend on our capacity to be active and alive, aware and authentic, congruent and committed at work. Yet we cannot achieve these personal goals without actively transforming the organizational structures, systems, cultures, processes, and techniques that put people to sleep and turn them into automatons or objects to satisfy corporate or bureaucratic ends.

Waking up is not effortless or risk-free. As we do so, we are compelled to honestly examine our choices, styles, and patterns; elicit tough, painful feedback from others; critically assess our commitments and the results we produce; and actively participate in critiquing and transforming the dysfunctional conditions under which we work. We are invited to grow up, take responsibility for everything and everyone we encounter, increase our skills, and deepen the honesty and empathy of our communications and relationships with others. We are asked to be fully present in every moment, including the painful, disappointing ones we would prefer not to experience.

If waking up is risky, arduous, and time consuming, why bother? Waking up allows us to reconnect our passion and values with our work. We are able to contribute more to others and create something larger than ourselves. We can learn, stretch, grow, and transform failures into successes. We can develop strategies for improving or transforming our work environments and making our organizations more collaborative and democratic. Most important, waking up allows us to define and create ourselves as active and alive human beings.

Why We Wrote This Book

This book is a wake-up call to transform our working lives. It is an invitation to become conscious of who we are and what we are doing so we can all be more aware, authentic, congruent, and committed in our work. It is a compilation of ideas and experiences, processes and techniques, stories and examples, theoretical analyses and practical advice. It is a challenge to you the readers to overcome the *internal* barriers to waking up and transform the *external* hierarchical, bureaucratic, and autocratic organizational practices that put you to sleep.

Over the last thirty-six years, we have designed and conducted thousands of trainings, facilitations, consultancies, coaching conferences, mediations, interventions, feedback sessions, retreats, change projects, organizational redesign efforts, strategic planning sessions, team building workshops, group meetings, and similar practices. In the process, we have worked with multinational corporate giants, family businesses, entrepreneurial start-ups, government departments, neighborhood schools, social service agencies, nonprofits, political advocacy groups, charitable foundations, and community organizations.

Yet we rarely find organizations, even among the most innovative and enlightened, that actively support *all* their employees in waking up and transforming the conditions under which they work. We rarely find organizations that *routinely* provide turnaround feedback; that offer collaborative coaching, strategic mentoring, and participatory performance assessment; that *actively* encourage courageous listening, paradoxical problem solving, supportive confrontation, and risky conflict resolution; and that *consciously* design their cultures, structures, and systems to deepen personal and organizational learning.

Waking people up, encouraging their self-actualization, and expanding opportunities for participation in decision making are not only important social values, they are ways of increasing motivation, improving productivity, raising quality, and solidifying customer partnerships. To achieve these goals, organizations are ultimately required to jettison their soporific hierarchical, bureaucratic, and autocratic practices, and create collaborative, team-based, democratic practices in their stead.

While hierarchical organizations require a degree of passivity among lower-ranking employees, democratic organizations demand an active, awake citizenry. To generate this level of participation, we need to redesign organizational processes, techniques, structures, systems, and cultures to encourage awareness and authenticity. It is our belief that organizational democracy is not simply an option for enlightened organizations, it is *essential* to waking up, to the self-actualization of individual employees and to the continued evolution of our political and social democracy.

We wrote this book as a companion volume to our earlier work, *The End of Management and the Rise of Organizational Democracy*, in which we call for organizational structures, systems, cultures, and processes that are participatory, collaborative, self-managing, and democratic. Our purpose in this book is to assist organizations, employees, teams, managers, and leaders in their efforts to break out of the trance created by working for others rather than for themselves; to develop their capacity for awareness and authenticity; and to renew their active sense of responsibility for jobs they perform but do not own.

We wrote this book to challenge everyone to become more conscious, aware, authentic, and responsible for their work environments. We wrote it to help employees design, build, reinforce, and defend the processes, techniques, cultures, structures, and systems that reward vitality, authenticity, and lifelong learning. We wrote it to advocate and promote the idea of organizational democracy as a substitute for hierarchical, bureaucratic, autocratic management-driven organizations. We wrote it to wake ourselves up, and cultivate awareness and authenticity in our own work lives.

It is difficult for anyone to clearly identify, openly discuss, or actively break the hypnotic grip of hierarchically induced apathy, passivity, cynicism, and despair once they have fallen into it. While observing the way we work is the first step in waking people up, it is also necessary to dismantle the aspects of organizations that put people to sleep, and to redesign their cultures, structures, and systems in ways that stimulate personal awareness, collaborative choice, and social responsibility.

We have all sat and watched as the truth was revealed to us— and refused to listen or understand. We have all denied what we implicitly knew was true because it was too painful or difficult to accept. We have all learned the hard way. It is therefore important to recognize at the beginning that no one can wake anyone up unless they are willing to be awakened, and that no one should be judged or censured for being unable to do so. Therefore, while we can assist people in bringing greater awareness and authenticity into their lives, it is important to do so with kindness and empathy rather than harshness and humiliation, and to act as we would like others to act toward us. Beyond this, we can concentrate on waking ourselves up and not merely speaking but *being* the truth. By being present and awake ourselves, we make it possible for others to do the same.

How the Book Is Structured

In the chapters that follow, we offer observations, advice, and examples to encourage you, the reader, to learn to recognize and act on what you already know to be true. We offer you assistance in giving and receiving feedback, in coaching and being coached, mentoring and being mentored, assessing performance and having your performance assessed. We offer a variety of techniques to guide you in developing the skills you need to make your work relationships more honest, open, respectful, and effective.

We also analyze the structures, systems, processes, and cultural practices that limit personal and organizational growth. We identify the behaviors that suppress awareness, creativity, and initiative and that fail to pass on the information everyone needs to develop their creativity, flexibility, leadership, and responsiveness. We recommend dozens of practical remedial activities, including strategies for encouraging the development of democratic organizations and waking even the most resistant people up.

Each section in the book stands alone and can be read in whatever order meets your needs. To aid you in your exploration, here is a brief description and outline of each section.

Context: Cultivating Awareness and Authenticity

The section considers the context in which we understand our work experiences, process our encounters, and interact with our colleagues. Our initial stimulus for personal and organizational learning is often simply a recognition that there is something we can still learn that will help us lead more satisfying work lives. Yet our desire to learn requires us to acknowledge our shortcomings and modify our attitudes and behaviors based on the feedback we receive. For this reason, the chapters in this section describe the context in which waking up at work occurs, and the difficulties encountered in shifting people's attitudes and behaviors. We provide tools to investigate the origins of these difficulties and the dysfunctional patterns we learned in families, schools, and peer groups. We reveal methods for discovering who we really are, and expose the relationship between what appear to be personal issues and organizational design.

Processes: Championing Congruity and Commitment

This section explores ways of transforming traditional organizational processes and using them to encourage people to wake up and cultivate their awareness and authenticity. These processes allow us to bridge the gap between the intention or willingness to change and the organizational efforts needed to support people in doing so. Waking people up through turnaround feedback, coaching, mentoring, and assessment requires the use of skills not usually taught to managers plus a willingness to make waking people up a priority in the allocation of scarce organizational resources and already over-committed work time.

The processes we recommend for supporting people in waking up include turnaround feedback, transformational coaching, strategic mentoring, and participatory assessment. We also discuss ways computer technology can be used to support these processes, including video feedback, virtual coaching, and e-mentoring.

Techniques: Encouraging Turnaround Experiences

Here, we focus on expanding and improving techniques that are commonly used to support personal change. We describe ways of adapting these methods to waking people up, encouraging them to learn from mistakes and become more responsible at work. We start with preventive measures and progress to increasingly difficult interventions as resistance to change becomes more intractable.

We focus on courageous listening, paradoxical problem solving, supportive confrontation, and risky conflict resolution. Each of these methods is redesigned and expanded to supplement turnaround feedback, transformational coaching, strategic mentoring, and participatory assessment. Each is also a useful skill in building organizational democracy.

Relationships: Sustaining Organizational Awareness and Authenticity

Finally, we consider the cultures, structures, and systems required to build and sustain organizational democracy. Hierarchical, bureaucratic, autocratic organizations put employees to sleep. To wake them up, organizations require collaborative, learning-oriented, inquiry-based cultures; synergistic, team-based structures; and integrative, value-driven systems—all of which must then be strategically integrated into a single democratic whole.

Acknowledgments

In preparing this book, our thinking has been guided by the many clients, students, and colleagues we have known as we have learned how people wake up, turn their lives around, and transform their organizations. We are grateful to each of them not only for helping us discover techniques and the reasons for embracing them, but for the courage they exhibited in being willing to change themselves and the way they work.

We would like to acknowledge all the people who, even in brief encounters, contributed in countless ways to waking us up. We want to thank those who cared enough to give us turnaround feedback, transformational coaching, strategic mentoring, and participatory assessment. Special thanks go to our mentor Warren Bennis and to Sidney Rittenberg, who helped us sharpen our ideas; to Marvin Treiger, our meditation coach; and to Monte Factor, our personal source of turnaround feedback. Our editor Susan Williams helped us conceptualize the book; our indexer Carolyn Thibault made the text more accessible; and our assistants, Solange Raro and Grace Silva, supported us throughout with loyalty and commitment. This book is dedicated to our agent Michael Cohn, who recently died, and believed in us from the beginning.

We invite you to join us now in a process of mutual self-discovery. We encourage you to open yourself to new ideas and take risks you may have avoided. In the end, waking up, receiving honest feedback, and improving our skills, attitudes, and behaviors are essential parts of life and not to be feared. We hope you will take a chance on discovering who you are, be willing to express yourself authentically with colleagues, and change whatever in your organization stands in your way.

We hope you will accept the responsibilities of organizational citizenship by becoming the best person you possibly can be at work and helping others do the same. Only in this way can you make fulfillment, service to others, growth, learning, happiness, and love a part of every working day. These achievements are the best reward we can give ourselves. They are the most valuable form of wealth and the true aim of every kind of work.

Santa Monica, California KENNETH CLOKE
November 2002 JOAN GOLDSMITH

The Authors

Kenneth Cloke is director of the Center for Dispute Resolution and a mediator, arbitrator, consultant and trainer. *Joan Goldsmith* is an organizational consultant, coach and educator specializing in leadership development, and organizational change.

Cloke and Goldsmith have drawn on more than thirty years of practical experience in consulting with hundreds of organizations in the United States and internationally, including Fortune 100 companies, government agencies, schools, and nonprofits. They are coauthors of five previous books, including *The End of Management and the Rise of Organizational Democracy* and *Resolving Conflicts at Work: A Complete Guide for Everyone on the Job,* both published by Jossey-Bass.

The best way to make your dreams come true is to wake up.

Paul Valery

The Art of
Waking People Up

Part I

Context
Cultivating Awareness and Authenticity

1

An Orientation to Awareness and Authenticity

*I consider many adults (including myself) are or have
been, more or less, in a hypnotic trance, induced in early
infancy: we remain in this state until—when we dead
awaken . . . we shall find that we have never lived.*

R. D. Laing

We have all encountered employees who seem barely awake,
who squander their work lives, who blind themselves to what
is taking place within and around them, who speak and act inau-
thentically, who do not care about what they do, how they do it, to
whom, or why. Indeed, many of our workplaces seem populated with
the living dead, zombies who wrap themselves in a hypnotic trance,
as psychiatrist R. D. Laing described, only to find that they have
numbed themselves so thoroughly that they are unable to really live.

This indolent, apathetic, somnolent state has countless faces. It
can be found in preoccupations with the past and unrealistic expectations for the future; in attitudes of denial, defensiveness, and disre-
gard for the present; in frustration over failed change efforts; in reduced
enthusiasm due to hierarchical privilege, bureaucratic indifference,
and autocratic contempt; in a variety of mesmerizing relationships,
processes, cultures, systems, structures, and attitudes that limit the
capacity to perceive and act based not only on what is taking place
within and around us and diminish who we are as human beings.

This *zombification* and atrophication of work life happens incrementally whenever people are punished for being aware and authentic and, as a result, become frustrated, give up, cease caring, and stop trying. It occurs when managers stop telling the truth and lie or keep silent about things that matter. It occurs when feedback is no longer oriented to how employees can succeed but to how they have failed—not just in their work but as human beings. It occurs when performance assessments become judgmental and hierarchical rather than supportive and participatory; when organizations separate honesty from kindness, integrity from advancement, and respect from communication.

Numbing oneself to experience is a natural response to unfulfilled expectations, unprocessed pain, unfinished grieving, unresolved conflict, and repetitive disappointment. When employees experience repeated losses, pain, conflicts, and disappointments, they often withdraw, shut down, or defend themselves from bruised feelings and unhappy thoughts. In doing so, they deaden themselves to experience and to the pain they would otherwise feel if they were fully awake. The extreme forms of this emotional state are catatonia and schizophrenia, but more familiar examples include apathy, distracted behavior, superficiality, equivocation, isolation, substance abuse, recurring illness, stress-related injuries, cynicism, excessive absenteeism, hypersensitivity, and unresolved conflicts.

When employees defend themselves against awareness and authenticity even in small ways, they diminish their capacity for growth, cease being fully alive and slip into a kind of unfulfilling stupor. How, in this state, is it possible for them to learn or change? What could conceivably motivate them to continue developing, sharpening, and expanding their skills? How do they ever overcome their tragedies or learn to celebrate their triumphs? How do they become responsible team members, improve the quality of their work, or risk changing what is not working?

In truth, their only real option in the face of these disabling experiences is to wake up and change their *attitude* toward what they have experienced. As they wake up, they increase their awareness, become more authentic, discover where their organization is not congruent with its professed values, and commit to improve their work processes, organizations, relationships, communities, and environments—not once or in isolation, but continually and collaboratively with others. This is how they actually transform their work lives.

As people wake up, they become increasingly conscious of the dysfunctional elements in their work environments and relationships and can see what is not working or might work better. They can then abandon the destructive patterns, adversarial attitudes, injured feelings, upsetting memories, and addictive behaviors that keep them mired in the past. They can release unrealistic expectations for the future and attitudes of defensiveness and denial regarding the past. They can take responsibility for what they do and who they are, for their behaviors and the results they produce. They can then assume the arduous task of transforming their personal, organizational, social, political, and economic lives and creating more satisfying, sustainable, and supportive work environments.

Resistance to Change

In spite of these possibilities, or perhaps because of them, it is rare that anyone welcomes opportunities to wake up, gladly seeks ways of stretching beyond what is safe, or enthusiastically embraces fundamental changes. We are often reluctant to push to the edge of our capacities, to experiment or try out new things. Instead, we resist, avoid, rationalize, and bolster our self-deception that things are fine as they are. As poet W. H. Auden poignantly noted:

> We would rather be ruined than changed,
> We would rather die in our dread
> Than climb the cross of the moment
> And let our illusions die.

Many of us resist change even when it is critical to our well-being; when the need to change is presented gently, empathetically, and with the best of intentions; when we understand that it could dramatically improve our lives. Instead, we become self-protective, accusatory, and suspicious and would rather retreat with our false ideas intact than climb "the cross of the moment" and let our comforting illusions die. Why? What are we so frightened of losing?

We may be frightened that change will deprive us of jobs or income, or eliminate our role or source of identity, or undercut our self-confidence, or unsettle a precarious idea about who we are. We may be convinced that we will never be understood or appreciated for who we are. We may distrust our organizational environments so much that we cannot imagine anything ever changing, except by getting worse. We may have unresolved insecurities or doubts from our families of origin that keep us locked in unhappy relationships and feeling doubtful about our capacities. We may simply lack the personal skills or organizational supports we need to risk doing something that could radically change our lives.

In fact, it is not *change* that we resist, but what change implies. We resist the loss of what is familiar, the uncertainty surrounding anything new, the insecurity about who we are when the things with which we have identified no longer define us. Waking up and cultivating awareness and authenticity reduce this resistance by revealing a deeper identity that is not bound up in the past or future, or in what is constantly changing.

The Limitations of Roles and Expectations

When we become frightened of these aspects of change, we defend ourselves against learning, resist receiving honest feedback, hide behind roles, become inauthentic, cease being fully awake, and grow insensitive to what is happening around and inside us. We fight to preserve what is familiar, thinking we are protecting our power or image. Yet in doing so, we diminish our capacity for honesty and empathy with ourselves and others. Eventually we become stuck and unable to grow. Whatever our role, at a subtle level, power, ego, and resistance to change are increased by identifying personally with it, while honesty, authenticity, and openness to change are diminished.

In truth, these self-defining roles do not exist—nor, at a human level, do organizations, job titles, hierarchies, or status. They are figments of our imaginations—constructs, hypnotic images, mirages, phantoms, fetishes, and hallucinations that distance us from what is real and from each other. *Every* role is inauthentic, simply because it captures only a part of what we do and largely ignores who we are. Yet we invest these images with the power to control our lives, twisting them gradually into conformity with other people's expectations and losing our capacity for self-definition.

In *Fraud*, a novel by Anita Brookner, a woman tells a friend, "Fraud was what was perpetrated on me by the expectations of others. They fashioned me in their own image, according to their needs." People become inauthentic and fraudulent by hiding the most interesting, human parts of themselves behind masks and roles, revealing only what they hope others will find acceptable. This is a kind of sleep from which anyone can awaken at any time, even after years of accommodation. To do so requires cultivating awareness, authenticity, congruence, and commitment in ourselves, in others, and in organizations.

However we describe ourselves, whatever roles we assume, they do not touch the deepest parts of ourselves. In addition, in all our descriptions, there is an "I" that is describing "Myself." Yet the one describing is not the same as the one described. If "I" am able to observe and describe "Myself" as though from outside, which one am "I"? Every role or description we use to describe ourselves seems solid, yet beneath it lies a thought, and beneath the thought lies a thinker. Waking up means discovering the thinker. As we do so, we accept responsibility for our choices and recognize that our power lies there, rather than in our roles and self-definitions.

Why Organizations Create Roles

Traditional organizations use roles to define and reinforce rigid hierarchies of power. They do little to support people in changing or acting in ways that are authentic, honest, immediate, collaborative, and democratic, because to do so would invite a rearrangement of power relationships. Hierarchical, bureaucratic, and authoritarian organizational models permit—and in some cases actively encourage—role rigidity and hypocrisy. These organizations are unwilling to admit or examine their faults publicly. They discourage honest communication, suppress creativity, and undermine teamwork and self-confidence. In the process they put people to sleep.

In the absence of honest feedback and continuous scrutiny, these organizations desperately seek to defend and perpetuate themselves, causing them to undermine the values they publicly proclaim. They espouse creativity yet reward bureaucracy, conservatism, and defensiveness. They urge risk taking but celebrate only those who increase or preserve their financial bottom line. They call for change yet reward caution, stasis, and denial. They advocate equality but radically limit the possibilities for personal and organizational growth for those at the bottom. Is it any wonder that people fall asleep rather than wake up and risk their livelihood championing values that, while publicly proclaimed, are privately punished?

Where are the great examples of hierarchical organizations exercising courageous moral leadership? Where are the profound apologies, the honest confessions, the open admissions of error? When did a corporate CEO or government official last publicly admit wrongdoing without being forced to do so by an angry citizenry, a judge, or a prying press? How often are corporations balanced and truthful in their advertising, politicians in discussing the merits of opposing candidates, or CEOs in responding to allegations of financial or social wrongdoing? Examples of these dishonesties can be found in the newspapers every day and are apparent to everyone who is willing to acknowledge that abuses *inevitably* flow from the inflexibility and concentration of organizational power. If we want people to wake up and be honest with themselves, we need to honestly reveal what stands in their way within organizational life, act to overcome it, and model the behaviors we publicly advocate, starting with ourselves.

Every day, employees are punished for giving or receiving honest feedback to those higher in rank than themselves. Or their criticisms are passed through a maze of bureaucratic filters and rationalizations that diminish their effectiveness. As a result, many learn the virtues of silence and go to sleep.

Yet organizations that resist honest feedback or penalize employees for delivering it limit their own capacity to adapt, learn, and evolve. They reduce the desire of employees to expand their motivation, increase their skills, and make important contributions to their organizations. They shortchange themselves and those who rely on them.

Employees are then forced to choose among upsetting, ultimately ineffective strategies and to decide whether to fight back, quit, avoid, or accommodate and do what they are told. Few recognize that there is another choice: they can cultivate awareness and authenticity in themselves and others and work strategically to build respect for these qualities within their organizations.

Cultivating Awareness

Everything we do is mediated through our minds, which are immensely powerful, richly complex mechanisms that feed us massive amounts of information regarding our environment and internal activities, all in the service of surviving and succeeding. Our socially constructed minds, however, have the curious capacity to interfere with themselves, to deny disagreeable information, defend against new ideas, consider themselves unworthy, alter facts out of fear, anger, or shame, and confuse the message with the messenger.

Our minds organize our experiences into two primary categories: those that induce pleasure so we want to repeat them, and those that induce pain so we want to avoid them. We use language to focus attention and point our awareness, often with great precision, in the direction of things, ideas, feelings, and experiences that induce pleasure. Yet the thing that points is not the same as the thing it points at. For centuries, Buddhists have distinguished the finger pointing at the moon from the moon itself. Ridiculously simple as this sounds, many of the problems we face at work originate in a fundamental confusion between the observer and the observed.

In receiving critical feedback, for example, we often confuse the finger pointing at us with the person pointing it, and as a result, minimize, justify, or deny the behavior they are trying to call to our attention. We dismiss them by castigating their methods or intentions. We resist their efforts to communicate, and become unable to observe ourselves, evaluate the information they offer, or improve our skills. Human beings are not the only animals that give each other feedback, but we may be the only ones who judge, devalue, insult, berate, humiliate, self-aggrandize, and lie to each other about who we are. We defend ourselves to such an extent that we fail to recognize our true selves. At the same time, our success and survival sensitively depend on our ability to be aware and authentic, to discover what is taking place around and inside us, and to learn from the feedback we receive from others.

Ultimately, waking up means self-examination—not as narcissism, but as though it were feedback from an outside observer. It means looking at what keeps us from looking, listening to the reasons we are unable to listen, and becoming aware of the distortions we create in our own awareness. As we become more awake, we are able to spend more time in the present, reduce our preoccupation with the past and the future, and magnify our ability to recognize, accept, and learn from our mistakes.

Often, when we perform some routine task such as driving on a freeway or engaging in repetitive labor at work, we slip into a reverie and cease being aware of what we are doing. We operate on autopilot. Suddenly, a car swerves in front of us, or a machine breaks down, or the unexpected occurs. Immediately, we wake up, become aware of what we are doing, and tune in to our environment. Yet even then, many of us prefer to remain half-asleep or search for scapegoats, excuses, or places to hide. With awareness, we become better able to face breakdowns, take responsibility for them when they occur, fix them quickly, and avoid long-term damage. Sleepwalking not only dims our ability to foresee and fix breakdowns, it leaves us more vulnerable to harm and less able to recover afterward.

When we protect ourselves from information that could fundamentally alter our ideas about ourselves and the world around us, we defend a fragile status quo and in the process become weaker and more vulnerable. We become unable to move beyond the polished images we hope others have of us—or, strangely, even the tarnished ones we have of ourselves, including the one that we are unworthy or unlovable. We tell stories about who we are and what we could be, do, or have if it were not for other people's perfidy or for conditions over which we have no control.

In the end, waking up is simply awareness. Awareness is openness to feedback, and feedback is information we can interpret in an infinite variety of ways. We have a choice. We can resist, deny, or defend ourselves against this information, or we can decide to learn from it, adapt, and evolve. We can use it to feel sorry for ourselves, or to castigate others, or to wake up and become stronger. It is up to us to attribute meaning, draw conclusions, and act on the information we receive.

Awareness is available to each of us at every moment. It exists only in the present. It is an intrinsic quality of mind that can move from place to place and increase or decrease in scope and intensity of concentration. It can take the form of a spotlight that identifies shifts in the foreground or a floodlight that emphasizes congruity in the background. Over time, it can be cultivated, exercised, and enhanced, just as it can be neglected, abandoned, and allowed to atrophy.

The first goal of waking up is simply to increase our awareness by maximizing our ability to use internal and external feedback, which consists of information we can use to improve our skills and performance. The second, deeper and more profound goal of waking up is to become more authentic, centered, skillful, and content with who we are as human beings. As Buddhist nun Pema Chodrun writes:

> Life's work is to wake up, to let the things that enter into the circle wake you up rather than put you to sleep. The only way to do this is to open, be curious, and develop some sense of sympathy for everything that comes along, to get to know its nature and let it teach you what it will. It's going to stick around until you learn your lesson, at any rate. You can leave your marriage, you can quit your job, you can only go where people are going to praise you, you can manipulate your world until you're blue in the face to try to make it always smooth, but the same old demons will always come up until finally you have learned your lesson, the lesson they came to teach you. Then those same demons will appear as friendly, warm-hearted companions on the path.

By being awake and aware in this way, we are able to discover the vibrancy and beauty that is naturally present in our day-to-day lives, and become clearer, more authentic human beings.

Cultivating Authenticity

Whenever we do something that lacks integrity or consciously harms another person, we become counterfeit and unbalanced. Whenever we collapse our identity into a role, or allow our self-worth to be crushed by someone else's negative opinion of who we are, or pretend to be someone we aren't, we become divided and less congruent. Whenever we reduce our awareness, operate on autopilot, or anesthetize ourselves against "the slings and arrows of outrageous fortune," we diminish our capacity to be authentic.

The joyful authenticity of children never fails to capture our attention or warm our hearts. Yet we rarely give ourselves the same opportunity to be joyful, impetuous, genuine, and playful at work. Instead, we retreat behind self-aggrandizing egos, dreary hierarchical responsibilities, scripted bureaucratic roles, and closely guarded communications. We *will* ourselves to ignore or suppress the parts of ourselves that are trying to be free. Unfortunately, the self that learns to survive in these conditions is a colorless being. We are like crabs who carry the shells we grow at work during the rest of our lives. How sad it is to realize how much of ourselves we set aside at work and how little we make available to others, or even to ourselves.

The difficulty is that, in the short term, living authentically requires *greater* energy and courage than retreating into dullness and insensitivity, particularly in organizations that place a premium on superficiality, posturing, and blind acquiescence. In rigidly hierarchical organizations, those who behave authentically risk being marginalized or losing their jobs. Inauthenticity is encouraged by the use of bureaucratic, superficial, tedious, worse-than-useless feedback systems that stimulate defensiveness and pretense, and are widely perceived as isolating, undermining, and threatening to self-confidence. Sadly, these workplaces are dangerous for those who want to learn from their mistakes. They actively reduce responsibility and discourage leadership. Yet it is clear from research and elementary logic that authenticity contributes directly to increased motivation, organizational capacity, and economic success.

We first become inauthentic by uncritically accepting other people's judgments about who we are. We are reduced in families and schools to a series of labels. We are "unpopular," "bad at math," "unable to carry a tune," "unable to handle stress," or "poor at follow through." These early examples of hierarchically imposed feedback reveal how easy it is to capitulate to someone else's image of who we are out of self-protection, laziness, or lack of self-confidence.

Yet the power of these judgments is not that we are told we are incapable of something, but that we believed it and stopped trying because we did not think we could succeed.

Yet negative assessments can be heard not as verdicts but as *challenges* that encourage us to prove them wrong. Thus every external version of who we are is false because it is merely some single person's version—yet true because it reveals an internal disabling belief that, once shattered, can wake us up and make us more curious about who we actually are. Because each of us can get better at anything we choose to do, the way we respond to feedback reveals more about our self-confidence and skill in interpreting critical input than it does about our innate abilities. We can all learn, improve, and change every aspect of our lives. All we have to do is want to do so.

Moreover, a primary characteristic of leadership is authenticity. We are all drawn to authentic leaders. We admire them, count on them, and wonder what mysterious quality attracts us to them. Yet their secret is easy to discover: they are clear about who they are. They are in touch with their own inner truths. Leadership is ubiquitous. It exists at every organizational level through a myriad of roles and a wide variety of expressions and modes of operating. To become leaders in our own work lives, each of us needs to develop our capacity for authenticity. Only when we wake up ourselves, develop a clear sense of who we are, and act with integrity, can we begin to ask the same of others.

Cultivating Congruence

Democratic organizations require employees who are not merely awake but willing to make their awareness and authenticity congruent with their values and take responsibility for improving their work lives. Awareness and authenticity allow us to translate our intentions into congruent behaviors and committed action. Until awareness translates into commitment and commitment into action, we can delude ourselves into thinking we are aware and authentic when we are actually only playing it safe. But in our willingness to risk change, it immediately becomes apparent how far we have traveled and how far we still have to go.

Congruence is a quality of connectedness or unity between our thoughts, feelings, words, tone of voice, body language, facial expressions, and actions. When we are congruent, others see us as credible, trustworthy, and understandable. They feel respected and responded to, and we feel open and connected. Lack of congruence, on the other hand, consists of sending mixed, contradictory signals. When people are perceived as incongruent, their relationships become frustrating. Their negotiations turn into a series of "power plays" and win-lose propositions with little opportunity for mutually satisfying collaborations and partnerships. Congruence is "walking the talk." When we are congruent, our behaviors match our values, we are honest with ourselves and others, we listen to feedback for indications that we are sending mixed signals, and we are willing to take committed action to avoid creating false impressions. We experience ourselves as integrated, whole, and deeply consistent.

When people lack congruence and failures occur at work, they resort to blame, lie about their roles, divert attention to other issues, silently remove themselves from the line of fire, accuse others of misunderstanding or miscommunication, go on the offensive, blame the system, deny involvement, belittle coworkers, subvert the process, and demean leaders as incompetents. On the other hand, when they are congruent there is no reason to dodge, deny, distance, or defend themselves against responsibility for what they did or failed to do, and no one left to blame.

Cultivating Committed Action

Commitment is an indicator of our proximity to the problem. The more removed we feel from a problem the less committed we are to solving it. If we are not concerned about processes, relationships, and values, we are not willing to participate in making them right. Commitment measures the degree of our authenticity and awareness, and is reflected in the actions we are willing to take. It signifies ownership—not simply of outcomes but of processes, relationships, and values.

In waking up, we recognize that every action is a choice and we own every one of our choices, including the choice of not choosing. Committed action involves taking responsibility for our choices and the effects they have on others and on our environment. Initially, it does not matter whether our choices are conscious or unconscious, well-intended or hostile, accidental or on purpose, petty or grand. What matters is that we own them and do not diminish or deny their consequences.

Eleanor Roosevelt reminds us that in a democracy, we are all responsible for our choices, which are the only accurate confirmation of our personal philosophy: "One's philosophy is not best expressed in words, it is expressed in the choices one makes. In the long run, we shape our lives and we shape ourselves. The process never ends until we die. And the choices we make are ultimately our responsibility."

Congruent, committed actions both require and reinforce awareness and authenticity. They encourage and express leadership and model for others how to be responsible and true to themselves. They encourage closure by allowing us to feel complete about what we want and what we have done. They help us discover who we actually are.

What Wakes Us Up

What, then, can be done to release ourselves and others from the hypnotic trance in which we spend much of our working lives? In truth, *anything* can wake us up at any time: a casual comment, a chance occurrence, a moment of idle reflection. Most of us, however, are awakened with a start by events that shock us out of our complacency, or by an experience of pain or suffering. For example we may be awakened by

- A *sudden awareness of death*. When we receive a clear warning of our imminent demise, as when we suffer a heart attack, or learn we have cancer, or hear about a tragic loss to someone close to us, or are touched by a collective tragedy such as occurred on September 11, 2001, we may realize that we have not lived our lives as we wanted.

- A *horrible humiliation*. When we suffer shame or humiliation as a result of some action we took that lacked integrity, we may recognize that our blunder asks us to empathize with the suffering of others and act more humanely.

- A *personal failure*. When we fail, or are tempted to sell our souls for transitory successes, we may find it better to fall short and retain our integrity than succeed by methods that we know are self-destructive.

- A *lover's rejection*. When someone we love leaves us and we feel rejected, we may learn that sadness and loss are not the end of loving, or that we gave our love to the wrong person, or that we were complicit in their departure, or that their leaving allows us to grow and explore new parts of ourselves, or that we can learn to be better partners in the future.

- A *loss of employment*. When we have been disciplined or fired from our jobs, we may find that we took the wrong job, or wonder why others were able to see it and we were not, or renew our determination to find work we love.

- An *unresolved conflict*. When we are angry and locked in conflict, we may suddenly realize that we have lost

our capacity for balance and empathy and discover that
beneath our conflict is a possibility of better communications, processes, relationships, and understandings.

Though waking up often produces pain, both for the one whose
honest feedback encouraged awareness and the one who woke up
after receiving it, this very pain can lead to a deeper and more profound pleasure. This pleasure arises partly from the realization that
whoever initiated the process cared enough about us to risk our
wrath or displeasure, and partly from the enhanced self-esteem we
feel when we listen to their feedback and become more congruent
and skillful in the ways we behave.

But it is not necessary to experience death, loss, or pain in order
to wake up. We can also do so through an experience of joy or pleasure. For example:

- A *moment of intense joy*. When we fall in love or experience some exquisite pleasure, we are reminded that our
  experience of life is shaped by our attitude toward it,
  which can be full of pain or pleasure, fear or adventure,
  sadness or joy.

- A *perception of beauty*. When we experience nature or
  are touched by a poem or work of art, we may catch a
  glimpse of the exquisite underlying beauty that sur-
  rounds us.

- A *deep meditation*. When we meditate, we may
  become intensely aware of the impermanence of
  life and the inevitability of change and wake up to
  living in the present.

- A *recognition of absurdity*. When we recognize that what
  is important at work, on a cosmic level, seems futile and
  absurd, we may surrender to a larger truth and

recognize that life and work do not have to have a purpose or make sense, but can be enjoyed and experienced
more deeply when we don't take them so seriously.

- A *spectacular success*. When we succeed or achieve an
  important goal or experience successive accomplishments, we may discover that it was not the destination
  but the journey that truly mattered.

- A *gift of honest feedback*. When someone gives us the
  gift of deeply honest feedback, we may discover that
  we have the ability to change the way we act and
  think and begin to live our lives more authentically,
  skillfully, and openly.

While these pleasures encourage awareness, every waking up is
also accompanied by pain caused partly by the death of a false idea
of who we are. Yet this very death gives rise to a new form of pleasure in the birth of a truer, more accurate and authentic way of life.
Often the thing we hold onto with all our might out of fear of loss
ends up being the very thing we most need to let go of if we want
to live more fully and without fear. Awareness and letting go are
thus entwined and inseparable.

Seven Openings for Waking Up at Work

We all need feedback, coaching, mentoring, and assessment at various points during our work lives. These processes are necessary
because our eyes focus outward rather than inward, because our language creates abstractions that separate us from direct experience,
because our actions rarely bring us what we really want, because we
try to hold on to pleasure and avoid pain, because we lie to ourselves
about who we are to overcome feelings of inadequacy, because what
we think we already know prevents us from learning anything new
or different.

Yet our work lives also include moments when we are more inclined to wake up and change the way we think and act. In these moments, we become more aware of our surroundings and are able to notice that our behaviors are not as effective as we would like them to be, that we are not getting where we want to go, that we can learn something new or improve our skills, that we can choose to turn our lives around. Seven of these moments occur in every work life:

- *Entry.* The first opening takes place when we are hired into a new job and our attitude is optimistic and recep-tive to learning. We are fresh, vulnerable, and unbur-dened with the preconceived notions that nearly always block listening. We are responsive to feedback and willing to learn new behaviors. As beginners, we do not think we know all the answers, and are willing to entertain novel ideas and correct our mistakes sim-ply to be accepted and succeed in a new environment.

- *Aspiration.* A second opportunity takes place when we consciously choose to learn and develop ourselves, or are promoted, or are given a challenging assignment, or simply desire to hone our talents and abilities. This can happen at any time in connection with any task. In doing so, we transcend lethargy, apathy, cynicism, and organizational cultures that reward minimal perfor-mance rather than maximal effort, and begin to see ourselves in a new light.

- *Feedback.* A third opportunity presents itself when we are given honest coaching, mentoring, or feedback by colleagues, or when we receive a performance evalua-tion or assessment that criticizes our work. It then becomes possible for us to identify what we can do bet-ter, clarify our goals, and develop the strategies and skills we need to succeed.

- *Change*. A fourth turning point appears when the rules of the game are changed and a new configuration of expectations, guidelines, and strategies is presented, for example, when a merger or consolidation takes place, or there is new leadership. Every change offers a chance to learn something new, if we can learn to recognize and exploit these opportunities.

- *Leadership*. A fifth opening arises when we watch leaders who model openness to learning, or when we become leaders ourselves. This opening occurs when we decide to take responsibility for our actions and inactions and the results we create, even by our subtlest intentions. Leadership is a relationship, both with others and with ourselves. Successful leadership starts by listening responsibly to what others want and learning from our mistakes.

- *Failure*. A sixth opportunity appears when we have failed, or are having problems or conflicts, or perceive that we are in trouble. Our difficulties can make us more rigid and entrenched, or they can teach us to set aside our defensiveness and search for fresh answers. When we adopt a learning approach, we can turn potential disasters into opportunities, achieve goals that seemed impossible and uncover countless ways of being more effective.

- *Success*. A seventh occasion arises when we think we are done, or have it made, or retire, or quit, or reach a peak of self-satisfaction, fulfillment, and achievement. We then have an opportunity to start all over again and reach new levels of experience and expertise. It is possible for us in these moments to explore parts of ourselves that we have suppressed or ignored, and return to being beginners.

Organizational Support

What can organizations do to support employees during these moments and encourage lifelong learning? When we arrive as new employees, they can clarify what is expected and orient us to a culture of learning. When promotions occur, they can provide training and learning programs so that employees in transition receive the tools needed for success. When we are given feedback or assessment, they can foster a learning orientation that makes it easier for us to choose growth over defensiveness. When change occurs, they can clarify the rules, promulgate them by consensus, and make us responsible for enforcement. When leadership is exercised, they can teach us to become leaders in our own lives. When mistakes are made, they can offer tangible support to those who are not meeting expectations, speak painful truths, and encourage us to learn, repair the damage, and adopt new strategies. When we retire or are successful, they can offer continuous learning opportunities, such as leadership development, cross-training, apprenticeship programs, horizontal career ladders, and incentives that invite us to accept new responsibilities and make fresh contributions.

The choices we make at each of these decision points can also be supported by subtle signals that are sent by leaders, managers, and supervisors and messages that are communicated through organizational culture. When organizations are well led and have cultures, structures, systems, and processes that encourage individual, team, and organizational learning, improvements that may have seemed impossible now appear almost inevitable and learning becomes limitless.

At each of these openings, we confront choices that either shrink or expand our lives. We can choose to ignore what we have been told, blame the messenger or the process, resist the information, and remain stuck in patterns that restrict our potential. Or we can choose to listen, become receptive, explore the information we are receiving, examine our intentions, methods, and results, and commit to our own renewal and regeneration. Only the second choice leads to awareness, authenticity, congruence, and commitment, each of which leads, in turn, to waking up and lifelong learning.

Turnaround Feedback, Coaching, Mentoring, and Assessment

Many of the opportunities for waking up occur at work as a result of feedback, coaching, mentoring, and performance assessment. The pain we experience in waking up, listening to information we do not want to hear, letting go of old behaviors, and acting in new, inexperienced ways makes delivery of honest turnaround feedback, coaching, mentoring, and assessment both essential and dangerous. Yet without honest turnaround processes, we can easily collude in our own stagnation, remain asleep, and continue along old trajectories that are demonstrably unsuccessful. Without turnaround feedback, coaching, mentoring, and assessment, it is difficult even to conceive of waking up, especially when hierarchy, fear, and the status quo lull us into complacency.

The processes, techniques, systems, and relationships we use to encourage awareness and organizational learning must therefore meet four criteria. First, they need to be at least as *honest* as the degree of resistance they seek to overcome. Second, they need to be at least as *complex*, integrated, and robust as the organizational purposes they support, the challenges they address, and the environments they influence. Third, they need to be at least as *rapid* in their ability to adapt, evolve, and develop methods of self-correction as the changes taking place in employees, organizations, the immediate environment, and the outside world. Fourth, they need to be at least as *participatory*, egalitarian, democratic, and collaborative as the relationships that are influenced by them.

In every workplace where learning is valued, employees need periodically to review and renew their work skills, honestly assess their strengths and weaknesses, collaboratively coach and mentor each other, constructively resolve their conflicts, and learn from their mistakes. This means that traditional, hierarchical organizational processes must be transformed by making them more honest, complex, rapid, and participatory. This means reinventing traditional improvement processes. It means developing *turnaround* feedback, *transformational* coaching, *strategic* mentoring, and *participatory* assessment processes that promote self-reflection, self-correction, collaboration, and continuous improvement. These new forms actively encourage people to wake up, turn their lives around, and cultivate awareness, authenticity, congruence, and commitment. How do they do so?

Feedback is a process by which information is transmitted or fed back to someone regarding their attitude, behavior, or performance. Traditional hierarchical feedback often results in increased resistance. *Turnaround* feedback is concerned not only with transmitting information regarding skills and achievements but with dismantling sources of resistance and identifying the defenses, knots, obstacles, misperceptions, and underlying dysfunctions that block improvement.

Coaching is a partnership in which feedback is used to improve the details of an employee's performance. *Transformational* coaches work to release their partners from the physical, mental, emotional, and spiritual confines that limit their capacity to succeed. Coaches often come from outside the hierarchy and are not entangled in the relationships or social networks of the person being coached. Some coaches are from completely different venues or fields, allowing them to bring an external perspective to the performance, while others are masters in their fields. Coaches do not do the actual work; they operate from the sidelines, observing the person being coached, feeding back what they see, and recommending a detailed course of action.

Mentoring is also a partnership, but often with someone from the same organization who is actively engaged in similar tasks. A mentor is like a master craftsman who develops the skills of an apprentice, someone who has proven skill and can provide guidance in relation to career goals, networking, and relationships. *Strategic* mentors are focused less on the details of performance than on creating overall strategies for success. They clarify the subtle political, social, and cultural influences on organizational relationships, develop strategies for navigating them, and link people with each other across organizational lines to achieve common, strategically integrated purposes.

Performance assessment is intended to provide employees with information about their successes and failures at work. *Participatory* assessment is intended to involve employees in their own improvement, self-correction, learning, and growth. Whatever undermines these outcomes is both personally and organizationally counterproductive and likely to increase resistance to change. For this reason, participatory assessment requires an active, egalitarian, democratic partnership between those who conduct assessments and those who receive them. Participatory assessments are therefore freer of judgments, labels, punishments, and undermining criticisms than hierarchical models, and should not be used to discipline employees. When discipline and assessment are merged there is every reason to resist, deny responsibility, and resent whatever feedback one is given. To encourage lifelong learning, a remedial intention is required on the part of the assessor together with a willingness to learn on the part of the assessed.

Lifelong Learning

As educational philosopher John Dewey pointed out decades ago, every experience persists into the future, leading to new experiences that either enhance or block future growth: "Just as no man lives or dies to himself, no experience lives and dies to itself. Wholly independent of desire or intent, every experience lives on in further experiences. Hence the central problem of an education based upon experience is to select the kind of present experiences that live fruitfully and creatively in subsequent experiences."

The learning continuum Dewey describes requires feedback, coaching, mentoring, and assessment processes that amplify learning experiences and encourage employees to proceed confidently into fresh encounters. While we can learn important lessons from every experience and each piece of feedback, certain experiences teach us deeply who we are and how to behave. It is these experiences that wake us up and invite us to see all of work as an opportunity for lifelong learning.

Few organizations communicate that lifelong learning is valued, unless it can be demonstrated to result in discernable competitive advantage or increase profitability. Few organizations devote significant resources to developing the natural intelligence and humanity of their employees. Few empower employees to challenge their authoritarian practices. Few actively encourage genuine risk-taking, play, creativity, and ownership—yet these are precisely the traits organizations need the most.

Organizations with leaders who are committed to lifelong learning encourage employees to welcome information that fuels their growth and development, *especially* when it is critical, unpleasant, or contradicts deeply held assumptions. They create cultures in which criticism is seen as the highest form of compliment, where mistakes are seen as natural and failure as essential to growth. At every moment in every working day, learning organizations challenge employees at every level to recognize that no matter how successful they have been, no matter how much they have achieved or think they know, there is always room to master the subtle, challenging, arduous, endlessly intriguing art of waking up.

2

The Art of Waking Up

*When I think about it, I must say that my education has
done me great harm in some respects. This reproach
applies to a multitude of people—that is to say, my parents, several relatives, individuals, visitors to my house,
various writers, a crowd of teachers—in short, this
reproach twists through society like a dagger. . . . I can
prove any time that my education tried to make another
person out of me than the one I became.*

Franz Kafka

Kafka's reproach extends not only to relatives and teachers but
to managers and supervisors who routinely try to make other
people out of employees than the ones they are and mold them to
fit preconceived notions of who they ought to be. When the mold
reinforces the needs of the organization or management and ignores
the needs of employees, it becomes oppressive to comply—and dangerous not to.

This managerial effort to mold employees to organizational ends
can have positive or negative purposes. The purpose is positive
when it shows employees how to succeed within a diverse organizational environment; when the employees' own unique, creative
natures are acknowledged and supported; when the organization
and its leaders are open to being equally molded by those lower in

the hierarchy; and when no one has to suppress who they are or what they think or feel out of fear or distrust.

On the other hand, the purpose turns negative when employees are required to conform to rules that restrict not only their behaviors but their cultures, identities, and characters; when they are required to surrender their dignity and freedom and then are treated as inferiors; when they are asked to deny who they are in order to uphold standards that are based not on shared values or human needs but on the desire of shareholders and officers to maximize their earnings through coercion and control; when rules and policies reflect only the wishes of upper management and not those in the lower ranks; and when upper management is allowed to behave differently as a result of its superior power or influence. The message sent to employees by these actions is that *who they are* is unacceptable and must be disguised or suppressed if they are to survive or succeed.

When directed to act in ways that suit organizational purposes but run counter to their own needs or desires, employees have four fundamental responses to choose from:

- *Silent obedience* and surrender of organizational responsibility, resulting in loss of energy, initiative, awareness, creativity, and active collaboration

- *Passive-aggressive acquiescence*, or "public compliance and private defiance," resulting in hypocrisy, silence, deceit, subtle forms of sabotage, suppressed rage, cynical obedience, and a seemingly endless cycle of unresolved conflicts

- *Active rebellion* and refusal to comply, resulting in discipline or termination, adversarial communications, and a hardening of positions on both sides

- *Strategic engagement* and commitment to waking up, both within oneself and collaboratively with others,

resulting in personal transformation, team commitment, and organizational learning

Among these choices, most employees opt for the first, slipping
easily into a culturally acceptable semiconsciousness disguised as
"meeting expectations." Many select the second, becoming cynical,
disaffected, and marginally recalcitrant. A few pick the third, revealing an underlying irreconcilability between themselves and the organization or its management. A small number choose the fourth,
deciding to act strategically to alter the conditions under which they,
their colleagues, the organization, and its leaders operate. In doing
so, this fourth group takes on the more difficult task of reducing the
role of hierarchy, bureaucracy, and autocracy while actively encouraging responsibility, risk taking, initiative, creativity, strategic thinking, honesty, leadership, and commitment—the very attributes
organizations need in order to be successful in the long run.

Waking up does not mean lying to ourselves about how wonderful our work lives are, or giving up because we lack equivalent
power, or retreating because the problems are too difficult or embedded to change. It means being honest and strategic at the same
time, focusing on what can be changed, both in ourselves and in
the organization, and committing to act with integrity and determination to expand everyone's skills and capacity. Of all the options
listed, the fourth is the most difficult to carry out in practice and
the easiest to misunderstand, because it sends two contradictory
messages at the same time: the rebellious *separating* message of opposition to negative conditions, and the obedient *unifying* message of
commitment to personal and organizational improvement.

Some Underlying Questions

Even in organizations whose cultures, values, and norms of behavior
support democracy and encourage participation, it is not possible to
wake up or act with awareness, authenticity, congruence, and com-

mitment without consequences. These consequences force us to recognize and respond to several underlying questions: How eager are we to increase our awareness and engagement at work? How prepared are we to act authentically and shift our attitude and behavior? How willing are we to make our actions congruent with our values? How ready are we to take risks and become responsible for what we create?

In considering these questions, we are forced to address their neglected opposites: Are we willing to live our lives without ever waking up? Are we willing to spend our work lives being who others want us to be and surrendering our right to live and work as we choose?

Clearly, the path to waking up requires us to overcome numerous hurdles—visible and invisible, harmless and perilous. Awareness and authenticity can appear frightening, especially when the rewards seem minimal, the penalties high, the path unfamiliar, and the outcomes uncertain. For this reason, most employees choose security over self-actualization and are frightened and hostile toward those who take a different path.

Though there are clearly risks involved in waking up and living authentically, there are far greater risks in failing to do so, including the risk of losing what is most important in life—our unique characters, our capacity for awareness, and our ability to engage in collaborative relationships with others. This deeper risk led the German writer Goethe to warn, "The dangers in life are infinite, and among them is *safety*" (emphasis added).

This suggests another set of underlying questions: What would it mean to be awake, aware, authentic, congruent, and committed every day at work? What would we do differently? What organizational cultures, structures, systems, processes, and techniques would we change? How would we go about changing them? How would we treat those with whom we disagree? How would we approach each task? How would our attitudes change? Who would we become as a result? These questions lead in turn to our two final questions: Why wait? And why not start now?

Clarifying the Goals

Our goal in waking ourselves and others up is not to produce conformity to some abstract, idealized managerial model of the perfect employee. Rather, it is to assist ourselves in becoming more fully, deeply, and authentically who we are, so we can bring more of *ourselves* to our work. It is to create relationships of trust, environments of learning, and organizational structures, systems, cultures, and processes that allow us to self-correct and achieve balance in our lives, and be able to learn from every work experience in ways that improve our capacity for perception, understanding, growth, learning, and change.

Actually, it is *precisely* our flaws, complexities, and diversities that make us empathetic, interesting, and adaptable. Our mistakes, glitches, and blemishes are enormous sources of creativity that can help us locate fresh solutions to seemingly intractable problems. The English novelist D. H. Lawrence attacked with a vengeance the simplistic approach to perfection that so often characterizes organizational efforts at personal improvement:

> The Perfectibility of Man! Ah heaven, what a dreary theme! The perfectibility of the Ford car! The perfectibility of which man? I am many men. Which of them are you going to perfect? I am not a mechanical contrivance. Education! Which of the various me's do you propose to educate, and which do you propose to suppress?
>
> The ideal self! Oh, but I have a strange and fugitive self shut out and howling like a wolf or a coyote under the ideal windows. See the red eyes? This is the self which is coming into his own.
>
> The perfectibility of man, dear God! When every man as long as he remains alive is himself a multitude of conflicting men. Which of these do you choose to perfect at the expense of every other?

The very goal of perfectibility emanates from a false assumption that who we are is inadequate. It assumes there is an abstract, ideal, rational state to which we should all conform; that it is important to suppress the parts of our selves that are not perfect; and that it is possible to do so over time without serious personal, organizational, and political consequences. Yet who among us is perfect? Isn't perfection itself a kind of imperfection and imperfection a kind of perfection? Who is qualified to define the ideal characteristics to which we all must conform? Do not advantages flow from the very flaws we try so hard to discourage? How do we become someone we are not without losing our souls and thereby becoming imperfect? And is not imperfection sometimes simply the voice of a new paradigm pointing to improvement and new possibilities?

Rather than aim at perfection or lofty, idealized, generic standards of behavior, a different approach would be for organizations to provide employees with the unique information, instructions, and support that allow them to do better at whatever it is they want to achieve. This means assisting them—not in accepting historically mandated conditions but in actively *transforming* these conditions and adapting them to their own visions, styles, and values. It means championing employees who do not conform to ideals of perfection but contribute in unique ways to their colleagues and organizations. It means encouraging people to see their imperfections as sources of learning, growth, and change. It means using turnaround feedback, coaching, mentoring, and assessment to wake people up, transform their organizations, and cultivate awareness and authenticity in their work.

By *turnaround* we mean using reconfigured organizational processes to take big risks and support change in big ways. By *transformation* we mean returning to who we are and becoming who we want to be. Turnaround and transformation are achieved by empowering employees to participate fully in making organizational decisions; by encouraging them to take responsibility for the choices they make; by not blaming others for their lack of awareness and authenticity but encouraging them to develop the skills they need to do whatever they choose to do; by bringing them into collaborative, democratic relationships with each other; and by making it possible for them to dedicate themselves to work passionately for what is most important to them.

This may sound easy but is extremely difficult in practice, because it comes with a price. To get there, it is necessary to drop the mask, cut the crap, lose the pose, and become deeply honest—first with ourselves, then with others. We are required to invite disagreeable news, encourage painful feedback, and learn to pick ourselves up by the bootstraps; to take the risk of discovering and being who we actually are—not in isolation, but collaboratively with others. Freedom in this sense is not exercised *against* others but *with* and *for* them.

Turning Ourselves Around

In rapidly changing work environments, innumerable innovations falter or fail because prudence prompts us to settle for incremental modifications and minor improvements when wholesale transformations are demanded—not only in the things we do but in the ways we do them. To produce transformational results, we require approaches that uncover the real issues, tell the truth, speak in ways people can hear, and support people in doing what they believe is right.

There is a fundamental difference between altering, improving, or correcting something and transforming it or turning it around. Turnaround and transformation are nonlinear, unpredictable, and discontinuous. They occur through choices, leaps of committed action, deep listening, subconscious perceptions, and instantaneous flashes of insight. They take place at a right angle to accepted truth, to what is, to who we think we are.

Sometimes what is turned around is very small and escapes notice because it is so obvious or has been accepted for so long.

Sometimes a personal trait is turned around that seemed unimportant at the time, or we assume it is already who we are, or we failed to notice or understand its significance. Sometimes we assume someone else is at fault, or that we are, and miss the fact that fault and blame have nothing to do with solving the problem, they simply keep us locked in patterns we do not like.

A turnaround is a crossroads, a qualitative shift in how we see or think about a problem or in the way we go about solving it. And we are always at such a crossroads at every moment in our lives. Sometimes the crossroads seems faint and distant until events bring it into focus, forcing us to act.

Because turning points are intrinsically unforeseeable, the turnaround approach to feedback, coaching, mentoring, and assessment demands an openness to the unexpected, a responsiveness to paradox and nuance, a search for hidden clues, and a willingness to be astonished. Fundamentally, it does not matter whether the shift is large or small. Small shifts can trigger enormous changes. The trick is to locate the levers, identify the catalysts, and allow learning to produce the acceleration and critical mass needed to break the grip of habit.

The role of turnaround processes and techniques is not only to provide people with the information, encouragement, and support they need to confront their problems, it is to give them the honesty they have a right to receive along with the empathy that allows them to hear it. It is to inspire them to throw away their ideational and emotional crutches and learn to walk on their own, with support from others.

Breaking the Cycle of Distrust

The foundation of all turnaround processes and techniques is trust. There will always be incidents that take people to the edge of their willingness and ability to trust each other. Those who deliver turnaround feedback, coaching, mentoring, and assessment need to build trust by being open and honest enough to relay information that is difficult to hear and empathetic enough to listen and learn. Those who receive it build trust by being willing to translate what they learn into committed action.

Once either side slips into distrust, a self-reinforcing downward spiral begins that seems impossible to escape. Whatever recommendation either side offers for reducing the distrust rings false to the other side. Distrust then feeds on distrust, creating a circular dynamic in which unmet expectations lead to distrust, which triggers self-protecting, trust-breaking behaviors in response. Each side views the other side's behaviors as hostile or disrespectful and adopts a self-protective stance that causes further distrust, as illustrated in Figure 2.1.

Figure 2.1. Cycle of Distrust.

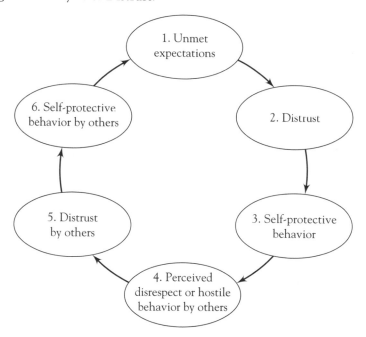

In this way, distrust becomes a vicious circle from which it seems impossible to escape. Yet turnaround processes and techniques create multiple turning points and openings through which trust can be regained. When we examine these turning points and openings closely, we discover a rich variety of methods for rebuilding trust in relationships. It is possible, for example, to rebuild trust by the following measures:

- Negotiating clear boundaries and respecting those created by others, whether or not they respect yours

- Speaking honestly and intimately about yourself and your mistakes

- Being as sincere and unlimited with apologies as you are with honest feedback

- Being consistent over time

- Being open about problems and flexible about solutions

- Empowering others to make decisions or making them collaboratively

- Jointly agreeing on a vision or shared values or goals for your relationship

- Making your actions congruous with your vision, values, and words

- Encouraging teamwork, collaboration, and participation

- Listening and empathizing with others even if they have not listened or empathized with you

- Being dependable in crises or hard times

- Participating in social interactions and sharing personal information about your life

- Offering to sacrifice something important to you to achieve a larger goal

- Treating everyone with *unconditional* respect

Trust is a choice in every relationship. None of these actions will guarantee the restoration of broken trust, but they will make it more difficult to maintain distrust and gradually diminish trust-breaking behavior. Residue from past experiences, fears about the future, and incongruent behaviors in the present fuel feelings of distrust and block successful feedback, coaching, mentoring, and assessments, spinning employees into a downward spiral of anger and pain. Trust is rebuilt by focusing not on what the other person did or did not do but on critiquing one's *own* behavior, improving one's trust*worthiness*, and focusing attention not on words and promises but on actions, attitudes, and ways of being.

Three Ways of Being

We all live and work in a world we cannot fully trust, and must choose between three fundamental options regarding how to live in such a world and handle our distrust. We can approach whatever happens that does not match our expectations with a *negative* attitude and treat it as a burden, or we can approach it with a *positive* attitude and affirm its beneficial features, or we can *transcend* these categories, reject both, and end the ceaseless, complicated interplay between them.

The transcendent approach integrates the negative truth of harsh reality with the positive truth of generous possibility. It acknowledges the presence of necessity and opportunity, frustration and dedication, inadequacy and abundance, disaster and opportunity that are present in all change efforts, while not becoming limited to either of them. It does not accept the world as it is but works to transform it. These three ways of being are contrasted in Table 2.1.

Table 2.1. Three Ways of Being.

Negative	Positive	Transcendent
Passive	Active	Engaged
Irresponsible	Responsible	Committed
Reactive	Proactive	Strategic
Uninterested	Involved	Intrigued
Asleep	Relaxed	Serene
Unaware	Aware	Alert
Impatient	Patient	Resolute
Self-centered	Other-centered	Interconnected
Dishonest	Honest	Have integrity
Resistant	Accepting	Enthusiastic
Stuck	Flexible	Agile
Alienated	Popular	Courageous
Confused	Clear	Confident

When we are negative or unhappy about life or its circumstances, it is easy to become apathetic or cynical and simply give up. When we are positive or happy, we easily become complacent and develop a stake in preserving the status quo. This causes us to fix problems superficially and become stuck or dulled to the creative, transcendent possibilities that come from fully exploring the sources of negativity. When we recognize the higher combined truth that lies hidden in both these alternatives, we start to recognize the presence of deeper problems, shift them at their source, and transcend the attitudes and ideas that got us into trouble in the first place. We can then move on to discover newer, higher orders of problems.

Taking a negative approach to problems is the first step in recognizing their presence, but it is one that easily leads to cynicism and apathy, which disarm change efforts and thereby perpetuate the problem. Taking a positive approach leads us to come up with alternatives, but it also easily results in denial that the problem is as important or destructive as it is, which leads us to fix it superficially. Taking a transcendent approach means seeing the problem in all its manifestations but not being discouraged by the seriousness or difficulty of the task ahead. This leads to an enhanced commitment to transcend the problem both internally within ourselves and externally within the organization or even in society as a whole.

We become far more powerful and effective in solving problems when we have already solved them within ourselves and are able to approach them from above; when we adopt an outlook that transcends negative and positive characterizations; when we create a context that is oriented toward the future and avoids getting stuck in the past.

At the same time, if we focus only on ourselves and ignore the external conditions that continually generate new problems, we will not succeed in overcoming them. We will merely escape the immediate need to face them and allow them to reappear in different guises. When we transform the systems that produced these problems and transcend our inner vulnerability to them, we more easily understand how we got into difficulty in the first place, how to collaborate in ending them, and how to avoid similar problems in the future.

The object of waking people up and using turnaround processes and techniques is ultimately to understand that our most difficult problems are *already* solved, transformed, and transcended when we approach them with awareness, authenticity, congruence, and commitment. This knowledge brings with it the realization that there is nothing that cannot be improved or made better through a combination of individual and collective awareness leading to committed action; that all of life is a process of waking up and turning around; and that everything that happens presents us with opportunities for transcendence.

3

Where It All Begins

*The richest source of family history you could find
anywhere in the world is the memory of your parents
and your grandparents—memories that will tell you
things you never knew or have long since forgotten
about yourself. . . . The giving and getting, the sense
of belonging and contributing to something larger than
yourself, to something that began before you were
born and will go on after you die, can make it possible
for you to accept life in a way that makes you wish
the whole world could realize how easy it is to feel as
you do, and wonder why they don't.*

Alex Haley

As novelist and family researcher Alex Haley revealed in his groundbreaking book, *Roots*, our family legacies and histories even several generations back significantly influence our lives in the present.

Our families, schools, and peers first taught us how to work hard for what we want, how to ask for what we need, how to collaborate with others, and how to handle critical feedback, coaching, mentoring, and assessment. We first developed self-awareness, a willingness to examine ourselves, and an openness to self-correction from our parents, aunts, uncles, teachers, friends, and siblings who cared enough to coach and mentor us. Our earliest experiences with feedback, coaching, mentoring, and assessment took place in our families of origin and in our schools and peer groups, where we learned how to react when other people became upset at what we said or did, when we made mistakes, or when things did not go our way.

We also learned early on, as most children do, how to slack off and pretend to be busy, how to suppress what we really think, how to pretend to listen, how to use anger and defensiveness to resist feedback, coaching, mentoring, and assessment, and how to fake change even when it was to our benefit. We learned how to kiss up to people in positions of power and authority, how to drag our feet and sneak out the back when there was work to be done, how to attack others with gossip and rumors, and how to undermine and subvert group effectiveness when we were not included.

Everyone arrives at work with rich family histories and experiences that directly and indirectly, consciously and unconsciously, influence the way they respond to a variety of workplace pressures. These prior experiences create archetypes, models, exemplars, symbols, and metaphors that reflect psychological patterns. These, in turn, are translated into ways of behaving and strengthened by repetition, rewards, punishments, and selective reinforcement.

For the most part, these early traces of childhood are lost from conscious awareness and are seldom openly recognized or discussed at work. Indeed, the unstated rule in most workplaces is that dysfunctional family patterns are not to be mentioned. Yet to the extent that they remain unexamined, they indirectly shape our responsive and compensating behaviors. If we critically examine our family patterns and the consequences that flow from them before offering or receiving feedback, coaching, mentoring, or assessment, we can gain insight and release from these unconscious archetypes. By doing so, we can discover the origin of many of our attitudes toward these turnaround processes, and the limits of our ability to apply them successfully.

The challenge we all face in waking up is not merely one of using our positive early experiences but digging deeper and directly confronting our negative family, school, and peer experiences that, until we address them, continue to dominate our lives. We need to design workplaces where honest conversations can be held regarding these experiences, so we can cease being controlled by them. As Carl Jung wrote, "One does not become enlightened by imagining figures of light, but by making the darkness conscious."

Options in Responding to Dysfunction

All dysfunctions seek to replicate themselves. Only equally dysfunctional responses can justify negative behavior, overcome guilt and shame, and rationalize the dysfunction by making it appear normal. Those who grew up in dysfunctional families or work in dysfunctional organizations usually feel they have limited options, which is one of the primary ways dysfunction expresses itself. The only choices these employees can see are those that, in one way or another, allow the dysfunction to continue. These include

- Denying the existence of the dysfunction and sweeping it under the rug

- Adapting, accommodating, and becoming dysfunctional themselves

- Becoming apathetic or cynical, going with the flow, and putting a minimum amount of energy and effort into work

- Gossiping, complaining, judging, spreading rumors, encouraging others to fight, or becoming professional victims

- Blaming or directing anger at those who are dysfunctional and taking time from creative efforts to engage in equally dysfunctional battles with them

- Choosing not to surround themselves with dysfunction
  and leaving

None of these responses eliminates the dysfunction, either in families, schools, peer groups, teams, organizations, or ourselves. Each of these choices traps us in something equally dysfunctional, or cheats us, our colleagues, and our organizations, out of growth and learning. In contrast to these patterned responses that allow the dysfunction to continue are strategies for escaping and recovering from it that do not replicate the dysfunction. These responses require courage, support, and determination to implement because they break with the past, prevent the destructive behavior from moving forward, and acknowledge the need for renewal and healing. These responses include

- Choosing, at whatever cost, not to become dysfunctional

- Seeking assistance from outside experts such as therapists, counselors, facilitators, and mediators in resisting the dysfunction

- Openly discussing the dysfunctionality and joining with others in a search for the underlying reasons that created it

- Negotiating agreements with those who engage in dysfunctional behaviors to marginalize their dysfunctionality

- Joining with others in groups to collaboratively address the dysfunction

- Choosing to limit or break contact with those who are toxic or who trigger dysfunctional reactions

- Using turnaround forms of feedback, coaching, mentoring, and assessment to better understand, oppose, and transcend the dysfunction.

Our choices fundamentally boil down to a shorter list: we can either tolerate the dysfunction and adapt our thinking and behavior to it, or we can act to change it by transforming the way we think and behave when we are in its presence. Whichever choice we make will be based partly on what we learned in our families of origin about our ability to overcome dysfunction, and partly on the availability and support for turnaround feedback, coaching, mentoring, and assessment within our organizations. When we successfully oppose dysfunctional behaviors—even in small ways—we feel more powerful in facing them in the future, and able to confront our next dysfunctional encounter with greater self-confidence.

Transcending Family Ruts

We all learned how to survive our families, schools, and peer groups and developed strengths that allowed us to succeed. We prize the skills that resulted in success and shun those that ended in failure. Yet we rarely recognize that our very strengths and successes created many of the weaknesses and failures we later experience in life; that they have actually kept us from learning new skills and developing alternative strategies for getting what we want.

Every strength thus conceals a corresponding weakness, and every successful pattern creates a resistance to doing things differently. We each develop an Achilles heel of vulnerability by relying on a single approach and turning it into a rut. Novelist Edith Wharton warns us of the danger of getting locked into ruts that inhibit us from exploring other possibilities in our lives:

> Years ago I said to myself: "There's no such thing as old age; there is only sorrow." I have learned with the passing of time that this, though true, is not the whole truth. The other producer of old age is habit: the deathly process of doing the same thing in the same way at the same hour day after day, first from carelessness, then from

inclination, at last from cowardice or inertia. Luckily the inconsequent life is not the only alternative; for caprice is as ruinous as routine. Habit is necessary; it is the habit of having habits, of turning a trail into a rut, that must be incessantly fought against if one is to remain alive.

As small children, we were completely dependent for survival on adults who withheld confidence-building love and life-giving resources when we disappointed them. Our parents and teachers communicated their desires, expectations, and demands through emotionally charged feedback, coaching, mentoring, and assessments, and we quickly discovered that it was better to mimic them or do what they wanted than challenge *their* ruts and place our survival in jeopardy.

Psychotherapist Steven Heller created an allegory to explain this dynamic. A young man must climb a mountain to get to where he needs to go in life. His parents tell him which path to take up the mountain and how many stones and what kinds of wood to carry in his backpack. As the mountain grows steeper he veers off these paths and starts to unload some of the rocks and wood from his pack, for which he is soundly criticized and punished. His parents are fearful for him, worried about possible mishaps, and convinced that the path they took and the stones and wood they carried are the only safe way to climb the mountain. Their desire for his success causes them to criticize his choices and influence him through negative feedback, coaching, mentoring, and assessment.

To reach our destination, we all need to find the path that is right for us, carry what we actually need, and unburden ourselves of unnecessary baggage. To do so, we must first listen to, then reject the overpowering influence of our parents and teachers, who traveled to a different location at a different time under different conditions. We have three choices for how we can proceed and decide what we will carry into our adult working lives:

- We can follow our parents' and teachers' advice and proceed step-by-step along the path they created.

- We can reject their advice and depart completely from their path and advice.

- We can assess whether their path and advice work for us and be willing to either abandon or follow it.

The first two choices are limiting because they do not allow us to select what is right for us and reject what is not. Perhaps their advice regarding the rocks is wrong but their warning about the wood is right. Neither blind acceptance nor blind rejection will lead us to the correct path. We discover the right way only by listening and learning from wise counsel and then trusting our own experience and inner voice.

Our early efforts to tailor who we are to parental expectations in order to survive produces obedience and conformity, followed by a deep, adolescent resistance to their input as we become increasingly independent. Yet our active resistance recreates and reinforces the very thing we are resisting, carrying it forward into future generations. Once we discover and decide to follow our own path we no longer need to resist their ideas because we have silenced our internal anxieties and fears about not conforming.

Many problems and dysfunctions at work result from our inability to escape this dialectic of conformity and resistance, and our consequent failure to discover our own path up the mountain. Whatever family patterns we cannot break, whatever rules we cannot question, whatever we are driven to resist or reject outright, whatever we blindly accept or affirm, we are condemned to repeat. To stop this cycle, we need to take the following steps:

- Wake up and recognize their existence.

- Take responsibility for their effects on ourselves and others.

- Learn what we can from the past and from others and decide to move beyond received wisdom.

- Find our own path up the mountain.

Although parents and teachers may no longer be active influences in the lives of employees, their roles and voices echo back through the archetypal parental roles played by their managers, on whom their economic survival seems to depend. We recently conducted a coaching session with Larry, a manager at a large aerospace corporation who wanted to become more effective in dealing with staff conflicts. We asked him about his approach in delivering controversial messages, honest feedback, and risky communications. He said he mostly avoided them. We asked why, and he said it was because he wanted to be liked. We asked why it was important to him to be liked, and he said he was afraid of doing the wrong thing and being fired. His fears took priority over speaking honestly, surfacing conflicts, confronting employees, and challenging those with whom he disagreed.

We asked Larry where this fear of doing the wrong thing originated and when it had begun, and he said it had started in his family of origin. He felt his family patterns were the deciding factor in his approach to delivering feedback and coaching to the people on his team. He grew up as a middle child between two aggressive brothers. He saw his older brother as a bully and his younger brother as a pampered baby. His goal was to avoid getting caught in between. He tried to make peace, get his older brother to approve of him, and convince his younger brother to give in so the conflict would go away.

As a manager, Larry experienced the same pressures he felt from his parents and brothers and felt trapped whenever there was conflict-laden information to deliver. At work, he kept trying to run away, placate the one who was most angry, and convince the other side to give in. If he had not been a manager, he might have received honest feedback about his communication style, but no one lower in the hierarchy wanted to risk giving him honest coaching, and his boss was pleased that Larry did what he asked. As a result, Larry continued to reward aggression, escalate emotions by pushing them below the surface, block collaboration and teamwork, and signal that no one should rock the boat.

We asked Larry if he would be willing to explain his family background to his staff and ask for their support by giving him honest feedback and coaching. He did so with great frankness and sincerity. Several employees spoke about how important it was for them to hear him take responsibility for his poor communications. Five employees volunteered to form a feedback and coaching team to support him by giving honest, constructive feedback when he needed it and designing an honest feedback process that would involve all team members. Morale skyrocketed as a result and conflicts based on miscommunication virtually disappeared.

Parents as Managers and Managers as Parents

Many of the supervisory activities engaged in by managers have their antecedents in the expectations and real-life activity of parents, elder siblings, and teachers, whose principal role was to give us feedback on everything we did and coach or mentor us through the early stages of life. For this reason, it is impossible to give or receive feedback, coaching, mentoring, or performance assessment without triggering unconscious childhood patterns and memories.

The lessons we learned at the hands of our first managers, our parents and teachers, included not only the successful behaviors they wanted us to learn, such as neatness and politeness, but the unsuccessful ones they were not even aware they were teaching. Many of us were taught by example how to selectively distribute resources based on subjective preferences, how to exclude those without power from planning and decision making, how to punish those who disobey, and how to lie to avoid punishment. Many learned how to pass the buck and deny responsibility, how to blame others, how to resist change and avoid conflict, and how to conceal what we really think and feel. Many of us learned how to undermine people's reputations through gossip and rumors, how to use anger, shame, and fear to get what we want, how to lift ourselves up by putting others down, and how to feel that whatever we do is not good enough. Mostly, we were taught not to honestly discuss or openly admit *any* of these lessons, especially in the presence of someone with power over our life.

As children, we were rarely encouraged to deliver upward feedback, coaching, mentoring, or assessment, or taught how to confront or mediate with parents and other authority figures, or how to work collaboratively with our opponents. Many of us were not asked what we thought, or allowed to make choices, or permitted to work at our own pace in our own way. Instead, we were chastised for disobeying orders, or having too much fun, or expressing displeasure with boring assignments. We were expected to stand in line, wait our turn, perform routine tasks in routine ways, and keep our creative and dissenting opinions to ourselves.

This lack of concern for who we were and what we wanted, thought, and felt was communicated far more forcefully than any information we learned in history, art, or mathematics. It was relayed not only by clear, overt, explicit rules but by confusing, secret, unspoken messages that were far more intricate and difficult to decipher, yet far more effective in altering our behaviors, thoughts, emotions, and attitudes. What was ultimately communicated through these experiences was a simple message: *it is easier and safer to be asleep than it is to be awake*.

These childhood experiences frightened many of us, leaving us with a sense of shame about who we were. It caused many of us to live less joyful, creative, and intentional lives. It led us to shut down, resist feedback from superiors, or submissively accept their judgments and evaluations. It resulted in many of us either blindly accepting or blanketly rejecting our manager's views, rather than discovering our own inner truths and finding our own way up the mountain.

These antiquated patterns not only threaten our chances for success, they strangle our spirits and personalities and dampen our ability to participate in democratic decision making—not only on our work teams and organizations but in our social and political life as well. The more authoritarian our family background, the more likely we are, in psychiatrist Erich Fromm's words, to develop a "fear of freedom," and the more accepting we are likely to be of authoritarian or dictatorial leaders. The experience of accommodating to the demands of authoritarian parents, teachers, and managers leads employees to pretend, as novelist Don Delillo chillingly describes, to be someone they are not: "You maintain a shifting distance between yourself and your job. There's a self-conscious space, a sense of formal play that is a sort of arrested panic, and maybe you show it in a forced gesture or a ritual clearing of the throat. Something out of childhood whistles through this space, a sense of games and half-made selves, but it's not that you're pretending to be someone else. You're pretending to be exactly who you are. That's the curious thing."

Ultimately, these family and school experiences reinforce hierarchical, bureaucratic, and autocratic patterns that undermine our capacity for independence, self-determination, critical thinking, collaboration, and dissent, all of which are *prerequisites* for personal awareness and authenticity, democratic self-government, and organizational self-management.

Four Steps to Breaking Patterns from the Past

As a result of these early experiences, many people spend much of their time on autopilot, simply trying to hold onto their jobs and protect the fragile identities they feel they need to survive. They avoid explicit and implicit feedback and do whatever is required to meet minimum work demands. The difficulty is that keeping silent, going to sleep, and doing the minimum create internal as well as external consequences. Ultimately, they result in a work life that is repressive, self-protective, and meaningless.

The degree to which we are able to question and avoid these survival strategies is the degree to which we have awakened. Our ability to wake up is supported by four basic steps that may appear simple but require considerable courage in practice:

1. Become aware of how your thinking, feeling, and acting is based on patterns from the past and how these patterns play out in the present.

2. Take responsibility for the effects these patterns have created on yourself, your organization, and others.

3. Decide to break these ancient patterns and work collaboratively to invent new ways of responding to problems and challenges.

4. Solicit honest feedback, coaching, mentoring, and assessment to identify and develop the skills, support, and strategies you need to succeed.

As we become more conscious of inherited patterns of thinking, feeling, and acting, we can assess our behavioral legacies and choose not to be controlled by them. As we take charge of our lives, we automatically become more responsible and satisfied at work and more conscious and effective organizational citizens. When the hidden, archetypal power of managers and organizations to act *in loco parentis* is broken and employees become self-reflecting and self-managing, everyone is finally able to grow up, learn from the past, design their own futures, and be fully responsible for their participation in the present.

How to Explore Family Issues at Work

Those who provide feedback, coaching, mentoring, and assessment rarely inquire more than superficially into the family backgrounds of those with whom they partner in these processes. But without addressing early family and peer experiences it is difficult for anyone who sincerely wants to change to recognize the source of their difficulties or learn how to unravel and become free of them. By seeking permission to ask questions that direct employees to inner truths about their past experiences, coaches and mentors can help them complete these experiences and move on.

For some this will seem like dangerous territory. Many will feel uncomfortable probing into family histories or believe they lack the skills to do so. Others will consider it an intrusion into intimate, non–work-related areas. This will be especially true for those who have not resolved their own family experiences. Yet by failing to examine and discuss these issues, we ignore the most important causal factors in shaping dysfunctional workplace attitudes, habits, and behaviors. Worse, we condemn people to continue blindly following their unconscious patterns.

It is always important to step lightly into these conversations. If the inquiry takes place privately, empathetically, and constructively in the context of trusting, ongoing feedback, coaching, or mentoring, it is possible to ask about family issues without sparking embarrassment, defensiveness, or resistance. If we probe gently, tentatively, and empathetically to assess our partner's level of comfort with this topic and receptivity to this line of inquiry, we can obtain permission to go a little further. We can, for example, simply ask whether it would be all right to ask about family history. The first part of the conversation might sound something like this:

> I would like to ask your permission to explore your background and family history. You have complete permission to say no. I have no desire to pry into your personal life, but think it would be useful, based on what you've told me, to ask some questions about family background that could give you some new insights and help me work with you more effectively. Would that be all right with you, or would you prefer not to discuss these issues?

Please let me know at any point if you would prefer not to discuss these issues further.

Afterward, the coach, mentor, or feedback deliverer can progressively ask more probing questions while sensitively monitoring verbal and nonverbal signals, stopping wherever there is resistance, and providing supportive feedback as important stories, insights, and revelations emerge. The coach, mentor, or feedback deliverer may decide it would be helpful to share personal family stories, if brief and relevant, as a way of equalizing the risk and encouraging trust. Here are some questions that are often useful to ask:

- Is there anything about this person or issue that reminds you of someone or some problem from your family or childhood? If so, how?

- How did you respond then? What happened when you did?

- Do you have any feelings or reactions left over from the past that are similar to those you are feeling now?

- From whom did you first learn how to behave at work? What did you learn?

- What were some of the unwritten rules and unspoken expectations about work that were communicated in your family of origin?

- Do you believe your family background has affected the way you are approaching the issues or problems you are facing today at work? How? What messages did your family communicate regarding this issue or problem?

- What was your sibling order? What was its impact on your attitudes and ideas about yourself? What is the sibling order of the person with whom you are experiencing problems?

- Have you ever found yourself in this position before? When? What was the outcome?

- Do you want to achieve a different result now? Why?

- What kind of relationship would you *like* to have with the person with whom you are experiencing problems? Why?

It may be useful for the coach, mentor, or feedback deliverer to assign homework that allows their partner to probe deeper into family issues. The coach may ask the employee to talk with parents or siblings and find out their version of what happened, or write down all the ways a difficult person or problem resembles someone at home, or keep a journal or diary and record insights and thoughts regarding the person or problem. A critical moment may come with the discovery of the origins of the unwanted, family-patterned dysfunctional behavior. With these new insights, it becomes possible to choose whether to continue unexamined patterns or adopt different ways of behaving. Someone who has a new perspective and decides to change can be asked what kind of support would be useful in completing the change process.

The last step in breaking family patterns involves making use of the insights that are gained. The coach, mentor, or feedback deliverer can recommend or offer support to keep the employee on track, and follow through to see whether the employee's responses to identified issues actually change. The employee can solicit on-the-spot feedback from friends and colleagues; identify words, signals, or gestures that colleagues can use to provide subtle reminders about backsliding; request periodic check-in sessions; and make open, public declarations that the dysfunctional behavior will no longer take place. It is useful for the employee to publicly request support from coworkers in making the change and feedback when old behavioral patterns surface. The process can be made more interesting by negotiating low-level prizes or rewards or agreeing on penalties for regression. In some cases, it's best for

the employee to relocate to a new area, or take on a new assignment, or find a new mentor or coach, or call in a mediator to help
resolve intractable issues.

Overcoming Overcompensations

Many of us overcompensate at work for what our families did or did
not do. We try to fulfill whatever needs our families failed to satisfy,
or hold back and defend ourselves if these needs were satisfied to
excess. If, for example, we grew up in a family in which there was a
great deal of yelling, we may learn to yell louder or withdraw during conflicts and be unable to respond skillfully when our manager
yells at us. If we grew up in a family where there was no yelling, we
may never have learned how to handle it, or be unable to hear
aggressive communications accurately at an emotional level. We
may be frightened of change as a result of childhood dislocations
and overcompensate by trying to control everything that could
threaten our stability.

The role of turnaround feedback, coaching, mentoring, and
assessment is to assist us in learning to overcome these deficiencies
without overcompensating, find a balance in our responses, and discover newer, better ways of acting in difficult situations. When we
overcome our tendency to react in the extreme, we avoid the twin
traps of over- and undercompensation—and the false pride and self-
blame that routinely fuel them.

It is important in waking up and encouraging others to do the
same that we acknowledge the impact these defining forces have on
our choices and ability to learn from experience. It is equally important that we feel supported in affirming these influences in our lives
while recognizing that we are far too complex to be defined by any
single element or factor. It then becomes possible for us to own our
families, histories, cultures, and sources of identity and at the same
time transcend them, for example, by

- Taking full responsibility for our family history and experience without blaming or excusing others for what they did or did not do

- Equally owning the positive and negative parts of our past without blaming or excusing ourselves for what we did or did not do

- Seeking balance without overcompensating for our strengths or weaknesses

- Transcending whatever we inherited, learned, or adopted as children

- Defining for ourselves who we are

- Choosing both to embrace and be free of the past, and decide to live in the present

Once we become clear about the origins of our behaviors, we can counterbalance our strengths and weaknesses, live according to our values, and discover more deeply who we actually are without overcompensating or denying our past. This means waking up and realizing that the dead, unexamined weight of personal history holds us back, while the moment-by-moment experience of who we are in the present wakes us up and frees us to be more aware, authentic, congruent, and committed.

The first genuine act of personal freedom is therefore the act of waking up. The second consists of using our internal awareness to transform the external conditions under which we live and work. The third consists of *transcending* the internal reflection those external conditions create within us by being authentic and helping others to do the same. Ultimately, the reason for transcending family, school, and peer experiences is to achieve a sense of identity, balance, and perspective. As we do so, we magnify our capacity to achieve the results we want, graduate from our families of origin, and become who we want to be. In other words, we finally grow up.

Finally Growing Up

Waking up means recognizing that we can learn something from everything that happens to us at work, even from our failures and catastrophes. While we have little choice about our past or the challenges we face at work, we do have a choice about the attitude and approach we bring to them. In this way, we can view every problem or conflict either as a failure and catastrophe or as an opportunity to learn and develop new skills.

When we see our disasters and catastrophes as lessons asking to be learned, we can recognize that they contain the secret of our unhappiness, together with a precise set of directions for successfully resolving them, both now and in the future. When we probe our problems and conflicts to discover what they have to teach us, we learn how to become free of them, improve our skills, and work far more effectively. It is up to us to identify these lessons and apply them to whatever circumstances we encounter.

When we allow painful experiences from the past to dominate and preoccupy our thoughts in the present, we deplete our energy and subvert our relationships. This continues until we self-critically examine these experiences and either release or transcend them. Many of us lug around heavy stacks of ancient, fetid, rotting, useless ledgers citing all the wrongs that have ever been done to us and cataloging all the reasons we were not at fault. While our families, friends, or colleagues may encourage us to keep these pointless histories alive, every single one without exception weighs us down, keeps us stuck, prevents us from being fully awake in the present, and thereby cheats us out of having a different future. Every one is an excuse for not waking up. As in the following story, we carry the past like a dead weight into the present:

Two Buddhist monks who had taken a vow never to touch a woman approached a river that had overrun its banks. They came across an elderly woman who was unable to get across. One of the monks picked her up and carried her to the other side. The two monks did not speak again for several miles. Finally, one of the monks couldn't keep silent any longer. "You took a vow never to touch a woman," he said. "Why did you break your vows?" The other monk answered: "I put her down several miles ago, but you are still carrying her!"

What is the point of carrying around what happened to us in the past? What are we so frightened of? What might we learn that we defend ourselves against so resolutely?

The answer, of course, is our desire to be well thought of, our vulnerability, our shame, our guilt, our pain, our love. We are afraid to let go of the past because we don't know how to live in the present, because we have accepted an image of ourselves as inadequate or unlovable, because we will have no one to focus on other than ourselves, because we are frightened of being alone, or being fired, or dying.

The phrases "waking up" and "turning around" thus contain a double meaning. They refer not only to waking up to what is around us and turning our lives around, but to discovering what is already *inside* us, to turning around and facing ourselves—and doing so not out of fear or shame or guilt or pain, but with honesty and integrity and an unconditional willingness to accept who we are. The Sufi poet Rumi wrote eloquently of finding such a place that was no longer bounded by judgments:

> Out beyond ideas of wrongdoing and rightdoing,
> there is a field. I'll meet you there.
> When the soul lies down in that field of grass,
> the world is much too full to talk about.

When we meet in Rumi's space full of silence, we discover ourselves and each other, and realize that we can direct the full force of our awareness, authenticity, congruence, and commitment to solving our problems and living our lives. In doing so, we discover that we are already and have always been at the top of the mountain, and that the only mountain that really matters is the one within.

Part II

Processes
Championing Congruity and Commitment

4

Turnaround Feedback

*Everyone must be aware of and be judged by every-
one else, and the opinions that the ignorant, dull, and
slow-witted hold about us are no less important than
the opinions of the bright, the enlightened, the refined.
This is because man is profoundly dependent on the
reflection of himself in another man's soul, be it even
the soul of an idiot.*

Witold Gombrowicz

Throughout our lives we receive enormous quantities of feedback. We are constantly being told by parents, peers, significant others, children, employers, coworkers, friends—even, as
Polish novelist Witold Gombrowicz realized, complete strangers—
what they think of our strengths, weaknesses, physical features, personalities, ideas, emotions, attitudes, habits, and behaviors. In
addition, our minds and bodies continually function as feedback
mechanisms, registering information about ourselves and our environment, how we rank in relation to others, and changes that could
destabilize or secure our precarious positions. With so much feedback, it's a wonder we make sense of it at all.

Yet feedback is pivotal to all learning, development, and growth.
Without feedback, we become stuck and soon begin to stagnate.

Because most of our work lives are spent in relationships with others, it is important for our development that they be able to learn from feedback as well. The question, therefore, is not whether to give and receive feedback but *how* to do so. We are not born with this knowledge. We need to learn how to separate what is useful in feedback from what is not, how to reveal kernels of truth hidden beneath layers of self-interest, and how to receive painful feedback without becoming angry, hurt, and defensive. We need to learn to nurture and support openness, trust, honesty, and authenticity, both in ourselves and others. And we need to design turnaround feedback processes that communicate needed information and encourage us to change our lives as a result.

We need feedback because we all want to be kind more than we want to be honest; because our intentions are often different from the effects we have on others; because some things are too important to discuss openly and at the same time too important not to; because secrets become less dangerous and easier to resolve when they are spoken. We need it because negativity replicates itself in silent, hidden places, and we either pass it back in the form of feedback or pass it on and give it permission to continue. We need it because what we do is not always in alignment with who we are. We need it because we wear masks to protect our most vulnerable parts and hide what is actually going on inside us. We need it because we suffer from self-doubt, poor self-esteem, and self-denial and consequently repress and externalize our emotions. We need it because self-protection is instinctual and we see the world egocentrically. We need it because we each perceive things differently and need to periodically calibrate the accuracy of our perceptions.

Unfortunately, we also erect barriers to receiving and acting on what we are told, partly because there is so much at stake and feedback undermines our ability to deny, rationalize, and delude ourselves into thinking everything we do is right. By defending ourselves and resisting feedback, we deprive ourselves of unique opportunities to grow and learn. By accepting it, we free ourselves from delusions and false expectations and are better able to discover who we are and where we fit in the world.

Varieties of Feedback

Feedback basically consists of any communication delivered to someone about how they are affecting us. Successful feedback focuses on behaviors and relationships they can do something about, rather than personalities or immutable traits they are powerless to change. Feedback is most effective when it is delivered informally as events occur, rather than formally in annual or semiannual reviews, assessments, or structured performance evaluations. If the information surprises us, it means our awareness has not been effective in detecting how other people are affected by us. Feedback is different from other forms of information that may at first glance seem similar:

- *Project evaluation*, which focuses on the tasks, processes, and outcomes of a particular project

- *Performance assessment*, which gives individuals an overall performance evaluation based on their skills and results

- *Process evaluation*, which shows teams ways of improving their work methods and processes

- *Role or job description appraisal*, which evaluates coworkers' roles and job descriptions in relation to each other and assess what is not working

- *Organizational audit or inventory*, which periodically assesses staff in relation to their past actions and results, current directions, and what they can contribute to achieving future goals or strategies

Feedback can be delivered in ways that are hierarchical or egalitarian, authoritarian or democratic, bureaucratic or informal. It can be given annually or episodically. It can be specific or open-ended, lengthy or quick, drawn from internal or external sources, performance-based or attitude-based, oriented toward blaming or toward learning. It can take the positive form of acknowledgment, in which people are recognized and complimented for their efforts, without a "yes, but . . ." attached to what is said. It can also take the negative form of criticism, in which people are reprimanded for their mistakes or errors, or the neutral form of information that is neither positive nor negative but focused on facts and behaviors. It can be delivered directly or indirectly, publicly or privately, angrily or lovingly, immediately or belatedly, specifically or generally, honestly or dishonestly. The most powerful form of feedback is what we call *turnaround* feedback, which compliments people for who they are while targeting their mistaken behaviors for honest analysis and transformational intervention.

Whatever we measure we notice. Whatever we notice we open to question. Whatever we open to question we become willing to change. Conversely, whatever we fail to measure we ignore, whatever we ignore we remove from questioning, and whatever we remove from questioning we allow to continue and feel powerless to change. By waking up and noticing what we are doing that is not effective, we initiate the process of changing it, and at the same time increase our ability to be honest, empathetic, congruent, and committed with others. By giving and receiving feedback, we build relationships based on openness, compassion, and integrity, creating trust and collaboration in the process.

Turnaround Quality Feedback

In delivering feedback, we can either play it safe and adopt an "I'll scratch your back if you scratch mine" approach to feedback, or we can take a risk and adopt an "I'll be deeply honest with you if you'll be equally honest with me" approach. By playing it safe and reducing the level of honesty, we can temporarily avoid having to change anything important. But for feedback to wake people up and motivate them to change, honesty in the *content* of what is offered and empathy in the *process* of delivering it are extremely important.

Inauthentic feedback can be distinguished from the turnaround variety by the degree of risk attached to it and the combination of honesty and empathy, precision and kindness, openness and gentleness with which it is delivered. Turnaround feedback ultimately stems from a desire to help someone wake up—not just because of the way they are behaving toward others, but because of the discomfort and unhappiness they are creating for *themselves*.

Turnaround feedback is therefore a manifestation of love, including "tough love," because it does not shrink from pointing out what is not working. It separates the person from the act, extending loving acceptance to the first and unyielding criticism to the second. It encourages integrity and ethical, value-based behavior. It is most effective when the person delivering it is deeply nonjudgmental yet honest and clear. For this reason, feedback is most powerful and most useful when it is

- Opened with a self-assessment by the person giving it

- Offered after getting permission from the person receiving it

- Assumed that constructive intent is present in the person delivering it

- Delivered with "I" statements so it is clear that the speaker owns the perceptions being offered

- Focused on communication and acts rather than on personalities or personal characteristics

- Presented as from a peer, even if it emanates from a different level in the organizational hierarchy

- Offered constructively, with practical suggestions and concrete ideas for improvement

- Specific and detailed, so the person receiving it is clear about the problem and can identify the solution

- Balanced and fair, so the person receiving it sees the whole picture, understands that their positive qualities are appreciated, and is able to place the criticism in a context of learning and improvement

- Communicated in real time without waiting until the event is long over

- Delivered without anger or judgment so the personal feelings of the deliverer are acknowledged or removed from the communication

- Oriented toward learning, growth, and change

- Clear about the consequences and results of not changing the behavior

- Accepted with sincere gratitude by the person who received it, so that at the end of the process it can be successfully implemented without injured feelings, anger, or resistance

The immediate goal of any feedback process is to enable both parties to become more successful listeners and learners. To do so, both need to disarm their egos so that better listening can take place. When feedback works, ideas are heard constructively and nonjudgmentally, and denial, resistance, withdrawal, fear, anger, and dissembling do not get in the way. The process should support ongoing learning and self-correction, build integrity and authenticity, and allow information to flow in both directions. The ultimate goal is to welcome and invite deeply honest feedback without waiting for others to offer it.

Yet multiple obstacles interfere with learning from feedback and translating it into improved behavior. We do not receive the same feedback from all sources at all times and places, and conflicting messages confuse us. We are highly susceptible to inaccurate feedback from others, which may reflect less who we are than the needs, desires, and expectations of the people delivering it. It takes enormous personal strength to separate what is useful in feedback from what is not and resist other people's false ideas about who we are or ought to be.

In addition, feedback is often a one-way street reflecting hierarchical power and status. It may be delivered hypocritically, without great care or concern for the person who receives it, and used to punish or humiliate anyone who criticizes those above them. It may actually tell us more about the person delivering it, or about our relationship and communication with them, than it does about ourselves.

For these reasons, feedback should be thought of not as accurate, objective information about who we are but as a mixture of subjective and objective data revealing how our attitudes and behaviors affect people differently. Those who deliver feedback may be jealous or angry at behaviors that insult or tempt them, and decide to use feedback to express their resentment. Personal loyalty may interfere with honesty, or people may alter or modify their feedback out of a sense of allegiance, making it harsher on those they do not like or support and gentler on those they do. Feedback may be delivered unequally and used to reinforce hierarchy or bureaucracy, undermining morale and obstructing the free flow of information. None of these uses of feedback encourages adaptation or learning based on accurate information. Each results in lost opportunities for improvement.

Reasons for Not Communicating Honestly

In spite of these risks, the greatest danger in delivering feedback does not arise from inaccuracy or subjectivity but from a reluctance to be honest about what exists. Some people have no difficulty delivering honest feedback, while others are more committed to politeness than to honesty. Some people are timid, quiet, or insecure, or have to be pushed into saying what they think, or have learned that it's best to keep their mouths shut. Some say: "Yes, things are great," when they are actually suffering or have severe problems that could be cured through feedback and critical insight. Some are simply afraid of communicating honestly.

Feedback is most effective when those delivering it are willing to be open, honest, and egalitarian in communicating what they actually think and feel. Doing so is dangerous, because it means running the risk of being disliked. Most of us want to be liked more than we want to be honest and lack the skills, empathy, or relational intimacy needed to deliver critical information without triggering defensiveness and resistance in others. Here are ten reasons people commonly cite for *not* communicating honestly:

1. We don't want to hurt their feelings.

2. They will misinterpret what we say.

3. They won't be receptive.

4. It will put our friendship at risk.

5. We will be open to retaliation or counterattack.

6. There's nothing in it for us.

7. It could backfire and the problem could get worse.

8. It could escalate and we don't like conflict.

9. We'll be out on a limb and won't be supported.

10. Nothing will change anyway.

Each of these reasons undermines integrity, saps self-confidence, and lessens our commitment to improvement and making a difference. Each reduces respect for the maturity and intelligence of the people with whom we are trying to communicate and renders feedback useless. Each of these ten reasons can be countered as follows:

1. It is possible to communicate honestly without hurting anyone's feelings.

2. We can communicate accurately so there is no misinterpretation.

3. They can't be receptive unless we try.

4. Without honesty, we can't have a genuine friendship.

5. If we act collaboratively, they won't respond defensively.

6. We increase self-esteem and opportunities for change through honest communication.

7. The problem will get worse if we don't communicate honestly. If we succeed, we won't have to be bothered by it any more.

8. If it escalates, we can use conflict resolution techniques to minimize and resolve the conflict.

9. If we risk being honest, others may take that risk also.

10. Things change when people communicate honestly with each other.

When we retreat from honest feedback, water it down, or make it useless, we cheat others out of any possibility of learning, turning their lives around, and becoming more skillful and successful. What is at stake in our honesty is both *their* opportunity to become better at what they do and *our* opportunity to act with integrity. If we communicate our feelings of love or friendship or sympathy, we can tell someone the truth in ways that allow them to learn.

Feedback Is Risky

Feedback is an inherently risky process, because other people can't ever completely know or understand us, because not everything other people want works for us, and because there is no such thing as disinterested feedback. We know the feedback we receive is accurate if it resonates with our inner sense of truth, if it is reinforced over time by different people who have no reason to lie to us, and if the person delivering it is clearly interested in our success and well-being.

Feedback is also risky because it can be used to suppress individuality and initiative. Every work of genius—every significant scientific, artistic, and social advancement—was opposed by people who did not understand it. Had these inventors listened to the feedback they received, they might have given up. Feedback is a kind of power that, in the absence of true humility, can easily be abused or used to instill uniformity and diminish diversity.

Employees are often given negative feedback for mistakes, failures, and glitches that were caused by the dysfunctional systems in which they operate, resulting in personal blame and a fresh round of organizational failures. Even well-intentioned critical feedback can hurt, causing people to close up and become less open, honest, and vulnerable than they were before.

The following primary risks of feedback can be countered by addressing them openly and adopting the measures indicated with each item:

- *The risk of arrogance.* Giving someone feedback with the assumption that we know how they should behave can be offset by negotiating with them as peers for more effective behaviors.

- *The risk of apathy.* A reluctance to give feedback because we do not care enough about the other person's growth and improvement can be countered by being curious about who they are and stimulating their interest through challenging learning opportunities.

- *The risk of judgment.* Judgments about who we are and what we have done can be shifted by listening more deeply, actively examining our assumptions, and asking questions about what we think we know.

- *The risk of creating a conspiracy of silence.* Adopting a conspiracy of silence or tacit agreement to forgo being honest can be broken by initiating open and honest communication.

- *The risk of triviality.* Keeping communications superficial and never addressing the real issues can be challenged by converting trivial interactions into deeper discussions, taking time, paying attention to larger issues, and focusing on the learning process.

- *The risk of focusing exclusively on the past.* Fixation on the past can be altered by focusing on the present or the future.

- *The risk of false objectivity.* An unwillingness to closely examine our biases can be countered by self-scrutiny and personal responsibility for creating more accurate perceptions of reality.

- *The risk of generality.* Depriving each other of specific examples of what was not successful reduces the possibility of learning, and can be opposed by citing specifics, details, and data for self-discovery.

- *The risk of unilateral action.* Feedback imposed without permission is an exercise of power over others and a kind of tyranny that can be shifted by creating a two-way process so people are more willing to participate.

- *The risk of excessive kindness.* Being excessively kind can be an act of cruelty, preventing someone from understanding how their actions affect others. This can be cured by honestly and empathetically communicating painful information, citing real examples and insisting on change.

Even when the person delivering the feedback uses these measures, there is an added difficulty that the recipients' natural protective reactions may lead them to experience feedback as simply another form of harassment. They may then see themselves as victims of someone's hostile intentions. It is easy to form a belief that our managers or coworkers are out to get us, intend us harm, or do not approve of who we are. By responding with denial, defensiveness, retreat, or counterattack, we reveal either that we lack the ability to hear and learn from critical feedback, or that they delivered it in ways that triggered our self-protective response.

When we perceive feedback as harassment and identify ourselves as victims, paradoxically we let ourselves off the hook. We can rightfully feel we are not to blame, rationalize our inactivity and defensiveness, garner sympathy, and use stories of victimization to turn others against our harasser. But by doing so, we cheat ourselves out of opportunities to learn and become more successful.

Tips About Feedback

The key to delivering and receiving critical feedback is for both parties to be clear that its sole purpose is to make us better at what we do. Here are some tips for those about to receive it:

Tips on Receiving Feedback

- Whenever possible take the first step and invite it.

- Adopt an open posture and use active, empathetic, and responsive listening techniques.

- Check it for accuracy against your own or other people's memories and experiences.

- Release your defensiveness and anger.

- Ask clarifying questions to make sure you understand it.

- Summarize the key points to show you have heard it.

- Identify practical solutions and behavior changes you can make.

- Ask for help and enlist collaboration in making desired changes.

- Take time to digest it and think about the interests of the person delivering it.

- Reframe it in your own words so it becomes yours.

- Express appreciation for the other person's honesty and caring.

- Ask them if it is acceptable for you to give them feedback in return.

Even if the feedback is wrong, ill-intentioned, and based on false premises and you know that what you did was right, you can still learn by listening to someone else describe what you did and what its impact was. This is especially true when you have ongoing relationships with others that depend on their trust and open communication.

If you are about to give someone feedback and are interested in maximizing their receptivity, here are some additional tips:

Tips on Delivering Feedback

- Establish an honest, trusting relationship by requesting feedback yourself and modeling how to receive it.

- Introduce the topic and set the mood for listening with a reassuring tone of voice and body signals.

- Ask for permission to deliver it. If permission is denied, ask for feedback regarding the reasons, elicit the other person's expectations, and model openness in listening.

- Share positives, and use "Yes, and" instead of "Yes, but" statements.

- Maintain eye contact if culturally appropriate to do so.

- Be direct, honest, empathic, and to the point.

- Use "I" statements and monitor your own emotional involvement.

- Ask for reactions, responses, agreements, and disagreements. Listen and ask for details.

- Test for understanding to see whether your message was received accurately.

- Jointly create or recommend a plan for improvement.

- Ask what you can do to help.

- Thank the person, acknowledge their willingness to listen and reinforce their feedback by summarizing any agreements you reached about what will be done differently, by whom, and by when.

In feedback, intention is more important than skill and it is possible to follow every one of these tips and still not be successful. If you are not clear about why you are offering or requesting feedback, or have mixed feelings about it, or your intentions are complex or contradictory, others will immediately sense that you are being hypocritical and back away. Conversely, if others become defensive or seem to be backing away even though you have followed all these tips, it may be because your intentions are mixed or not completely clear.

Team Feedback

Teams are intimate working relationships in which coworkers depend sensitively on feedback from others for their success. As a result, even petty frictions, miscommunications, misunderstandings, and dysfunctions can cause teams to experience drag and turbulence and lose their synergy, trust, and morale. Insignificant conflicts can accumulate to the point that emotions escalate beyond control and work grinds to a halt.

For these reasons, it is useful to periodically clear the air of issues that have simmered beneath the surface through a team feedback process in which team members give feedback to each other. In conducting these sessions, we often use the feedback and assessment instruments shown in Exhibits 4.1 and 4.2. We start by asking

Exhibit 4.1. Supporting Team Process.

Please score yourself and others on the following behaviors, ranking each from 1 to 5: 1 = Never; 2 = Rarely; 3 = Sometimes; 4 = Often; 5 = Always.

Supporting Behaviors	Self	Others
1. Volunteering for roles		
2. Encouraging others		
3. Speaking honestly		
4. Asking for feedback		
5. Supporting the agenda		
6. Bringing team back to the agenda		
7. Monitoring time limits		
8. Inviting others to speak		
9. Summarizing results		
10. Acknowledging others		
11. Being on time		
12. Bringing materials or refreshments		
13. Mediating conflicts		
14. Requesting clarification		
15. Being open to others' ideas		
16. Inviting others into discussion		
17. Suggesting positive processes		
18. Sharing real thoughts and feelings		
19. Sharing information		
20. Encouraging fun		

Exhibit 4.2. Blocking Team Process.

Please score yourself and others on the following behaviors, ranking each from 1 to 5: 1 = Never; 2 = Rarely; 3 = Sometimes; 4 = Often; 5 = Always.

Blocking Behaviors	Self	Others
1. Interrupting discussion		
2. Starting side conversations		
3. Making sarcastic comments		
4. Building negative attitude		
5. Ignoring others' comments		
6. Being argumentative		
7. Making negative facial gestures		
8. Dominating discussion		
9. Withdrawing from discussion		
10. Making tangential remarks		
11. Manipulating for personal agenda		
12. Resisting consensus		
13. Forming divisions within the team		
14. Downplaying others' contributions		
15. Sitting apart		
16. Arriving late		
17. Leaving early		
18. Being unwilling to clarify		
19. Being defensive		
20. Rejecting feedback		

participants to record any observations of their own behaviors or those of others that either support or undermine the team process. These assessments provide a basis for discussion and feedback with teammates. Like all frameworks, these follow a prototype that can easily be revised to reflect a team's unique circumstances.

After completing these assessments, we ask team members to identify any insights they had while filling them out. We then ask the team leader to identify any of her own personal behaviors that either support or block the team process. The team leader then asks

every team member to give her feedback one at a time on her observations about herself. If she is very tough on herself, the team will
always come to her defense. If she lets herself off the hook or engages
in behaviors that undermine the team process and does not men-
tion them, the team will identify these problems for her. Thus an
opportunity is created for deeper discussion and group intervention.
After everyone has finished giving feedback to the team leader it
becomes the next person's turn, and so on until everyone is finished.
Afterward, we ask everyone to evaluate the process, encourage them
to model transparency and openness in future communications, and
acknowledge them for their receptivity and honesty.

A Script for Managers Seeking Feedback

When managers request feedback from their subordinates, fear of
retaliation often blocks honest, critical communication and deprives
managers of information that could improve their performance.
When we advise managers on ways of eliciting useful feedback from
their subordinates, we often recommend that they prepare a script
outlining what they want to say and the questions they want to ask.
Here is an example:

> Thank you for being willing to meet with me. I would
> like your feedback on how I am doing as your manager. I
> really want to hear your honest opinion, and don't want
> you to feel you can't communicate any criticisms or prob-
> lems you may have with the way I am performing. I want
> to assure you that this conversation is completely confi-
> dential and off the record because I really want to know
> what you think, no matter how negative it may be, and I
> promise you that I will support and protect you in doing
> so. Is that acceptable to you? Thank you.
>
> To start with, I would like to ask you a couple of ques-
> tions. While I will be writing down your answers, this is

only for my own learning and not for any other purpose.
Here are my questions:

- What am I doing that is successful?

- How could I improve my performance?

- What specific ideas or suggestions do you have for
  how I could improve?

- How could I support you more effectively?

- Would you be willing to support me in improving? How?

- Is there anything else you would like to add?

Thank you again for being willing to answer these
questions. I appreciate your honesty and forthrightness
and invite you to continue giving me feedback whenever
you see some way I might improve.

It is best not to adhere to this script word for word, but to create your own relaxed, comfortable, smooth conversation. The body
signals and nonverbal messages you receive can deepen your understanding of what you are being told. You can use these questions to
develop and extend the feedback process so it continues to deepen
and enrich the relationship between you.

Video Feedback

Another way of creating powerful, direct turnaround results is
through video feedback. Video feedback allows us to see how we
look to others and how we exist in reality, rather than as we imagine ourselves in our mind's eye. This helps prevent our escape into
defensiveness and denial. The camera does not lie, as we can hear
from the following response of a thirty-three-year-old manager to
seeing herself on tape:

[Watching the videotape,] it became clear that I still basically operate as a child in the world, expecting others to

be right and strong, and me to be wrong and inadequate.
I spend much of my time at work trying to conceal my
insecurity and emptiness. . . . What troubles me is that
no matter what my achievements are, I still act like they
are insignificant, because I *feel* insignificant and inferior,
as a child does in a world inhabited by superior and successful grown-ups.

Video feedback is especially useful for revealing personal behaviors and interpersonal dynamics that occur during meetings and discussions. There is a richness of analysis that comes from watching
what appears on the videotape from a distance, as opposed to what
we are able to notice in the moment. Most people who receive
video feedback discover a gap between their inner image and their
outer reality. One woman we coached put it this way:

I think of myself as a kid, maybe sixteen or seventeen; I
guess I dress that way too. But when I was first videotaped in a meeting with my staff, I realized I was on the
other side of the desk from people looking at me for
answers! I didn't feel like a woman, but there I was—
the manager.

This woman, seeing the dichotomy between her self-perception
and the perception of others, was able to probe deeper into the
causes of her reluctance to act as an adult at work. She used the
objective evidence of the videotape together with feedback from
her colleagues to change her style and assume responsibility for her
role and communication patterns.

We all grow up with images from popular culture of movie or
rock stars who personify womanhood and manhood. With these
images, we try to insulate ourselves against any feedback that might
distinguish us from our fantasies. Even when the evidence appears
through video feedback, it is still hard to accept.

Where do these images come from that tell us what we ought to look like? We want to believe we actually *are* the ideal self we see so clearly in our mind's eye and have a hard time accepting ourselves as we are rather than as we want to be. Our stake in maintaining a favorable image of ourselves blocks us from developing our strengths. Rather than creating a unique image that authentically reflects who we are, we guard ourselves against information that might contradict our fantasies. No wonder we are so surprised when we first see ourselves on videotape!

The first step in creating an authentic sense of ourselves is reclaiming what is ours, as distinct from what belongs to others. We videotaped an employee and her manager while they spoke to help them separate reality from the fantasies they had of each other. The employee was surprised by seeing herself appear more self-possessed than she felt:

> I had a very vain reaction to myself. *[laughter]* I remember being very uncomfortable . . . but my reaction now *[on seeing the videotape]* was, "You came across pretty well." The thing that surprised me, I guess, is that I have a feeling that my self-consciousness shows. As a matter of fact, it didn't. I really felt that I was the most unself-conscious person. I just thought I looked more relaxed than other people.

The roles we play at work are masks we can use to hide our emotions from our managers, coworkers, and even ourselves. After we've been playing these roles for a while, the gap between who we are and who we pretend to be widens. We begin to *become* our masks, revealing even less to others and missing opportunities for empathy and personal connection. A developing leader of a large manufacturing company described this gap using pronouns that divided his true self from the person he observed on tape:

When I'm not on the spot talking, I always think that
my voice is reaching a pitch. . . . And your voice, it contracts inside and you can feel this pressure and this desperate talking. But on videotape I look calm. And when
I've been videotaped speaking, you're so nervous, trying
to say relevant things and you're on the spot all the time,
but it's amazing what defenses you've become adapted to,
and on the outside you look calm.

It is a continual struggle to maintain a hold on reality in a society where the distinction between reality and fantasy is so routinely
and effectively blurred. The myth of a "normal life" and the leadership models offered by the mass media deny our real workplace
experiences and diminish who we are.

This gap between inner feelings and outer presentation isolates
us from others and from authenticity. We assume others will understand how we feel and respond to our needs, yet we keep our most
vulnerable feelings hidden. When someone we want to reach is
unable to read our minds or meet our secret expectations we feel
hurt and rejected. How sad it is not to share our deepest selves or
allow others to touch us.

Using video feedback makes it possible for us to confirm how
we appear to others and know ourselves a little better. Video
feedback helps us wake up, connect with who we actually are,
and build more realistic self-images and authentic relationships
with others.

Questions to Prompt Self-Reflection

The value of video feedback lies not only in viewing ourselves but
in reflecting on what we see—either alone, with others, or with a
personal coach. Here are some questions coaches can ask that were
created by our friend and colleague, psychiatrist Dr. Norman Paul,

who has used video feedback for years to reveal hidden emotional issues to his clients and foster more realistic self-images:

- As you review the video, if you look at yourself as if you were a stranger, what do you notice? How are you different?

- If you look at yourself knowing it is you, who do you resemble in your family? What do you like or dislike about the person you see on the video?

- How is that person conning himself or herself?

- If you were to coach this person, what advice would you give?

These questions allow video subjects to step outside their defensiveness and analyze themselves as though they were strangers. It allows them to recognize their family patterns and see that these patterns have led them into personal beliefs that are untrue or even destructive.

When an interaction between two members of a team is video-taped, we have created some additional questions that can be used to assist them in analyzing their discussion, conflict, or meeting, including these:

- What surprised you most about what you saw in yourself? About what you saw in others?

- What communication problems do you see between these people? What is not working in their relationship?

- What do you think they are trying to say to each other? What are they trying *not* to say? What does each person most want to hear?

- What coaching would you give them?

- What emotions is each person feeling that they are not communicating directly? Is there defensiveness? Anger? Shame? Guilt? Pain?

- What did others do or say that might have triggered this emotional response?

- What does each person need to take responsibility for in this communication? In this relationship?

- What does each person really want from this relationship?

- What is each person contributing to the communication or the conflict?

- What is not being discussed that needs to be put on the table?

- What would it take for these people to get along?

- What is one thing you would like to hear the other person say?

- What is one thing you would like to be acknowledged or recognized for by the other person?

These questions allow groups and teams to create a more accurate image of themselves and their relationship and determine what each one is contributing or doing to undermine it, without either building themselves up or putting themselves down. They allow participants to choose the kind of relationships they *want* to have with each other and act strategically on the basis of who they are in ways that nurture the relationships they want.

Chekhov wrote, "Man will become better only when you make him see what he is like." Yet men's—and women's—self-images turn out not only to be grossly inaccurate, but flexible, malleable, and adaptable through a combination of awareness, experience, insight, intention, and authenticity. Video feedback allows us to see that we can change our colleagues' behaviors and impressions of us by altering our *attitudes*, changing what we say and do, and paying attention to what we are communicating beneath the surface.

Feedback is ultimately a set of questions we all need to answer for ourselves. Put more simply, it is a way of waking ourselves up and cultivating awareness, authenticity, congruence, and commitment in all our work. It increases our ability to see ourselves as others see us, and to discover and be who we actually are.

5

Transformational Coaching

[Coach John Wooden and I] startled each other, I think. Our backgrounds were so different, I a child of the city and proudly black, he a country child from middle America, and a deacon in his church—and we were thirty-seven years apart in age. Yet there was an immediate simpatico between our temperaments and a kind of pragmatic idealism that we shared, although I couldn't have put that into words back then. I just knew I was drawn to whatever he had. . . .

I don't know why fate placed me in his hands, but I'm grateful that it did. My relationship with him has been one of the most significant of my life. He believed in what he was doing and in what we were doing together. He had faith in us as players and as people. He was about winning basketball and winning as human beings. The consummate teacher, he taught us that doing the best you are capable of is victory enough, and that you can't walk until you can crawl, that gentle but profound truth about growing up.

Kareem Abdul-Jabbar

The aim of transformational coaching is not merely to assist people in becoming more skillful and successful, but to encourage them to believe in themselves, in who they are and who they can become. As basketball great Kareem Abdul-Jabbar so beautifully describes, a transformational coach enables players to achieve results beyond what they thought were possible; to develop untapped capacities; to cultivate awareness, authenticity, congruence, and commitment; and to produce not only winning performances, but *themselves* as winning human beings. These outcomes require a transformational approach to coaching.

Coaching has become an accepted, highly effective method for improving individual performance at work and increasing motivation and job satisfaction. A large body of literature and a growing population of professional coaches and coaching associations are emerging to assist organizations in providing these services. As work has become more complex and organizations become more interested in retaining talented employees, coaching has developed into an accepted method for improving employee skills and capacity and meeting rapidly changing organizational demands.

Many human resources departments now have dedicated staff who assess coaching needs, contract with outside coaches, develop in-house services, and train staff to serve as peer coaches. Many corporations, government agencies, and nonprofit organizations with limited resources recruit retired executives and volunteers with special skills to coach their employees.

Unfortunately, nearly all these programs focus on incremental improvements in individual performance or minor modifications in communication and behavior. They concentrate almost exclusively on results, rather than on the human beings who produce them. Although these efforts are positive and, in most cases, useful for all concerned, we believe it is possible to go beyond these efforts and deliver a different kind of coaching that focuses on *transformational* change—both in the individuals being coached and in the teams and organizations of which they are a part.

At work, as in sports, transformational coaches challenge players by asking them for more than seems humanly possible. At the same time, they are supportive and communicate that winning means doing the best one can. They are integrative and assist individuals in seeing themselves as part of a larger team effort. They are positive and do not punish people with negativity. They are focused and shift attention from blaming to a creative search for solutions. They are empathetic and listen to deeper human meanings. They believe in the synergistic capacity of the people they coach to become greater than the sum of their parts.

The job of a transformational coach is not to perform the work or motivate the performance but to remind those they coach of the innate abilities and motivation they already possess. Transformational coaches connect people with one another as members of a single team, allowing them to take coordinated, harmonious action. They remind people of their commitment to each other and of the power of collaboration so they can do better together than they can working alone. They discover and communicate the special capacities and talents of each person, empowering them to contribute in unique ways to the larger effort. For this reason, their purpose necessarily extends beyond improved performance to changing the lives of those they coach.

Coaching Is a Voluntary Relationship

Transformational coaching is an intimate, interactive, mutually supportive relationship between chosen partners who are prepared to improve in significant ways. Both parties are responsible for making the relationship work and producing satisfying results for each other. Successful coaching requires a positive attitude toward mistakes and an open attitude toward learning on both sides.

Ultimately, transformational coaching is a choice. Its power stems not from coercion but from voluntary commitment. A coach cannot make a difference unless the person being coached agrees to listen and act on the coach's advice. For the relationship to work, both parties have to freely choose each other. Thus the first goal of coaching is for the performer to accept the coach. In our practice, if a supervisor directs a subordinate to be coached by us, we begin by giving the employee permission to reject us and either find another coach or agree to coach *us* on how we can better address their needs.

Great coaches use the coaching process to transform *themselves* and discover new methods, insights, approaches, and opportunities for growth from the people they coach. This commitment to mutual learning removes the aura of judgment and one-sidedness from their observations and advice. If a performer resists, refuses to accept advice, or is unable to implement a suggestion, the coach can use this as an opportunity to develop new ways of communicating, overcoming defensiveness, and identifying more targeted suggestions. In return, the coach's clarity, intention, power of observation, and personal commitment to improving the coaching relationship have an enormous impact on whether the process will be successful.

Coaches Are on the Sidelines

Transformational coaches are rarely in the direct chain of command of those they coach and more often come from the outside. They may be external consultants, human resources professionals, or peers drawn from any part of the organization. Their influence is based entirely on the depth and quality of their commitment to the coaching relationship, and on the ability of the performer to translate their ideas into improved performance. Both of these goals require that the coach be on the sidelines, which is why coaching takes place off the field, outside the boundaries of actual performance.

The best coaches have no vested interest in the organization, its culture, or the specifics of achievement. Their outside position enables them to detect subtle dynamics that are often hidden from those on the inside. They can then question what may seem obvious to those performing the work and challenge accepted wisdom about how to solve problems.

To preserve a unique, personally supportive outsider's point of view, we often advise coaches "not to drink the water"—that is, to put some degree of distance between their coaching relationship and the demands of the organization that hired them. For this reason, successful coaching makes extensive use of independent consultants and in-house resources from different departments, regions, and teams whose reporting lines do not overlap with those of the person being coached.

Once the individual or team being coached is immersed in action, they become so intent on performing that they cannot see how they might improve. Coaches therefore stay one step removed from the rush of immediate demands, but in close enough communication to fully understand the pressures, diverse requests, time constraints, and needs of those being coached.

Coaches listen for passion, values, and commitment, observe their translation into action, and speak in ways that close the gap between them. In effect, coaches give performers permission to act on their passion, values, and commitments and bring more of themselves to their work.

Early in the coaching relationship, it is useful for those being coached to make these passions, values, and commitments explicit to their coaches, and vice versa. The coach can then direct a light—sometimes a spotlight, sometimes a floodlight, sometimes a laser—on these qualities, focusing on them at critical moments. It may even appear that the coach is more passionate and committed than the player, but the coach is only recalling and returning attention to the performer's first principles at critical decision points when attention is diverted by the press of more immediate demands.

Six Steps to Transformational Coaching

Many of the difficulties people face at work do not result from their individual actions or personalities. Rather, their problems are relational and systemic and cannot be corrected in isolation from the rest of the team, or even from the organization as a whole. To help one, it is often necessary to help all. In this sense, transformational coaching means addressing problems *holistically* and overcoming organizational obstacles along with the underlying issues that generated them.

Transformational coaching requires looking beneath the surface, waking people up, and challenging them to change—not in minor ways that bypass their fundamental issues but in life-altering ways that allow them to leave their old patterns behind and discover deeper, more authentic ways of being.

Transformational coaching requires both the coach and the performer to be awake. This means both participants need to have a strong sense of who they are, clearly articulate the goals they want to achieve, and commit to reaching consensus on a coaching contract or plan. There is no set pattern to transformational coaching. The following six steps, however, provide a framework for guiding the parties toward successful results.

1. Conduct a *Ruthless* Self-Assessment

Transformational coaching is a process that begins with a ruthless, unflinching self-assessment by the coach. The object of this self-assessment is to assist the coach in becoming clear and conscious about his or her personal goals. The coach begins by uncovering expectations, fears, strengths, and weaknesses, along with whatever extraneous baggage he or she may bring to the relationship. We suggest the coach begin by answering the following questions:

- Why did I decide to become a coach? What's really in it for me?

- What are my strengths as a coach? What are my weaknesses?

- What are the expectations of those who engaged my services? What are my expectations of myself?

- What are my anxieties, fears, and uncertainties about the process?

- What is my mandate for the coaching process? What are my short- and long-term goals?

- Have I communicated my mandate, goals, and expectations to the person I will be coaching? If not, why not?

- How do I feel about the person I will be coaching? Have we agreed on the process, mandate, goals, and expectations? If not, why not?

- Do I have any biases, prejudices, or negative history with the person, or disappointments regarding the team, task, or position, or unrealistic expectations regarding the coaching?

- What is the time deadline for performance? What are the limits on available resources? Can I meet these constraints?

- Is there any resistance or confusion on my part, or on the part of the person I will be coaching? Where is it coming from? What could I do to eliminate it?

- Who can be my "shadow coach" and sounding board for issues or problems that arise?

These questions can prepare the coach for stumbling blocks to successful coaching, identify areas of sensitivity, and stimulate self-learning. We often serve as "shadow coaches," working confidentially

out of the limelight to coach other coaches. Shadow coaching supports coaches in seeing their own counterproductive behaviors and
overcoming bottlenecks. Shadow coaches provide advice regarding
rough spots and safe spaces to reveal self-doubts; they help expose
unique possibilities and personal issues, and support the coach in
debriefing and learning from the experience. Coaches can make
excellent use of shadow coaches by sharing the results of their self-
assessment and asking for advice.

At the beginning, the person being coached also completes a
self-assessment. Here are some questions to start the transformational process by confronting some difficult issues:

- Why did I decide to be coached? What's really in it for me?

- What do I expect to get out of a coaching relationship?
  What are my goals? How might coaching be useful to me?

- How do I evaluate my own performance? What are my
  strengths? What are my weaknesses? What are my
  expectations of myself?

- Is there anything that frightens me or makes me hesi-
  tant to enter into a coaching relationship? Do I have
  any anxieties, fears, or uncertainties about teachers,
  authority figures, or coaches?

- Have I fully communicated what I really want to my
  coach? If not, why not?

- Do I have any biases, prejudices, or negative history
  with the prospective coach, or with the team, group,
  task, position, or outcomes that will be affected by
  the coaching?

- Is there any resistance or confusion on my part to being
  coached? Where is it coming from? What do I need to
  do to explore and eliminate it?

- What specifically do I want to stop, start, or do better? Why do I want to stop, start, or do better in these areas?

- Why haven't I done so until now? What makes me want to start doing so now? Why do I think coaching will help?

- How will others know whether I have succeeded?

- How could I sabotage myself and not do it? How could I allow others to sabotage me?

- How could I support myself? How could I get support from others?

- What's in it for me to actually do it? What will it mean if I don't?

- Am I ready for my work life to be transformed by coaching? If so, why? How? If not, why not?

- What are my long-range goals for the coaching process?

These self-assessment questions may be difficult to answer, but they will allow those being coached to become clear about their reasons for entering the coaching relationship and recognize that there are internal as well as external barriers to successful performance.

2. Negotiate a Values-Based, Transformational Coaching Relationship

The next step in coaching is to negotiate a clear set of goals and expectations for the relationship. Successful coaching relationships are built through small, subtle communications and collaboratively negotiated agreements that build trust and partnership. These agreements are introduced by the coach at the very first meeting. In transformational coaching, both parties agree to be honest, open, and willing to listen to each other. They define a set of values they will honor, such as shared decision making, honest communications, and commitment to resolve their disagreements.

By reaching consensus on a set of shared values, the parties commit to standards that will allow them to take greater risks and move the coaching process in a transformational direction. Values are builders of integrity and responsibility, authors of optimism and self-esteem, and definers of who we are. They are made manifest and alive through action. The simple act of opening a dialogue regarding ethics, values, and integrity automatically calls attention to the ways people act in contradiction to their values, places a value on having values, and prompts self-correction.

Once a foundation for the coaching relationship is grounded in shared values, the coach initiates a collaborative negotiation to define the parameters of the coaching relationship, and identifies what both parties can do to make it mutually supportive and successful. We advocate drafting a coaching contract that makes explicit the values, expectations, goals, and processes that fuel the relationship. Coaching contracts are reached by the following actions:

- Clarifying goals and expectations, surfacing doubts, and negotiating ground rules

- Asking both parties to indicate what they want from the coaching experience and what they can provide

- Coming to agreement on roles and responsibilities and writing them down

- Clearly communicating each person's explicit needs

- Identifying the skills and styles that work best for each person

- Discussing fears, vulnerabilities, and worst-case scenarios, and identifying how they might be overcome

- Digging deeply into what needs to be transformed; asking honest, empathetic, probing questions; and giving feedback to each other on the answers without necessarily trying to solve the problem

- Agreeing to work together to overcome obstacles and to learn as much as possible from each other

- Committing to give each other feedback about what does not work in the coaching process and evaluating results in action

- Reviewing these agreements, identifying next steps, and confirming each party's commitment to working together

After these steps are taken, a coaching contract is then drawn up and signed by both parties—and others where appropriate. This agreement may contain a time line identifying specific actions to be taken and milestones to mark significant improvements. Reaching consensus on the contract and ground rules builds trust between coaching partners by making their expectations clear and increasing their comfort with the process. Coaching contracts are not fixed in stone and can be renegotiated at any point.

3. Create a Constructive Coaching Environment

After conducting a self-assessment and negotiating expectations, the coach and the employee work together to create an informal, constructive environment that will nurture and support their relationship. The coach observes the employee in action to become familiar with the practical issues and problems that need to be addressed and asks others for their ideas and input.

Both parties set aside ample time for each coaching session, making sure there are no interruptions so the coach can give full attention to the performer. This means turning pagers, cell phones, and computers off and leaving instructions not to be interrupted. They find a location for the coaching session that allows them to sit across from one another in an informal atmosphere. The coach does not sit behind a desk. Instead, they meet informally so they can listen carefully, communicate openly, and watch for subtle shifts in body language, facial expression, and mood. Occasionally the coach asks to meet or even work for a while in the employee's work space to see what it looks and feels like and what can be learned in this environment. In general, the coach puts a high priority on the employee's success and makes sure the employee knows it.

In arranging the session, the coach clarifies its goals and outlines any preparations the employee should make: questions to consider, tests to take, materials to read, or tasks to perform. The coach inquires whether the employee has any questions or requests prior to the session and asks the employee to bring the self-assessment and goals for the coaching process to the first meeting. The coach reflects on his or her own self-assessment and goals and considers whether and how to share them.

Before the session, the coach uses empathy to consider what goals and desires for accomplishment the employee is likely to bring to the session. The coach also assesses the employee's current strengths and weaknesses before considering the kind of assistance coaching might provide. The coach uses the insights achieved through empathy not as final answers, but to help design follow-up questions for clarification.

At the session, the coach welcomes the employee as a respected colleague, takes time to make a personal connection, and encourages the employee to take an active role in framing the conversation. Together, they create a common, agreed-upon agenda proposed by the employee, with additional issues proposed by the coach. The coach summarizes the employee's concerns to provide encouragement and make it clear that these concerns have been heard.

The coach analyzes, describes, and asks questions about the employee's performance in a balanced way, including what could be considered "personal" or private issues that could have an impact on the employee's success. In doing so, the coach makes it clear that the purpose of these questions is to assist the employee in improving. It is important that the process be controlled, safe, and constructive so that the content can be creative, open, and risky, and begin to address transformational issues.

The real work of coaching consists of developing the employee's capacity—not merely for improvement but for transformation. Incremental changes require little commitment, but transformational changes demand dedication and a willingness to take risks.

4. Balance Positive Reinforcement with Critical Insight

Good coaching focuses on the strengths of the performer and reinforces the positive aspects of the performance while not diminishing or soft-pedaling its negative aspects. The coach acknowledges the employee's positive qualities, outstanding personal attributes, and successes. This acknowledgment must be sincere and not appear to be a manipulation in preparation for subsequent negative feedback. The coach selectively reinforces the employee's strengths and looks for concrete steps that will continue to build on these positive qualities and develop them further.

It is important that the employee acknowledge these successes, strengths, and accomplishments and identify ways of continuing to build on them. Positive reinforcement is a process of give-and-take ending with the performer's assumption of responsibility for improvement. This requires that positive reinforcement should be focused on the *person*, while critical insight is directed at the *problem*. The object of transformational coaching is not to make people doubt their ability to change or the validity of who they are. Rather, it is to separate their self-esteem from the behaviors that have prevented them from being successful. When employees are told, "You are doing a good job, but . . ." all they hear is the "but," and ignore whatever follows. Instead, coaches can just give positive reinforcement and say nothing afterward that diminishes or disqualifies it.

Later, they can offer critical insight without having to preface it with a qualification that can easily be discounted as insincere.

5. Provide Turnaround Feedback

Turnaround feedback is perhaps the most hazardous and consequential step in the coaching process. It requires honesty, sensitivity, and a willingness to work through issues until they have been understood, owned, and overcome. Genuine turnaround feedback generates significant shifts, not only in individual performance but in team and organizational culture. This feedback can help employees realize that they can make mistakes and still receive active support and nonjudgmental coaching, rather than public humiliation, silent hostility, and blame.

After gathering information from colleagues, supervisors, subordinates, customers, and clients, the coach makes an independent assessment and points to lessons that can be learned and areas for future growth. Concurrently, the coach assesses the attitude with which the feedback was received and reflects on that as well. Finally, the coach asks for feedback on the coaching itself as a way of modeling receptivity and encouraging trust.

In giving feedback, the coach specifies instances of problem behaviors, attitudes, and ideas. Concrete information and real examples allow performers to discover what needs changing and how to change it. To provide useful feedback, the coach avoids generalized judgments about the personality or motivation of the person being coached and approaches the feedback session with a goal of *mutual* development. In doing so, the coach

- Starts by describing the performer's behavior in specific, nonjudgmental terms

- Shares perceptions of the effects a specific behavior is having on the performer and the performer's work, organization, coworkers, and potential for career advancement

- Focuses on the problem as an "it" rather than as a "you"

- Asks the performer to identify the assumptions and intentions that underlie the behavior

- When appropriate, clarifies discrepancies between intentions and effects

- Shows how the performer's true intentions were not realized in the actions

- Identifies options and alternative behaviors that will express the performer's true intentions

- Works with the performer to identify specific steps that would have been more successful

- Identifies next steps the performer will take and how the coach will provide support, with a target date for the completion of each action

In addition, it is possible to use technology and electronic communications to vastly improve the quality and timeliness of the coaching process. Coaching through e-mail provide opportunities for instant messaging that can be used as an adjunct to personal meetings, telephone calls, videoconferencing, and other forms of communication, making it possible to provide "virtual coaching" on demand. For a template-based approach that allows coaches to lead employees through a personal change process, see *The Compass*, written and published by Joan MacIntosh and the Grove Consultants.

6. Move Toward Closure

After both parties have fully discussed the feedback, coaching contract, personal development plan, and other issues on which they are working, they identify specific actions the performer will take to increase effectiveness in implementing these plans. It is then appropriate to bring closure to the session by encouraging continued learning, growth, and a willingness to accept transformational coaching in the future.

To bring closure, the coach may review the expectations and coaching contract to identify the goals that were achieved, successful aspects of the coaching process, and ways it still might be improved. The coach models taking ownership of the lessons that were learned and being responsible for implementation and improvement. To encourage the performer to become independent and learn that continuing growth is possible without coaching, the coach

- Summarizes the history and milestones of the coaching relationship

- Makes recommendations for future improvements and next steps

- Asks the performer to summarize the areas that still need improvement and the actions that will be taken to address them

- Expresses confidence in the ability of the person being coached to succeed without coaching

- Acknowledges and compliments the performer for being courageous and willing to critique past attitudes, behaviors, and ideas, and for offering the coach feedback on the coaching process

- Appreciates the time and effort the performer put into the process, indicates what it has meant to the coach personally, and wishes the performer well

At the end of the coaching relationship, both parties may feel sad about the loss of their partnership. As they reach closure, they may want to recognize through a ceremony or ritual the *equality* that now characterizes their relationship and the ability of the employee to succeed independently. As the coach relinquishes that role, the employee develops a self-image as competent, skillful, capable of self-reliance, and able to use personal intuition and talent without looking to a coach to shore them up or step in and solve problems externally.

In the actual experience of coaching, each situation is unique. There are thousands of approaches to coaching and the steps we have just outlined may be more useful in a somewhat different order. They may occur within a single session or it may take multiple meetings to assist the employee in coming to a deep understanding of even a single incident. The diversity of issues and flow of the process offer a steady stream of surprises, challenges, and opportunities. Each coaching partnership should be given adequate opportunity to develop its own unique approach.

Turnaround Feedback Supports Transformational Coaching

Once employees become open to receiving feedback and decide to change, coaching shifts direction and provides them with the support they need to perform and continue making course corrections. In general, feedback is oriented toward achieving insight and awareness, while coaching is oriented toward making concrete behavioral changes. Whereas feedback is often received passively, coaching requires active participation and interaction on the part of the performer. Feedback wakes people up to the reality of what they are doing that is unsuccessful. Coaching wakes them up to their potential for success and shows them how to achieve it.

The complex, complementary interplay between turnaround feedback and transformational coaching is illustrated in the coaching we provided to a senior manager in a large service organization. His aggressive style was quite successful in delivering bottom-line results, but unsuccessful in that it created a great deal of conflict with staff, other managers, union leadership, and his own supervisor. His employees gave him an "unsatisfactory" rating, and it quickly became clear that unless he changed his management, communications, and decision-making style, he would not last in his position and the organization would pay a stiff price for his failure.

We began by conducting interviews with his staff. We analyzed the data and gave him coaching based on the feedback we received. We delivered some pretty tough feedback in an effort to wake him up. The information was definitely of "turnaround" quality. By confronting it, he was able to see what he was doing that was causing him to be unsuccessful and began to change his behavior. The points italicized in the following paragraphs represent the feedback his staff gave him. The comments in regular text indicate our observations and the coaching we gave him.

• *You respond to criticism by blaming others or shifting attention to their faults.* No matter what the issue, it's not about them or what they do, it's about how you handle it. It's easy to slip into criticizing what other people do, but that lets you off the hook, since it keeps you from recognizing that you can improve the way you handle *whatever* they do. Try to ignore the specifics of their behavior and focus only on the success or failure of your response to what they did. If you push too hard for what you want you may get it and lose your relationship, which is more important. If you focus on building better relationships, you will eventually get what you want.

• *You always tell us "I tried that and it didn't work," no matter what we suggest. We get very discouraged in making suggestions for improvement.* The fact that earlier efforts failed means nothing. Try asking instead, "How can we do it so it *will* work?" Then let them try it and learn from their experiences. The earlier efforts may have failed because the timing or mood wasn't right, or because the intention behind it was untrusting and suspicious, or because there wasn't adequate commitment, or because the real issues hadn't surfaced yet, or because the process was flawed, or for a thousand other reasons. We suggest you not ask if something is right or true. Instead ask what is right or true *about* it. Don't ask what went wrong, find out what you can learn from what happened. Go out of your way to seek out those with whom you disagree and ask them what you can do to improve your skills. After every conversation ask for feedback about how you did or what you might do better. Take notes, commit to work on it, and get back to them to find out how much you improved.

• *You don't pay any attention to what we've said, and we feel ignored or unheard.* If they don't feel heard, it's not their fault. It means you haven't listened well enough. The next time you hear a criticism, try *not* responding, except with a clarifying question, such as: "What did I do that caused you to feel that way?" or "Please tell me more," or "What can I do to solve that problem?" Don't slip into feeling sorry for yourself. If you buy it, others will too and you will lose the power of selfless action. Don't talk about what other people did or ought to do. Focus on what you plan to do instead. Drop the past completely and speak only about the present or the future. It's not about fault, it's about *improvement.* Start with the assumption that if there is a problem, you created it yourself; that you chose every one of the results you see now. Then let it all go, because blaming doesn't help unless you want to get stuck. Leadership is not about fault but about creating a sense of collective responsibility that lies beyond fault.

• *Interactions with you are too emotional. You get so defensive that we can't discuss the problem or solve it.* The criticisms staff bring *to* you are not directed *at* you, they're directed *toward* improvement. You are not the problem—and neither are they. The problem is an "it" or a "we," not a "you," an "I," or a "them." When you personalize it, the issue becomes emotional and about rejection and loyalty. When you depersonalize it, the issue shrinks and becomes merely an obstacle that is vulnerable to a good strategy. Try using a different pronoun and approach the next problem as an "it" or a "we." Then ask for feedback about how you did or what you might do better. Take notes and work on it.

• *You act like you own the problem and that the solution has to be yours. We want to be part of the process of making it happen.* If you own the solution, by definition you also own the problem. If what you want is collaboration and partnership, try *not* fixing the problem by yourself. If every time a child is asked to do the dishes a parent steps in and does them instead, the child never learns how to take responsibility. And yes, if the child does the washing, in the beginning the dishes will not be as clean as the parent wants. Dirty dishes are not the problem. The problem is how to transfer ownership of the dishes and responsibility for cleanliness from the parent to the child. Neither yelling nor abdication nor doing them yourself will achieve this goal.

We coached this manager, who had been highly defensive and resistant to change, for four months. At each session we selected one of these points of feedback, focused on the underlying issues that led to the feedback, and brainstormed ways he could respond. After four months, the manager was able to integrate the feedback into a new style and set of behaviors. While he continued to have problems, his employees eventually gave him a "satisfactory" evaluation as a team leader.

Strategies for Transformational Empowerment

Ultimately, transformational coaching consists of empowering employees to transform themselves. This means taking a strategic approach to the performance of those they coach and considering how the outside world influences performance through subtle and implicit expectations, demands, assumptions, rules, and hidden agendas that disempower the performer.

By confidentially interviewing employees, peers, supervisors, subordinates, and customers, coaches can gain a deeper appreciation of their realities and can develop strategies to promote transformation through empowerment. These interviews also allow coaches to develop a network of relationships they can use later to support employee empowerment.

A critical element in transformational coaching is the development of empowerment strategies that gradually shift leadership and control from the coach to the performer. A performer who sets the agenda, raises issues, and identifies what to do takes charge of the change process and will continue learning after the relationship is over. Jan Carlzon, CEO of SAS Airlines, uses a sports analogy to illustrate this point:

> In the game of soccer, the coach is a leader whose job it is to select the right players. He must also ensure that his team goes onto the field in the best condition to play a good game. On the field, there is a team captain, analogous to a manager, with the authority to issue orders on the field and to change plays during the course of the game. But most important are the individual players, each of whom becomes his own boss during the game.
>
> Imagine a situation in which a soccer player breaks away toward an open goal and suddenly abandons the ball to run back to the bench and ask the coach for the order to kick the ball into the goal. Before he can run back to the ball, he has lost not only the ball but also the game.

Often the first place where the performer experiences empowerment is in the coaching relationship. Transformational coaching therefore begins with the coach empowering the performer to set or alter the coaching agenda. A clear example of a performer setting the coaching agenda can be found in the following e-mail message from a manager we coached at a large urban museum:

> Hi—I hope I have not been overloading you with too much information. I did get a chance to speak with my boss again and I have two topics that I'd like to discuss with you tomorrow:
>
> How can I work with my boss to position the Research and Collections branch in the best way in the New

Museum in general, both inside and outside the Museum, with the board and with the leadership team?

How can we best use our differing personalities and strengths to deal most effectively with people? What strategies will work best in different kinds of situations and what methods can I use to develop and evaluate and refine our strategies?

As a result of this message, we encouraged her to continue redefining our coaching relationship, create an agenda for our next session, and manage the relationship with us. She extended her capacity for taking the initiative from coaching to her relationships at work, and evidenced a new level of maturity, responsibility, and leadership that won her a significant promotion and acknowledgment from her colleagues.

One strategy for encouraging empowerment and increasing the pace of change over time is to schedule regular check-in dates to register how well the advice is working, whether it is perceived as being successful, whether problems have arisen that require it to be revised or tweaked, and whether the performer is acting in an empowered fashion. This allows the coach to assess the clarity, self-confidence, initiative, ownership, and commitment of the performer in implementing new ideas without needing to be coached.

At the end of the coaching relationship, the coach assists the performer in overcoming obstacles to ending the relationship and seeing that it is no longer necessary. We call this the "Dumbo Effect," after the children's story about an elephant with long ears who believed he could fly, but only if he held a feather in his trunk. After losing his feather in mid-flight, Dumbo realized that his belief in the power of the feather was merely a way of convincing himself he could fly when, deep down, he did not think he could. Coaching is like Dumbo's feather, and as people learn to fly on their own, it is time to withdraw and let them see that they can rely on themselves.

Being coached is like having a best friend, teacher, trainer, wilderness guide, and personal consultant all wrapped into one, who shows you exactly how to do what you want to do and how to avoid what is getting in the way. A woman leader we coached described the benefits this way:

> I found coaching very, very helpful in many ways: clarifying (or moving down the road to greater clarity on) a set of goals and an overall vision for my career and life: practical, yet also reflecting and defined by my values and passion; seeing more clearly the ways in which how I view my past and current experiences has defined and in key areas constrained my thinking about my future and what possibilities I might investigate and pursue; developing a road map of where I want to go and what I'll need to find out to get there. It made my life and goals, and my potential, more real—and concretized my role in taking and exercising the leadership to create the life and career I want.

Transformational coaches work to create relationships that can tolerate difficult feedback, that enable both the coach and the performer to discover new areas for growth, and that collaboratively create the strategies needed to get there. Sometimes this means integrating potentially offensive information into the coaching process. Often the feedback, coaching observations, and suggestions for improvement are difficult to hear, and the greater the transformation demanded, the greater the resistance to listening or following coaching advice. If the coach can build a trusting, empowering relationship with the performer before delivering potentially threatening information, the chances increase that it will be heard and implemented. But coaches who are unwilling to deliver difficult, transformational advice face an even greater risk: that of being superficial, glossing over difficult behaviors, and missing unique opportunities to solve problems at a deeper level.

Effective transformational coaches take time to learn from problems and play with alternative solutions. They respond spontaneously based on their intuition, explore issues out of pure curiosity, and resist the immediate imposition of patchwork solutions. Rather than "fixing" people, transformational coaches use problems to discover insights, intentions, and better ways of solving them.

Transformational coaching teaches people how to cope with challenges and continue growing. It focuses on waking them up to their personal strengths and weaknesses and helping them become more aware and authentic in every part of their work lives. The challenge of transformational coaching is to enable employees to expand their capacity to embrace problems, form collaborative partnerships, find creative solutions, and explore not merely the questions that emerge from the coaching process and the answers to which they lead but *themselves* and their relationships as the ultimate source of all questions and all answers.

6

Strategic Mentoring

Every action, thought, and feeling is motivated by an
intention, and that intention is a cause that exists as
one with an effect. If we participate in the cause, it is
not possible for us not to participate in the effect. In
the most profound way, we are held responsible for
our every action, thought, and feeling, which is to
say, for our every intention. . . . It is, therefore, wise
for us to become aware of the many intentions that
inform our experience, to sort out which intentions
produce which effects, and to choose our intentions
according to the effects that we desire to produce.

Gary Zukav

The designation *mentor* conjures images from legend and literature of a master steeped in wisdom, an older, accomplished role
model who is able to marshal networks, resources, contacts, and
experience to assist younger, less experienced apprentices in interpreting the confusing rules and conflicting messages that compli-
cate life and learning secret strategies for overcoming the obstacles
that block success.

We all need mentors, not only to make connections with people we might otherwise never meet but to help us become more
strategic; in other words, to show us how to link our intentions with

the outcomes we want. As philosopher and writer Gary Zukav wisely points out, this means being strategic about our intentions. Organizational mentors use their vast experience, seniority, contacts, and understanding of the intricacies, subtleties, and complexities of organizational politics and culture to reveal the hidden meaning of communications, create links with people beyond our reach, guide us through the labyrinths of power, and teach us strategies for intentional success.

Very simply, strategic mentors encourage us to wake up and craft a carefully planned approach to purposeful self-development. By sharing their experience, discernment, and insight, they increase our capacity to learn. They show us how to cultivate awareness and authenticity in ourselves and others. They do so by allowing a part of what they discovered and who they became to be passed on, through us, to future generations.

What Is Strategic Mentoring?

The main purpose of conventional mentoring is to help individual employees climb the organizational career ladder. The main purpose of *strategic* mentoring is to wake employees up to the full strategic possibilities that flow from using their intentions as well as their talents—not in isolation or adversarial competition, but in collaboration with their coworkers and fellow team members to achieve goals that benefit everyone.

What are strategies, and how do mentors use them? Strategies are

- Ways of moving from vision to reality, from goals to achievement
- Road maps that provide directions rather than descriptions
- Guidelines for the allocation of resources
- Projections over time

- Ways of overcoming specific, clearly identified barriers

- Sources of multiple tactics, both direct and indirect

- Ways of integrating process, relationships, and content

- Frameworks for practice that are practical and holistic

Mentors use strategy to position employees for success. For example, military historian B. H. Liddell Hart wrote, regarding strategy in warfare, "The true aim of strategy is not to battle but rather to achieve a situation so advantageous which, if it does not of itself bring the enemy to surrender, would produce a sure victory in the battlefield."

Strategic mentoring, for this reason, is closely linked to turn-around feedback, transformational coaching, and participatory assessment. When mentoring is strategic, synergy can be created among and between these processes. Strategic mentoring therefore extends beyond the employee to encourage the development of *learning organizations* in which each employee's success is seen as connected to the success of others. In this way, the potential for success is enhanced for everyone, all-round development is supported, and work is seen as an opportunity for learning, skill building, and personal growth.

The strategic element in mentoring was described by *New York Times* reporter Jonathan Mandell, who asked a number of young writers to comment on their experiences in a mentoring program for beginning playwrights:

> Mentor playwright Charles Fuller, author of "A Soldier's Play" . . . has doubts: "I don't know if there is a whole lot you can teach someone about writing plays. I'm not sure that's possible." But, he continued, that is not what programs like the Cherry Lane Alternative Mentor Project can best offer anyway. "What a writer needs," he said, "is

not, 'Cross your T's and dot your I's' but: 'Hey, don't let this get you down. It's just a play.' Some people get so tense and anxiety-ridden that they can't get the work done. I think a lot of what Chris [mentee Christopher Shinn, author of 'Four'] needed was somebody to talk to about the work, and about what he was going to go through."

To Mr. Shinn that meant: the actors who would make up their own lines, the agent he wanted to fire, the rehearsals where nothing went right, the silly newspaper interviews.

"I already knew how to write plays," Mr. Shinn said, agreeing with his mentor. "But I didn't know how to be a playwright. Charles prepared me for the humiliation of being a playwright."

Through mentoring, these young playwrights learned the difference between skill and comprehension, between intentions and effects, between the act of writing and being a writer. These lessons have parallels in all tasks, job descriptions, and organizational functions. But what exactly is mentoring? How does it differ from feedback and coaching? And why does it need to be strategic?

Mentoring is similar to coaching, yet differs in important respects. While coaching focuses on performance, mentoring addresses the context in which the performance takes place. Coaching targets specific behaviors while mentoring concentrates on the attitudes, ideas, assumptions, and feelings that precede behavior. Mentoring seeks to improve employees' understanding of who they are and what they do. It helps them see how they might improve their attitudes and respond more strategically to the inevitable anxieties, humiliations, and defeats that accompany performance. Strategic mentoring speaks to *being* rather than doing, to altering relationships rather than implementing tactics. The mentors' goal is not merely for their mentees to succeed, but for them to develop the ability to transcend the conditions that hold them back.

While feedback supports employees in understanding how they are performing and coaching helps them improve, mentoring has a somewhat different (though occasionally overlapping) function. It is certainly possible for mentors to provide feedback or serve as coaches, advisers, or problem solvers. But mentors also help employees develop long-range strategies to implement their values, advance their careers, and navigate complex organizational waters. While feedback focuses on what *was* and coaching focuses on what *is*, mentoring focuses on what *could be*, motivating employees to move to more advanced levels to acting, thinking, and being. Mentoring is less oriented to action than are feedback and coaching, and more oriented to cultivating the awareness, attitudes, intentions, and relationships that ensure success.

For example, we recently observed a brilliant mentor at work in a large entertainment industry conglomerate. The chairman of the company, Pete, a Caucasian man, took an interest in Al, an African American regional vice president of sales and marketing many layers beneath him in the organization. Al was one of the few managers of color at the vice presidential level. When we asked Al about the extent of diversity among his peers, he replied, "You're looking at it."

Pete had a strong commitment to encouraging diversity in the organization—so much so that he denied a bonus to a senior executive for filling seven management positions without appointing a single diverse candidate. Without wanting to appear as if he were jumping layers of hierarchy by coaching Al himself, Pete asked us to convey a message that for Al to move to the next level in the company he needed experience in a broader range of departments. Pete offered to partner with us and look for opportunities that would allow Al to advance.

We suggested that Pete agree to mentor Al directly. Pete, as mentor rather than chairman, asked Al about his interests and where he wanted to go in the company. He gave Al some feedback on his goals, indicating several that were not high enough. He made some recommendations about changes in style, strategies for relating to colleagues, and ways of positioning himself for advancement.

Al asked Pete how he had become the organization's top leader. He asked for Pete's views on where and how he could be most useful in the organization. They agreed to partner in a project to improve sales in the region. Pete was willing to speak at a luncheon hosted by Al for key customers. He agreed to listen to the concerns of Al's customers regarding product delivery and services and to speak at a showcase event with Al to highlight their partnership in meeting customer needs. Pete also agreed to Al's request that he meet with the regional sales and marketing team to show his appreciation for their efforts. Jim, Al's direct supervisor, was informed of their conversation and supported their mentoring partnership.

After his mentoring session with Pete, Al's confidence increased dramatically. The performance results in his region showed immediate, significant improvement at a time of economic recession when other regions were not increasing their sales. Pete and Al's story reveals how mentoring can improve organizational equity, fairness, diversity, and democracy by assisting employees in overcoming racial barriers, leading to partnerships across traditional hierarchical organizational lines.

The Uses of Mentoring

Mentors can be used to meet multiple organizational demands. They can assist managers who have just joined the organization or been promoted to a new level in learning the ropes. When a new initiative is introduced, mentors can support managers in implementing it more effectively. Mentors can be useful when standards for performance are raised or higher levels of competency are required. They can help create shifts in organizational culture, as often takes place with mergers or changes in leadership. They can be used to smooth the transition to new ways of working, as with self-managing teams.

As an example of what mentoring can achieve, a comparison of pre- and post-program results in an Air Force mentoring program revealed dramatic improvements. The study, reported by the Gallup organization, showed that 81.9 percent of those being mentored received above average or excellent performance evaluations after completing the mentoring process, compared with only 40.9 percent before. Self-confidence in relation to promotion increased from 63.6 percent before to 90.9 percent afterward, and decision-making ability improved from 81.9 percent to 95.5 percent after introducing the program. In addition, 95.5 percent planned to continue in the organization after mentoring, as opposed to 72.7 percent before.

In spite of these dramatic results, most organizations offer mentoring only to upper-level managers. Worse, they overly restrict what mentors can and cannot do, or only half-heartedly support programs, or undermine their effectiveness by mandating, selecting, or assigning mentors from above.

We find it is always best when mentees are allowed to choose their mentors, when mentors are asked to volunteer, and when release time is provided to support the program. When the mentoring relationship is voluntary on both sides, interactions become more open and it is easier to build trust and true partnership. Many organizations use mentoring questionnaires not only to provide each side with information about potential partners detailing their expectations, styles, mentoring goals, and experiences but to make the mentoring relationship more voluntary.

Mentoring can provide critical assistance to new employees at every organizational level from custodian to CEO. It can be used proactively to assist employees who are candidates for promotion or have been named in succession planning. It can support team members in cross-training and apprenticeship programs. It can help employees who have good skills but are experiencing performance or behavioral problems. And it can be used to reduce attrition following significant losses, calamities, or periods of rapid organizational change.

As the tempo and complexity of technological advancement, organizational change, and employee turnover increase at a dizzying pace, many seasoned employees find they lack the skills and experiences needed for success. In some fast-paced organizations, reverse mentoring or "mentoring-up" programs are used to invert the usual pattern of elders' mentoring youth and provide senior staff with access to the superior technological and creative thinking skills of younger employees.

Mentors as Strategic Partners

In all collaborative ventures, whether in teams, networks, advocacy groups, task forces, or organizations as a whole, mentoring encourages employees to take risks and accept new challenges. Mentors reduce the loneliness and stress of isolated employees and not only create lasting partnerships with those who desperately need assistance but enrich their own lives and careers as well. The pleasure of watching a mentee reach a personal goal, achieve recognition, or solve a difficult problem is deeply satisfying to the mentor as well as to the mentee, and a contribution to the organization as a whole.

As mentors make the secrets of their success transparent and accessible, clarify confusing cultural norms, impart personal wisdom, and transform esoteric knowledge into strategic opportunity, they discover a richness in their role and learn to put their accumulated experience to use. We interviewed a number of peer mentors in a team environment who described their experiences as follows:

> "As our relationship unfolded I realized more and more what I knew and what I had to offer."

> "When she grew so that she could take on a new, higher-level position, I found new aspects of myself that I could contribute to her being successful."

> "I think I understand the culture of the organization and enjoy passing that information on to new members."

"I think I give the people I mentor some insight into the organization. When I first came here, human resources offered me a mentor, which was very helpful to me. She took me to lunch, and we talked about the issues I was facing and how I could learn how to get along with my coworkers."

"As senior members of the division, people are looking for leadership and guidance from us. I've enjoyed making a contribution to my mentees. Also, I've learned from my errors and mistakes and been able to pass it on."

The mentoring process can be used to assist not only individuals but entire teams and departments, allowing them to hone and perfect their collective skills, improve their capacity for self-management, spot problems in their relationships and processes, and position the team or department strategically within the organization. Team mentoring can assist organizations in overcoming the constricting effects of hierarchical and bureaucratic barriers to collaboration, thereby allowing the diverse ideas, skills, and experiences of team members to be put to strategic advantage.

In one organization with which we worked, mentoring was used to support team members in shifting from an extremely hierarchical environment to a self-managing one. As they made this shift, they integrated new staff into the team process. Every new employee was allowed to select a mentor from team members who had volunteered to serve, and each team was allowed to select a mentor for their group as a whole. These mentors were given several days of training to develop their skills in listening, feedback, strategic planning, conflict resolution, and changing organizational culture. Within five years of the program's inception, 100 percent of the mentors and mentees were still with the organization, and both groups reported that mentoring had immensely improved their individual and team outlook and motivation. More significantly, each team had been transformed into an engine of strategic advantage for the benefit of the organization as a whole.

What Makes Mentoring Strategic

The focus of strategic mentoring is not only on developing mentees as individuals but on improving the entire context and range of relationships in which they operate. Often, what appear to be personal or individual problems are actually by-products of organizational breakdown. For example, a strategic mentor may address what seem to be individual limitations on a mentee's capacity for success that are actually caused by the inability of a team to reach consensus, or the failure of a division to develop a clear customer focus, or a lack of agreement on organizational values. This lack of organizational focus requires mentors to work not only with their mentees but with others in the organization who are blocking their mentees' success, in order to develop strategies for that can bring about necessary organizational changes.

Every organization creates subtle, complex cultures, structures, systems, processes, and relationships that require interpretation by mentors to reveal what makes them tick. As employees come to understand these elements, they are able to develop strategies that allow them to achieve broader access and more far-reaching goals. In this sense, mentors are *interpreters* who both translate the unspoken language of the organization and provide a Rosetta Stone to crack the mysteries of organizational language. They are *political strategists* who reveal fruitful ways of transforming the organization as a whole.

For these reasons, strategic mentoring requires training and a range of supports and assistance throughout the process, in which both sides raise questions and discuss common problems. By working together, they are able to clarify the mentoring program's relationship to other organizational processes and reveal its relationship to organizational values, mission, vision, strategy, and goals.

Following training, mentors should be permitted to define and implement the program as they see fit, without interference or control from above. Throughout the strategic mentoring process, mentors commonly meet as a group in informal conversation to discuss common problems, share creative ways of addressing their mentees' needs, support one another in developing skills and techniques in waking people up, and identifying strategic or systemic changes they want to recommend to the organization as a whole.

The Stages of Strategic Mentoring

The strategic mentoring process starts with mentors and mentees collaboratively defining their relationship, developing a clear understanding of the differences in their personalities and communication styles, sharing criteria for success, and defining the boundaries and possibilities of working together. Mentors and mentees review their visions and long-term career goals, team relationships, and attitudes and beliefs regarding the organization as a whole. Mentors may empathize and recall having once been in their mentees' positions. They may clarify their reasons for becoming mentors, what they want and do not want from the relationship, the level of commitment they intend to bring, and areas in which they are unclear or confused. We recommend that they ask themselves the questions outlined for coaches in the last chapter.

During performance, strategic mentors serve as keepers of the flame, reminding mentees of their values, goals, and intentions and relating them to their strategies, behaviors, and effects. Values, goals, and intentions should not be set in stone, but should be revisited and revised as conditions change. Mentors are a visible reminder both of widespread commitment to do better, and of the need to measure every performance against strategic objectives.

As targeted goals are achieved, strategic mentors encourage their mentees to solicit feedback and coaching from customers, colleagues, and anyone who may have an interest in their performance. They may suggest ways of building more successful relationships, improving performance, or fine-tuning long-term strategies. They may assist in behind-the-scenes problem solving, analyzing organizational culture, building leadership and team skills, or preparing for dialogue, negotiation, or conflict resolution.

At some point, the formal part of the mentoring process comes to a close and mentors complete the experience by encouraging mentees to recognize that they are capable of standing alone, managing their own development, and making decisions without their mentor's support. While they may continue to have informal contact for years, the mentoring relationship is brought to an empowering end so it does not turn into a crutch, a dependency, or a burden for both.

In reaching closure, mentors and mentees mutually agree that they have completed the mentoring process and that it is time to move on. At the close of the process, as with transformational coaching, they review and evaluate what they did, identify their achievements, acknowledge their successes, and discuss their plans for the future. If they can each acknowledge what they contributed and gained from the process, no residue of debt or dependency will be left, and both will be in a position to take what they learned into future relationships.

E-Mentoring

Computer technology has created a new medium of communication with its own positive and negative features. E-mail has led both to more advanced forms of communication and unimagined opportunities for misunderstanding and miscommunication. Mentoring, like all relationships, develops over time as people learn more about each other and grow to trust one another. E-mentoring requires even greater knowledge and trust because the opportunities for misunderstanding and miscommunication are far greater.

The two principal dangers of electronic communication and e-relationships are that without face-to-face contact, understanding will diminish and instantaneous *flaming*—sending intemperate and insulting messages—will become more common. On one hand, electronic communication allows mentors to instantly intervene, track developments, network enormous databases, and connect people directly with one another across the globe, while on the other hand, trust and personal contact can be lost or misused.

The electronic medium permits rapid emotional responses to be prepared without listening and forwarded without much reflection. In addition, mentors may not be able to keep their e-mail communications confidential; if legal issues develop, such messages can be resurrected and subpoenaed. Also, a focus or fascination with "high-tech" communications often outshines the need for an equal focus on "high-touch" communications. It can be difficult in e-mentoring to identify what needs to be done or pick the best way of assisting someone whose success may depend on subtle, indirect messages that cannot be transmitted electronically.

By itself, e-mentoring is not enough, but in conjunction with other methods it can significantly enhance the mentoring relationship. As an adjunct to direct face-to-face communication, e-mentoring invites rapid interventions and communications that might otherwise take hours from a busy schedule. On the receiving end, mentees can analyze advice and integrate it into their lives at convenient hours without having to respond in person to visual and personal prompting by their mentors. In organizations where mentoring is viewed as secondary to getting the work done, e-mentoring can take only minutes a day, allowing greater economy in solving problems that do not require delicacy or finesse.

Tools for Successful Mentors

The most powerful and effective tool in strategic mentoring is the unique, personal character of the mentor, whose awareness, authenticity, wisdom, integrity, experience, and insight nurture others and help them improve their work lives. Mentors require a high level of self-awareness, insight, and understanding regarding their own strengths, weaknesses, and personal agendas, which always profoundly shape the mentoring process.

Every mentor brings a unique personal history to the mentoring process that makes it both unpredictable and endlessly creative. This history includes weaknesses and personal failures that, if shared, can contribute in important ways to a mentee's growth and understanding. Someone who has never reflected on failure may actually be less successful in mentoring than someone who is able to understand what it feels like to fail and has used that experience to overcome ego and self-doubt. It may prevent them from "over-mentoring" and interfering with the ability of their mentees to discover for themselves the best path to take, the skills they need to travel it, and the best way of evaluating the insights their mentors impart along the way.

Another common tool for successful mentoring is networking, in which mentors use their relationships and accumulated experiences to assist mentees in solving problems, accessing resources, opening opportunities, and achieving goals. Here are two typical comments by mentors regarding this aspect of their relationships:

> "My past experience will be very valuable, so I can teach others how to step back and how to step in, how to listen and how to be aggressive or assertive when necessary, and how to connect with the right people who can help them get it done."

> "My personal relationships with my colleagues and senior management are good. I get along well with others and have good communication skills. I want to build a bridge for the people I mentor to the decision makers in our shop."

An essential tool for strategic mentors is emotional intelligence. It is critical that mentors be awake, emotionally available, and aware of the subtle, deeper meanings of sensitive emotional communications that are often critical to the mentoring process. Emotional intelligence includes the capacity for empathy, considering "How would I feel if it were me?" and supporting mentees in increasing their emotional awareness, sensitivity, and discernment as they work through their intense emotions.

Along with emotional intelligence comes another subtle, strategic mentoring tool, which is patience. Patient mentors are careful not to push too fast. They do not set goals that are too high for their mentees to achieve, and they avoid overinterpreting their mentees' actions. Instead, they ask curious questions that elicit an accurate definition of problems and do not immediately jump to solutions. Once a problem has been deeply understood and fully explored, solutions emerge naturally, and mentees are able to discover and own them without requiring a mentor's guidance.

Successful mentors recognize that every strategic decision regarding performance must be made by their mentees *alone*. They are aware of the danger of becoming too invested in their mentee's success. This natural tendency of mentors to become parental figures creates a risk that they will smother their fledgling mentees' capacity for self-reliance. It is not unusual for mentees to become dependent, or for mentors to elicit obedience, deference, and subservience rather than intelligence, self-confidence, and independence. Like parents, strategic mentors are most successful when their mentees achieve their goals and develop their skills without receiving any overt, discernable support—in other words, when they have completely internalized their mentor's advice and skills and are able to succeed on their own without external support. The object of strategic mentoring is thus for the mentor to become increasingly invisible and irrelevant to the mentee.

For this reason, strategic mentors do not try to control their mentees or encourage them to uncritically implement ideas advocated by others. They do not try to predict the future or control the environment or take failures too seriously. While mentors make recommendations and give advice, they also are willing to let it go, remain silent, and allow mentees to make their own decisions, experience their own mistakes, and discover their own path through the maze.

Understanding Organizational Culture

When we ask mentees what skills their mentors possess that prove most useful, many cite their mentor's ability to read and interpret the confusing language of organizational culture. Organizational culture can provide a rich, supportive environment for growth, or it can obstruct the ability of employees to achieve their goals and solve their problems. When hidden organizational norms, behaviors, attitudes, and customs are exposed, mentees are able to make better decisions and adapt more quickly. They can become part of the culture and use it to achieve their goal or mobilize to change it when it blocks their learning or development.

Because organizational culture is always in flux, no fixed description or final catalogue of its elements can be codified. Effective mentors therefore not only expose the hidden rules of the culture but provide their mentees with tools for analyzing and navigating it on their own.

Cultural anthropologist Edward T. Hall has outlined the elements of culture in his classic book, *The Silent Language*. We have applied Hall's schema to the key elements in organizational culture and the primary strategic initiatives mentees can take to become fluent in organizational culture and maneuver through it to achieve their goals. Cultures, including organizational cultures, contain rules for

- *Interacting with the environment.* Mentees need to be completely familiar with their organizational environment, including its actual and potential marketplaces, internal political and social forces, customer demographics and needs, strategic possibilities and potential limits.

- *Associating with others.* Knowledge of how people in the organization coalesce, gather in affinity groups, organize to achieve goals, and get work done promotes the development of strategies and alliances that can support mentees in achieving their goals.

- *Subsisting.* Understanding how the culture rewards, compensates, and supports people and determines the ways they subsist inside the organization can encourage mentees to take strategic risks.

- *Understanding gender and other biases.* Understanding the cultural biases, prejudices, attitudes, and rules regarding gender, race, ethnicity, sexual orientation, age, and disability inside the organization can increase the freedom to operate without the constraints these biases impose.

- *Navigating territoriality.* Mapping the cultural forces that determine how boundaries and space are established and what it means when these lines are crossed can provide key information in negotiating limits and navigating organizational space required for achieving mentees' ends.

- *Monitoring temporality.* Understanding organizational time and how it is thought of and used can provide important information regarding expectations, work habits, behaviors, time-based communications, and allocation of temporal resources.

- *Learning.* Cultural attitudes toward learning can be open or closed, supportive or dysfunctional, individualistic or team-based in their ability to contribute to growth and development, as well as to the organization as a whole.

- *Playing.* Play and humor, including an understanding of what people laugh at and what they find in bad taste, gives information that is useful in solving problems and creating better relationships without violating hidden rules.

- *Using property.* A knowledge of cultural rules regarding possession, exchange, and use of personal and organizational property, including various forms of intangible property, can prevent transgression of invisible boundaries.

- *Fighting*. A subtle knowledge of how people engage in conflict and what they do when differences become irreconcilable is an important element in organizational culture. As mentees become adept at understanding and resolving conflicts, their ability to achieve other goals also increases.

Navigating these elements is extremely fluid, subtle, and dependent on personal experience, so that the process of understanding how to respond to organizational culture never ends. It is therefore clear that the need for mentoring never ends. Rather, it is *transcended* through a strategic development of the mentee's skills and confidence and the creation of an independent network of successful and empowering relationships. A mentee who reaches this new, transcendent level in the mentoring process graduates from mentee to mentor. Thus the mentoring relationship is successively outgrown as it becomes increasingly unnecessary in addressing one level of problem, and is continually renewed in addressing higher-level problems.

Mentors are not only leaders, they are also best friends. They do not simply point the way as disinterested observers, they offer advice as colleagues based on their own experience. They can never anticipate the precise terrain their mentees will be required to traverse or the challenges they will be required to face. Novelist Albert Camus wrote a request to a friend in words that apply equally to strategic mentoring: "Don't walk in front of me, I may not follow. Don't walk behind me, I may not lead. Just walk beside me and be my friend." Sound advice in any relationship.

7

Participatory Assessment

The conventional approach to performance assess-
ment stands condemned as a personnel method. It
places the manager in the untenable position of judg-
ing the personal worth of his subordinates, and of
action on these judgements. No manager possesses,
nor could he acquire, the skill necessary to carry out
this responsibility effectively. Few would even be will-
ing to accept it if they were fully aware of the implica-
tions involved. . . . A sounder approach, which
places the major responsibility on the subordinate for
establishing performance goals and appraising progress
toward them, avoids the major weaknesses of the old
plan and benefits the organization by stimulating the
development of the subordinate.

Douglas McGregor

McGregor's critique of performance assessment is as valid today as it was when he wrote it in 1957. While many organizations have dramatically improved their performance assessment systems since then, most have missed the more profound implications of McGregor's critique. The problem is not simply that organizations take a hierarchical, top-down approach to assessment, but that they do not involve the people who are being appraised in defining the criteria and designing the processes by which they are to be evaluated. They fail to include employees in assessing their progress in meeting assessment criteria, or ensuring that their assessments are conducted in an egalitarian, collaborative, mutually supportive way.

None of us, McGregor believed, has the right or the capacity to judge others. Moreover, performance assessment inevitably becomes counterproductive when we try to use it to coerce people into change. Telling employees how they ought to behave is far less effective than *inviting* them to become active participants in assessing their own behavior, aiding them in understanding how they can improve, and inspiring them to commit themselves to doing so.

For this reason, it is always a mistake to assign managers the task of enforcing performance standards through hierarchical or undemocratic assessment systems. Managers fall into the trap of creating unilateral, objective, generic standards for other people's performance, appraising them against those standards, disciplining those who fail to meet them, and periodically instilling fear by raising the bar in an effort to increase output and efficiency. Hierarchical assessment systems are based on the following implicit, demonstrably false assumptions:

- Imposing external standards of competence on employees, assessing performance against them, punishing those who do not meet them, and using fear as a motivator is the best way of improving the quality of their work.

- Assessment standards reliably measure fitness and ability to do a particular job, display a set of skills, or exhibit mastery of a body of knowledge.

- The benefits of this approach outweigh any damage they may cause to employee morale and motivation to change.

Although some writers have argued that the entire effort to assess and correct employee performance should be scrapped, we believe there are valid reasons for critiquing behavior in the service of learning. We advocate transforming traditional performance assessment systems by making them participatory and egalitarian, assessing everyone, using subjective as well as objective measures, encouraging improvement and learning rather than documenting static skills and conformity, and making those assessed active participants in designing and implementing the entire process.

Assessment should be dedicated to discovering why performance was inadequate in the first place and measuring effects in the real world, rather than creating complex written criteria or ideal scenarios. It should support active participation rather than passive analysis. It should clarify the elements of successful performance and the concrete steps required for improvement. It should encourage diverse and creative responses and reward rather than penalize a willingness to push back and disagree. It should promote responsibility and collaboration rather than conformity and obedience.

The sole purpose of assessment should be to improve performance. This means everyone in the organization should be responsible for inviting assessment, selecting criteria, defining the process, maintaining records, tracking progress, and achieving results. It means inviting full participation and clearly articulating the purpose and values of the process so everyone is clear about the potential uses of the information they are providing. If an *evaluation* is needed to support staffing or compensation decisions or document discipline or termination, it should be conducted separately from a performance assessment that is dedicated solely to improvement. Any confusion about the purpose or values of the process will result in its reduced effectiveness, because employees will disguise or cover up errors rather than acknowledging them.

Values—Integrating Theory and Practice

Values are priorities that highlight what we care about and place limits on what we will and will not do. They are ways of bringing behaviors into alignment with ideals and integrating theory with practice. Every performance assessment is based in values.

When assessment standards are created without employee input, imposed without debate, interpreted bureaucratically, enforced by superiors, and blindly acquiesced in by subordinates, the process results in employees' feeling bad about themselves, judged according to values not their own, and consequently unmotivated to change. On the other hand, when these values are made explicit through participatory assessment, standards are negotiated and adopted by consensus, interpreted flexibly, and employees are encouraged to evaluate each other, all participants feel better about themselves, support the process, and are motivated to change, because outcomes reflect shared values, ideals, and standards.

In participatory assessment, performance is analyzed in relation to explicit values that are agreed upon by participants. These include values such as *listening* in customer satisfaction, *quality* in service, *collaboration* in teamwork, or *commitment* in follow through. With this analysis, discrepancies between values-in-theory and values-in-practice can be identified, agreed upon, and used to improve performance by asking a few simple preliminary questions such as, What are your values? How do they apply to your work? How can you know whether you are successful in applying them? Is there any difference between your espoused values and what you actually do? Are the effects you see consistent with your intentions? These and similar questions allow employees to become more aware and authentic and close the gap between declaring values and implementing them.

Effective assessments not only improve employees' ability to perform their work but increase their energy and self-confidence as a springboard to improvement.

We are far more effective in achieving these results and solving a wide range of performance problems when we approach the assessment process democratically, with egalitarian values that are not distorted by superiorities of wealth, power, or position. By doing so, we communicate that improvement is everyone's responsibility, that no one is above criticism, and that the success of the whole depends on the success of each of its parts.

The Complexity of Experience: What Are We Assessing?

Many organizations have adopted a simplistic approach to assessment, thinking they can predict and perfect behaviors by measuring them. Most assessment instruments divide organic, holistic, fluid, environmentally sensitive, personally unique actions into concise, measurable bits consisting of job descriptions, lists of duties, and goals for the year. Then they compare one against the other to highlight places where individual performance falls short. Yet these measurable bits are rarely adequate to evaluate the complex interaction of motivation, intuition, creativity, interpersonal relationships, personal leadership, and teamwork that contribute to achieving even the simplest performance goals.

In addition, these assessment instruments tend to identify and measure *minimal* standards of performance and ignore maximal standards that rely on inspiration, a desire for excellence, sensitivity to details, or unique personal skills. Minimalist approaches encourage employees to aim for a predetermined floor and stop trying, rather than reach for a ceiling that is always rising and a little beyond reach.

Traditional performance assessments are, by design, abstract, objective managerial devices for evaluating a solitary employee's interdependent work results, all within highly subjective, managerially determined parameters. This allows managers to reward employees who are skilled in currying favor or in meeting predetermined, externally designed, semipermanent, artificially frozen bureaucratic standards. It allows managers to punish employees who work creatively, define their own standards, learn in unique ways, disagree with their superiors, or value collaborative relationships over conformity to abstract standards.

In many organizations, the process is seen as ending when employees sign a form indicating that they physically received the results of their assessment, leaving all continued learning and correction of mistakes entirely to them, backed up by an implicit threat of discipline or discharge if minimal standards are not met.

Yet we know that learning is a continuous, unbroken process that requires commitment, ongoing effort, dialogue, support, collaboration, creativity, and planning. Any organization that wants to use performance assessment to increase productivity, quality, and customer satisfaction will not succeed unless the entire process from start to finish promotes participation, rewards flexibility and learning, and makes improvement an integral part of organizational life.

What and how we assess determines what we get. For example, a number of volunteers in a recent study by Jeffrey Stanton and Amanda Julian were asked to perform a simple task and instructed that both quality and quantity would be important elements in their final assessment. Yet participants were able to observe as they performed the task that their assessors were actually measuring either quality or quantity. Researchers discovered that when participants believed their assessors were measuring only quality, quantity declined, and when they thought quantity was being measured, quality declined. It is therefore important for organizations not only to identify what will be measured but to actually measure what they really want to achieve. This means shifting the focus from satisfying minimal standardized requirements to achieving maximal and unique personal, team, and organizational goals.

Cultural Diversity and Assessment

The cultural background of employees, including their race, nationality, gender, age, sexual orientation, political beliefs, social class, hierarchical status, personal values, and similar factors can skew the assessment process and reduce its ability to foster learning and improvement. Traditional forms of assessment often contain hidden cultural biases. If nothing else, they fail to account for the fact that the person being tested may come from a culture that approaches assessment, learning, and problem solving differently from what the assessment process dictates, and may be justly suspicious of what can be perceived as a hostile organizational culture.

Most of us are oblivious to our own cultural background. We experience cultural bias as a fish experiences water, without even being aware of its all-defining presence. When we have an opportunity to step outside our cultural context and observe it, we become conscious of its power and can then choose to reduce, change, or eliminate it.

One of the advantages of participatory assessment is that it allows employees to clarify the cultural context of performance and encourages diverse cultural expectations and biases to be openly discussed, collaboratively negotiated, and jointly resolved. It encourages participants to understand and support cultural diversity and makes respect for diversity a value within the organization.

When we refer to cultural diversity, we refer not only to race, gender, and sexual orientation but also to a variety of unique styles, personalities, ideas, perceptions, and ways of working. For example, we worked with a nationally known engineering company where several Japanese American managers had been routinely passed over for promotion and given poor marks in performance assessment based on their lack of aggressiveness in pursuing business and career opportunities. What had not been acknowledged was that in Japanese culture, aggressive self-advancement and putting oneself forward for promotion were considered highly improper and a sign of egotistical, anti-team behavior. These behaviors, consistent with Japanese culture, were measured against standards that had been distorted not only by the North American culture of those conducting the assessment but by a closed, hierarchical organizational culture that made it impossible to air, discuss, or resolve these issues.

Every performance assessment is a process that requires an observer, and there is no such thing as neutral observation. The act of observation changes anything sensitive that is being observed. In addition, observers always bring *themselves* to the observation, and who they are has an impact on what they are able to observe and evaluate. The information they receive about the person being assessed is filtered through a set of lenses that shape their perception.

For this reason, performance assessments *cannot* be made culturally neutral or culture-free. An effective, fair assessment process is therefore one that is participatory, collaborative, equitable, and negotiated, so that it is inclusive and congruent with the cultures of both assessor and assessed. Equity and universal participation in assessment encourages increased diversity in hiring, promotions, and assignments, which in turn strengthens organizational effectiveness and adaptability. When cultural diversity becomes an integral part of the participatory assessment process, employees can be asked to reflect on the elements from their backgrounds, cultural expectations, and values that have influenced their performance. They can then find ways of succeeding that do not require them to betray or be loyal to their cultural heritage or to adopt a uniform, nondiverse cultural standard that requires assimilation and conformity.

Creating a Context: Linking Learning and Assessment

The starting point in developing an effective assessment system is for the employees to each identify their needs as learners, the needs of their coworkers, and the needs of the organization that are impacted by their efforts. These assessments promote self-esteem as a buttress to learning. A 1973 report issued by the U.S. Office of Education Study Commission on the Undergraduate Education and Preparation of Teachers made the following recommendations regarding assessment:

> A major function of assessment is to assist individuals in moving from childhood to adulthood as whole people.

It should encourage a growing sense of self; it should give a person the ability to hold a job that allows him to both support himself and to feel that he is doing something worth doing. It should give him a capacity to understand and, to some degree, control the major physical and social forces affecting his life. Assessment is a personal process that implies an acquisition of self-knowledge and of what is generally called abstract learning, it is also a social and political process.

In participatory assessment, the assessor needs to respect the dignity of each of the employees being assessed, respond to their individual intellectual, social, spiritual, and physical needs, commit to their learning, and provide the organizational support they need to succeed. The assessor should see the assessment process as encouraging lifelong learning, as a beginning rather than an end, and as a change strategy rather than as a pointless, frequently counterproductive bureaucratic formality.

For example, we worked with the CEO of a small consulting firm who was angered by the failure of his leadership team to generate business and produce revenue. In his view, the team was neither finding clients nor selling business. His assessment process consisted of telling them they were failing and demanding that they bring in more business or they would all be fired. He tried to shame them into compliance rather than invite them to collaborate in solving the problem. As a result, they grew demoralized, withdrew, and resisted making any change in their activities. We suggested he ask the leadership team to conduct their own participatory assessment.

We began by posing the following questions: What have we done that has been successful? How have we failed to generate business? How can we target our efforts? What are we willing to do to increase revenue? As a result of their active participation in the assessment process, the team that had resisted change was now unanimous in supporting new initiatives. They all shared their performance weaknesses and potential contributions, created strategies to support each other, targeted new clients, delineated a time line, and affirmed their individual and joint commitment to producing results. Everyone's attitudes changed and there was a burst of creativity that came from working together to solve the problem. With joint strategies that were owned by everyone, the CEO felt less alone, frustrated, angry, and desperate, and everyone's numbers went up.

Designing Participatory Assessment Systems

In most organizations, it is best to begin designing a participatory assessment system by critiquing the old process and completely redesigning it. This may mean interviewing employees, hiring consultants, or conducting focus groups to discover what was wrong or ineffective about the old system, what information was missed using traditional processes, and how the entire system might be redesigned to capture the information that is needed for success and put it to strategic use.

Any performance assessment system that is designed by employees to evaluate themselves will be viewed as fairer and more accurate than one that is designed by managers to evaluate their subordinates. For this reason, *every* employee should be involved in the redesign process, especially those with performance problems. They should agree on a single set of values, principles, and evaluative measures for everyone. This single system can then be customized, input can be elicited from internal and external customers, and the design can be fine-tuned through consensus decision making.

Universal participation allows a wide variety of methods to be used to address the diverse goals of the process. It lets multiple processes with divergent angles of vision and points of focus be used to tackle different problems while leaving ample room for uniqueness and diversity. It permits personal feedback and project evaluation to be separated from performance assessment and allows each of these processes to be kept simple, short, nonbureaucratic, self-managing, and user-friendly.

It is rare that any assessment yields identical results from every participant, so a mechanism is needed to address inconsistent assessments and evaluate commonalities and differences. In participatory assessment, as in 360-degree feedback, areas of contradiction can be thoroughly explored and used as an occasion for dialogue and problem solving. Indeed, the most important outcome of the assessment process may not be a document but a dialogue triggered by discrepancies and agreements between diverse assessors. For example, if an employee receives a high rating in teamwork from her supervisor and a low rating from her peers, a conversation is initiated to find out why and correct the problem.

Participatory assessors take responsibility for discovering and elucidating problems and continuing after the assessment is over to improve the long-term performance of the people they assess. They share what was learned and the commitments that were made, not only with individual performers but with their teams, internal customers, and generically with the organization as a whole. This allows individual learning to feed organizational learning, so that the assessment process can itself be assessed and improved over time.

Six Steps to Participatory Assessment

The following six steps are designed to take an employee from setting initial goals to clarifying competencies and committing to achieve them.

1. The assessed employee identifies applicable standards and goals for personal development, enhanced performance, and improved relationships with colleagues and customers based on a rubric that clearly identifies the skills required at each level of performance. A facilitator or designated assessment coordinator provides feedback and suggests changes, refinements, and additions to these goals that are either accepted, modified, or rejected by the employee. If the employee rejects necessary

changes, the facilitator reorients and adopts a different method, such as courageous listening, paradoxical problem solving, or conflict resolution.

2. The facilitator and the employee agree on the issues to be addressed, the assessment questions, and together request feedback from colleagues based on the 360-degree feedback model described in the next section.

3. The facilitator and the employee then analyze the results from the feedback and agree on the main conclusions. Where discrepancies, contradictions, or unresolved issues emerge, the facilitator and the employee agree on what they will do to explore, understand, and resolve them.

4. The employee identifies personal strengths and weaknesses based on the results. The facilitator provides additional feedback on strengths and weaknesses and makes recommendations, including training programs, coaching, or mentoring to support improvement.

5. The facilitator and the employee agree on what the employee will do to achieve greater competency in each area of assessment, and on what the facilitator will do to make certain that specific, concrete, ongoing support is provided.

6. The facilitator and the employee review what they agreed to do and expressly commit to achieving it. They set timetables and benchmarks and agree to meet periodically to check progress. They agree on what and how to communicate results with team members and internal customers, and give each other feedback on how they performed their roles during this process.

360-Degree Assessments

Every assessment is biased or shaped by the experiences and background of the assessor. For this reason, probably the most effective, equitable, and least distorted method of evaluating employee performance is the 360-degree assessment process depicted in Figure 7.1, in which each relevant experience and level within the organization contributes to the overall assessment. The 360-degree approach thus includes

- *Self-assessment.* All employees honestly assess their own personal performance.

- *Team or peer assessment.* All team members or peers look at how every other member of the team or peer can improve.

- *Vertical assessment.* Supervisors assess those who work under them, and are assessed by those they supervise.

- *Customer or client assessment.* Every organization asks its internal, and sometimes its external, customers or clients to assess what is working and what isn't, and what can be done to improve it.

The true purpose of the 360-degree process is not merely to gather information but to compare and merge diverse inputs based on slightly different angles of perception so that richer, deeper, more complex information emerges from the process. This realization may trigger a deeper conversation, face-to-face dialogue, team intervention, peer coaching, or mediation to solve the problem.

Figure 7.1. 360-Degree Assessment.

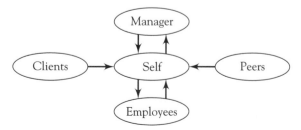

The main goals of the 360-degree assessment process are to

- Capture and communicate the effectiveness of an employee's overall performance as an iterative process.

- Encourage individuals, teams, departments, and programs to learn, experiment, and improve their performance.

- Increase organizational learning, intelligence, and adaptation.

- Encourage cross-organizational dialogue and responsibility for improvement, proactive prevention, and collaborative problem solving.

- Center performance on customer or client needs and expectations.

- Invite people in the organization to see participatory assessment as embedded in organizational values and culture, rather than as add-ons.

- Collect, discuss, and disseminate information in ways that lead to action.

At a substantive level, agreement on the main areas that will be assessed and the steps that will be taken to improve performance in each area are key results of the process. To achieve these results, assessment instruments need to be simplified and the process needs to be brief. For example, here are some generic performance criteria that were developed collaboratively in an organization we advised:

- *Task or technical competence.* Level of skill in performing required work.

- *Adaptability, resourcefulness, and initiative.* Adapting to new challenges, discovering resources, and taking initiative or exercising judgment without waiting for detailed instructions.

- *Responsibility and dependability.* Taking responsibility and following through to make sure the job is done correctly.

- *Relationship building and process skills.* Working collaboratively with others and using team processes to help others work together more effectively.

- *Respect for others and support for diversity.* Respecting and getting along with others and being able to work in a diverse environment.

- *Communication, negotiation, and conflict resolution skills.* Communicating clearly and effectively, negotiating collaboratively, and resolving conflicts among coworkers.

- *Leadership and mentoring skills.* Being a leader and assisting others in becoming leaders themselves.

The value of these criteria, to which others can be added, is that they identify a small, manageable number of skills that focus the participatory assessment process. By tightly targeting particular skills, the process becomes less time consuming and more focused on results. It is ideal if employees, managers, team members, and customers can keep the written portion of the assessment process as brief as possible and expand the amount of time spent in longer, open discussions of results that explore uniformities, discrepancies, and contradictions in the information received.

Discipline and Termination

If turnaround feedback, transformational coaching, strategic mentoring, and participatory assessment are unable to stimulate improvement and an employee's performance remains inadequate, the next step may be to initiate a different kind of assessment process that could result in discipline or termination. Reaching this point, however, usually means that feedback, coaching, mentoring, and assessment were not used correctly, or were not effective for reasons that deserve close examination.

The failure could be due to the use of traditional hierarchical processes that proved futile, or to miscommunications or insufficient participation. It may be that performance goals were set too high, or training was inadequate, or expectations were unclear or poorly communicated. It could mean the employee is in the wrong job, or might not be skilled enough to meet legitimate demands, or has given up and chosen not to improve. It may be that no one was courageous or cared enough to provide the employee with deeply honest turnaround feedback. Perhaps the manager was not skilled in penetrating the employee's defensiveness, or the employee was upset by an unresolved conflict with a coworker that was never mediated, or the manager was too autocratic, or there were unresolved personal issues from home. Failure could stem from a thousand reasons that have nothing whatsoever to do with the employee's innate ability to learn how to perform satisfactorily.

To address these shortcomings, it may be necessary to revert to discipline or termination. The first step in doing so is for the people responsible for imposing discipline to critique *themselves* and ask whether they genuinely did all they could. They should look to see if they communicated effectively, gave the employee the benefit of deeply honest turnaround feedback, and were willing to listen courageously to the employee's problems. Did they supportively confront the employee about specific behavior? Did they precisely define what was not working? Did they use risky methods of conflict resolution to address underlying issues? If the answer is no to any of these inquiries, it is not yet time to initiate discipline.

Unfortunately, managers who impose discipline and discharge rarely communicate deeply, empathetically, and honestly enough with nonperforming employees. This causes them to spend more time, energy, money, and resources getting rid of employees than finding out what went wrong, fixing it, and investing in future learning and development. As a result, employees are almost always shocked that they are being disciplined or fired, even after they have received years of warnings about marginal or substandard performance. In fact, their years of poor performance may have led them to assume that their poor performance could continue, that they had management's implied permission to perform as they always did.

The purpose of supportive confrontation is to finally challenge this assumption. It is common for those in positions of organizational authority to equivocate and pussyfoot around disciplinary issues out of a fear of confrontation or desire to avoid grievance and arbitration. By so doing, they cheat employees out of finally realizing that their behaviors are unacceptable and deciding to either leave or improve.

In the participatory assessment process, employees are directly told by their peers exactly what standards have to be met for them to succeed and the consequences that will occur as a result of falling short. Here are some questions that can be used to test an employee's perceptions regarding organizational standards, and what will happen if they are not met:

- If you were the manager of this organization, what level of performance or behavior would you expect from an employee in your position?

- Do you think the organization has a right to expect employees to meet minimal standards?

- What do you believe those standards are? Do you think they should be any different from what they are?

- Would you like to know in more detail what they are or why they were set?

- What impact do you think the failure to meet these standards will have on the team? On the organization?

- Do you believe you have met those standards?

- How could we test to make sure you have met them?

- What kind of support do you feel you need in order to meet these standards?

- What do you think should happen to any employee who fails to meet these standards?

- If you were a manager, how many warnings would you give an employee who failed to meet these standards prior to termination?

- What do you think is going to happen to you if you continue along this path?

- What would need to be done for any discipline or discharge to feel fair to you?

- What do you want to happen? What are you prepared to do to make sure it does happen?

- Are you sure you really want this job? Do you think you might be in the wrong position?

- If you really want this job, what are you prepared to do to keep it?

- How long should it take for you to meet these standards? What should happen if you don't?

- Would you like some feedback from me on what you have said in response to these questions?

The point of these questions is to wake employees up so they will stop fooling themselves with denials, rationalizations, defenses, judgments, and excuses. The intent is to encourage them to honestly recognize the consequences if they do not admit and correct their problems. It is never necessary to act unfairly or autocratically, or refuse to listen, or be unable to bend, or be afraid to act out of fear of hurting someone's feelings. The point of this process is not to inflict unnecessary pain but to try to jointly solve a problem. In truth, it is no favor to keep employees locked in positions where they cannot succeed. Indeed, we have seen several employees voluntarily resign after being asked these questions, as they realized they were in the wrong job.

Twelve Criteria for Just Cause

Once it has been decided to discipline an employee, it is important to do so based on principles and values that everyone can accept as fair and equitable, with the idea in mind of using the disciplinary process to improve performance. Over time, labor arbitrators have developed a set of criteria for employee discipline that are commonly referred to as *just cause* standards. It is our belief that for the disciplinary process to be considered fair and just, the following twelve criteria should be met:

- The rule or expectation is clear and reasonable.

- The investigation was fair and objective.

- The employee knows or should have known of the rule or expectation.

- The rule or expectation is job-related.

- The evidence of noncompliance is substantial.

- The rule or expectation has been applied to all employees equally without discrimination.

- The employee has been notified of the problem.

- The employee had a reasonable opportunity to correct the problem.

- The employee has been supported in correcting the problem.

- The discipline has been progressive and incremental, moving from oral to written warning and suspension before termination, except for serious infractions.

- The discipline takes into account the employee's entire record.

- The discipline is proportionate to the severity of the problem.

The best outcome of any disciplinary process is for the employee to either correct the problem or recognize the impossibility of the situation and leave voluntarily, with dignity and a positive employment record, rather than suffer the stigma and defeat of termination. To encourage organizational learning, those who make the decision to terminate should interview the employee extensively and seriously investigate all the employee's claims and defenses. They should review why the employee was hired in the first place, examine in detail the reasons feedback was not effective in turning around the behavior, and provide feedback to those whose earlier decisions or feedback were ineffective.

Many employees who are fired for poor performance ought never to have been hired, while others had managers who made it impossible to succeed or were constrained by organizational policies that undermined their commitment—none of which is their fault. Exit interviews allow the organization to identify what went wrong, improve internal processes, and discover what actually happened, even if it is after the fact. Miscommunications, ineffective processes, and dysfunctional relationships can be revealed and addressed independently of anything the employee does or does not choose to do. For real organizational learning to take place, however, none of these mistakes should be attributed to or excused by the actions or character of the employee.

Waking people up and providing them with turnaround feedback, transformational coaching, strategic mentoring, and participatory assessment is based on an assumption: that individual and organizational learning can be enhanced by open and honest communication, collaborative team relationships, and participation in the whole process of improvement. There is no reason why this same assumption cannot be applied to make certain that there is just cause for discipline or termination, and that one last effort be made to wake someone up. To do so effectively, we require not only the processes we have outlined in this part of the book but the techniques described in the next part.

Part III

Techniques
Encouraging Turnaround Experiences

8

Courageous Listening

Now, how to listen? It is harder than you think. . . .
Listening, not talking, is the gifted and great role, and
the imaginative role. And the true listener is much
more beloved, magnetic, than the talker, and she is
more effective, and learns more and does more good.
And so try listening; to those who love you and those
who don't, to those who bore you, to your enemies. It
will work a small miracle. And perhaps a great one.

Brenda Ueland

Waking up means discovering how to be present in all our conversations and relationships. The more awareness we bring, the more we are able to see and hear. Being fully present means listening as though our lives depend on what we are about to hear—and may change dramatically as a result of hearing it. To listen in this way—not only to what we know but to what we do not know—requires tremendous energy, and sometimes great courage. It takes courage to listen without self-delusion or self-denial both to what is and to what might be; to who others are and to who we might become.

Courageous listening concentrates on openings and possibilities; on opportunities for learning, transformation, and transcendence;

on prospects for self-actualization and self-realization; on intellectual curiosity, emotional vulnerability, and opening one's heart. These require courage because real listening takes us deeper and asks us to risk discovering something new—both about others and about ourselves. Courageous listening fuels creativity and synergy. It makes small miracles happen—as writer Brenda Ueland recognized—and perhaps great ones too.

The Sufi poet Rumi wrote, "The tongue has one customer, the ear." When we recognize this fundamental truth, listening becomes simple and also courageous. We begin by listening to what is said *without* words, to who the speaker is, to what the speaker wants or needs or fears or loves but does not feel comfortable talking about. We use empathy to locate the listener's ears and listen with them to what we are about to say.

We bring empathy and commitment to our listening by avoiding constricting judgments and defensiveness, openly and honestly addressing what is not working, and being kind and respectful, simply by the way we listen. We listen compassionately to what lies beneath someone's angry words, locating their pain, caring, and desire for it to be over. We focus our listening on reaching a complete understanding—not merely of what is being said, but who is saying it and why.

The Elements of Communication

Listening is as much a part of communication as speaking. Communication is fundamentally an exchange of information or data, together with a transmission of *meaning* between a speaker and a listener. Communication is often thought of as consisting of an articulate speaker who uses the correct words to convey a clear message through an appropriate medium of expression to a listener who receives the information accurately. In some communication models, the listener completes this circuit by giving the speaker feedback about whether the content of the communication was received. Figure 8.1 shows a

Figure 8.1. Traditional Diagram of Communications.

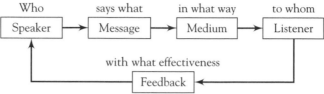

diagram commonly used to identify the indispensable elements that make up any communication.

This model is limited, however, because it does not reveal the critical role context plays in shaping the meaning of what is said and heard. Communication frequently occurs without words, or the words are interpreted as having a different meaning from the one that was intended. A shift occurs in understanding because the context in which the communication took place provides much of its true meaning and subtly shapes what the listener understands. A more accurate communication model needs to display speaking and listening as contained within a larger circle representing the context of the communication, as depicted in Figure 8.2.

Our awareness of context allows us to become more skillful, both in what we say and in what we are able to hear, thereby increasing

Figure 8.2. Communications and Context.

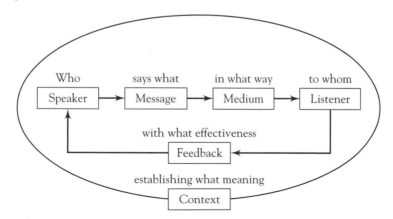

our ability to recognize the deeper, more profound meaning of the communication. A simple "hello," for example, can be delivered as an angry declaration or a seductive invitation—not just by tone of voice and body language, but by context and environment. For example, here are several ways of interpreting the same sentence:

I'm glad to see you.	(Even if no one else is.)
I'm *glad* to see you.	(What made you think I wouldn't be?)
I'm glad to *see* you.	(Instead of just talking to you on the phone.)
I'm glad to see *you*.	(But not the shlubb you came with.)
I'm glad to *see you*.	(It's wonderful to be with you.)
I'm glad to see you.	(So stop asking me if I am.)
I'm . . . glad-to-see-you.	(Are you glad to see me?)
I'm . . . glad . . . to . . . see . . . you.	(I'm drunk or I don't really mean it.)
I'm glad . . . to see you.	(As an afterthought.)
I'm glad-to-see *you*.	(Me Tarzan, you Jane.)

This example is drawn from Rudy Rucker's *Mind Tools*. Clearly, tone of voice, emphasis, and context are critical elements in interpreting the meaning of the communication. Even the most casual workplace communications in giving feedback, coaching, mentoring, and assessment contain elements that are ignored because we have not listened courageously enough. The success of these turnaround processes depends on increased awareness of these deeper layers of meaning.

This means we can improve organizational communications by managing the context in which they take place. When we listen deeply even to ordinary, unexceptional communications, we discover that speakers and listeners come from very different contexts and perspectives and mean entirely different things than might be deduced by adopting a literal interpretation of what they say. In similar ways, organizational structures, systems, cultures, processes, roles, expectations, and relationships all have a defining impact on communications. Of these, perhaps the most powerful is organizational hierarchy.

How Listening Is Distorted by Organizational Hierarchy

All workplace communications take place inside organizations, but what are organizations? Clearly, organizations are made up of people, property, and equipment. But they also consist of communications, processes, and relationships, all of which depend sensitively on listening. As a result, we are led to ask: What kind of communications are likely to improve processes and strengthen collaborative relationships? The answer is communications that are based on shared values and intentions, that identify common problems, and that move toward collaborative solutions. As we wrote in *The End of Management and the Rise of Organizational Democracy*:

> Hierarchies, bureaucracies, and autocracies create unnatural inequalities in power, privilege, and status between managers and employees. These inequalities transform organizational communications into one-way streets that permit management and staff to misconstrue each other's meaning and intent and allow even carefully crafted communications to be chronically miscommunicated. They encourage both sides to ask questions that are closed and pointed as opposed to open and curious, and to ignore answers they do not like. They allow managers to make statements that turn into lectures, requests that feel like demands, questions that seem like

interrogations, promises that are contingent on obedience,
and offers of support that are hollow or meaningless.

Inside hierarchies, any communications that are directed from
the top to the bottom will be subtly altered each time they are
transmitted, requiring them to be drastically simplified in order to
arrive without distortion. As a result, those at the bottom will be
forced to guess about their real meaning and substitute rumors and
gossip for genuine information. There will be too many communications trying to get from the bottom of the organization to the top
and only a few will finally make it—and these will have to be combined and simplified to the point of being practically useless.

As a result, the top will predictably be out of touch with the bottom and make critical decisions based on inaccurate data, causing
those at the bottom to question the judgment of those at the top.
While most communications regarding problems emanate from the
bottom, most decisions regarding how to solve them emanate from
the top. This separation results in those at the top making incor-
rect, costly, and untimely decisions, and those at the bottom feeling disempowered, distrusted, and disrespected.

In hierarchies, communications are unevenly distributed throughout the organization. Any manager can alter the meaning of a communication on its way up or down the hierarchy by blocking or
delaying it, treating it as more or less important, or subtly distorting its
meaning. In hierarchical environments, vertical departments are often
in competition with one another over resources. Managers become
increasingly competitive as they apply for promotion into fewer and
fewer positions. As this dynamic unfolds, there is a likelihood of distortion and a compelling motive to mold communications to gain
personal or departmental advantage. This encourages rumors and
miscommunications to spread and common purposes to be forgotten.

Each distinct department and managerial level will predictably
reinterpret, or *refract* incoming messages to match their own expectations, perceptions, histories, and desires. If a message from below

is critical of a department or its manager, it is more likely to be blocked or edited than if its content is favorable. In this way, there will be a bias toward passing on good news regarding colleagues and bad news regarding competitors.

Each of these miscommunications will predictably result in small-scale personal animosities, cross-departmental hostilities, feelings of rejection and disapproval, resistance to change, distrust, unresolved conflict, loss of morale, and other destructive outcomes that continue far into the future. On a large scale, they lead to paralysis and dysfunctions so severe they can cause entire organizations to fail.

The Elements of Communication

There is only one way to measure the effectiveness of any communication: did the listener understand what the speaker intended to communicate? If the answer is no, the communication was ineffective, and the speaker needs to consider what might be done to make it more effective. Turnaround processes such as feedback, coaching, mentoring, and assessment stand or fall on what listeners actually understand. This depends partly on the degree of awareness and attention the speaker gives—not only to the words but to the invisible elements that influence the listeners' interpretation of the communication. These elements include

- *Literal meaning.* Apart from context, what is the content or meaning of what is being communicated?

- *Environment.* What are the surroundings, the environment, history, structure, and system within which the communication takes place?

- *Process.* How is the message communicated? What is the tone? What is the energy level? What is the content of the method and medium being used?

- *Relationship*. What is the relationship between the speaker and the listener? What is their past history? What do they expect from each other in the future?

- *Understanding*. How much of what is being communicated does the listener actually understand?

- *Intention*. What effect on the listener is intended by the speaker? How much of what the speaker intends is actually understood by the listener?

- *Emotional effect*. What is the emotional effect of the communication on the listener, regardless of what was intended?

- *Acceptance*. Which parts of the communication are acceptable to the listener and which are not?

- *Awareness*. What level of awareness of the meaning and intention of the speaker is present in the listener?

- *Congruence*. Are these elements congruent with one another, or do they broadcast mixed messages?

To successfully receive or deliver turnaround feedback, transformational coaching, strategic mentoring, or participatory assessment, both parties need to monitor and understand the context in which their communications take place. For example, if a person receiving feedback is unclear or unaware of the intent of the speaker, or unable to work through the emotional impact of the communication, or perceives a lack of congruence with earlier communications, it will be difficult to hear what is being said.

On the other hand, if the context is one in which the employee *wants* to improve, there is a greater chance of recognizing that the performance or behavior is less effective than it could be. If the employee's coworkers create a context of empathy and affection, they can provide transformational coaching and discuss the actions or comments that are upsetting them. They can then be open and honest about the problems they want to address without triggering a defensive response.

One way to counter these possibilities is to listen for what doesn't fit, to pay attention not only to what the problem is but to why it hasn't been corrected. The most subtle information lies beneath the surface of the communication. The deeper the listening, the greater the courage required to hear it.

Listening as a Human Being

Most people are considered successful at work if they get things done and produce results. Yet our success directly depends on our ability to listen and learn. Someone can be highly competent in getting things done, but if they are unable to listen they will ultimately do the wrong thing.

As playwright George Bernard Shaw wrote, "The biggest problem with communication is the illusion that it has been accomplished." At work, the quality of listening differs based on our roles and relationships to others. We listen differently to superiors and subordinates, customers, and peers. When we listen to our children, we do so as parents rather than as peers. We (hopefully) listen to our spouses and significant others as committed partners, but we may also listen to them as unforgiving judges, self-denying rescuers, starved romantics, exacting slave-masters, or lonely, frightened children.

The illusion Shaw described is accentuated when we listen or speak within a role and allow the role to define us. When we listen within a role we are able to hear what is said, which is physiological, but we often miss what is *meant*, which is psychological. In the former, we understand the surface content of the statement and go through the motions of acknowledging it, but are so focused on performing our role that we miss the hidden issues, underlying emotions, nuances, and deeper meaning of the communication. We are unable to put ourselves in the speakers' shoes and cannot hear what they are saying from their point of view, or with their interests foremost in our minds.

When we listen within a role, we focus on finding the kind of information that will allow us to perform our designated functions. As parents, we listen for indications of safety or proper behavior rather than to childlike feelings, desires, and meanings we have forgotten how to understand. As managers, we listen for facts, which are often oriented to making sure nothing goes wrong so we won't appear incompetent in the eyes of upper management. As feedback providers, coaches, mentors, and assessors, we listen for ways of correcting an employee's behaviors and actions rather than understanding them. Whatever our role, we need to listen for feelings and the underlying meaning of what is being said if we want to understand the deeper truth of the communication. When we listen for facts without paying attention to emotions and meaning we hear less than half the story. What do you listen for? Here are a few possibilities:

- Interpretations
- Roles
- Intentions
- Interests and positions
- Dreams and visions
- Fears
- Humiliations
- Defensiveness
- Denial
- Metaphors
- Universality
- Cries for help
- Openings to dialogue or negotiation
- Requests for acknowledgment

- Expectations
- Modes of perception
- Emotions and feelings
- Wishes, passions, and desires
- Family patterns
- Stereotypes of others
- Self-esteem
- Resistance
- Prejudices
- Apologies
- Uniqueness
- Expressions of guilt
- Desire for forgiveness or reconciliation
- Need for support

In delivering feedback, coaching, mentoring, and assessment, there is a danger in listening for, or with the goal of finding, solutions and fixing things. In courageous listening, we listen with the goal of improving our ability to listen without having any goals. This means staying with the person and the problem and trying to learn more about both before rushing off to find solutions. Listening to the problem and allowing the person to describe it fully allows them to learn from it themselves and discover their own solutions. When we are unable to resist the tendency to solve other people's problems, we rob them of the opportunity to learn, invent, and own their solutions.

Fundamentally, no one wants to be listened to by someone in a role. Everyone wants to be listened to by a human being. The human qualities of openness and curiosity, empathy and compassion, reflection and feedback are all that are required for communications to succeed. Listening as a human being is not being passive, inert, or inactive, but active, empathetic, and responsive. It is a *relationship*—not only with the speaker but with ourselves and our own future possibilities.

Active, Empathetic, and Responsive Listening

Few managers or employees have been trained in the art of listening, or exhibit high levels of skill at gathering information outside their roles. Here are some methods people at work can use to encourage active, empathic, and responsive listening. Many will seem obvious and well known, yet they are infrequently practiced. We share them as reminders of how we can all improve our skills and become better listeners:

- *Encouraging.* Pose encouraging questions and comments to support someone in sharing their feelings, perceptions, and attitudes: "Please tell me more." "I'm interested in what you are thinking and feeling." "I would like to know how you feel." "I hear what you are saying."

- *Soliciting.* Ask soliciting questions to identify possible solutions: "I would like your advice about how we can resolve this." "Can you tell me what you think should be done?" "What do you mean by that?" (Followed by "Why?") "Tell me more about what you want." "What would you like to see happen?"

- *Clarifying.* As the discussion unfolds, ask questions that clarify the points being made and send a signal that you are interested in the speaker and what is being said. Communicate that you would like more information. Ask questions that elicit greater detail and meaning: "When did this happen?" "Who else was involved?" "What did it mean to you?"

- *Normalizing.* As feelings are expressed or opinions are offered, communicate that it is natural and normal to have these feelings, and allow people to feel accepted while expressing difficult emotions or critical thoughts: "Many people feel the way you do. . . ."

- *Acknowledging.* Invite continued openness by acknowledging ideas and feelings as they are being expressed, thereby giving permission for greater depth of communication: "I can see you are feeling really angry right now." "I can appreciate why you feel that way."

- *Empathizing.* Put yourself in the other person's shoes by trying on the perceptions and feelings the other person is expressing. Look into your own experience and find a time when you might have had a similar reaction, and refer to something similar in your own life: "I can appreciate why you feel that way." "I have felt something similar and I understand." But be careful not to say, "I know exactly how you feel." You don't.

- *Mirroring.* Mirroring reflects back the emotions, affect, demeanor, body language, tone of voice, and metaphors used by the speaker. Its purpose is to encourage the feeling that the speaker has a companion in emotion, rather than an objective listener. If the speaker takes a defensive posture, take one yourself, then move to an open one. If the speaker talks about feeling "trapped," ask "What would open the door to a solution?"

- *Reframing.* Reframing translates "you" statements into "I" statements and identifies reasons for your disagreement so the problem can be solved. Instead of saying, "You are a gossip," try saying, "I felt betrayed when you told Sally what I asked you to keep private, because it made me look like I don't like her." Reframing preserves or strengthens the emotional meaning of the statement while altering its form from an accusation or insult to a confession or request. It shifts the focus from what you did to what I experienced to disarm defensiveness and solve the problem. A template would be to say "So you felt [fill in] when I [fill in] because [fill in]. Is that right?" For example, "It seems to make you angry when I criticize your performance at team meetings because you would rather I discuss it privately with you first. Is that right?"

- *Summarizing.* If you want to let someone know they have been heard, summarize what was said in your own words: "Let me see if I understand what you just said. . . . Is that correct?" This form of feedback allows them to confirm or change their communication. It also lets them know you are interested in what they are saying and have grasped the essentials of the communication. Summarizing at the end lets you see whether

you both have the same perception of what was said
and decided.

- *Validating.* It is important to validate specific things the
  other person said or did, or something you learned, or
  something they contributed to the conversation: "I
  appreciate your willingness to be here." "I learned a
  great deal from what you said." "I know it took a lot for
  you to be as open as you were and I want to acknowledge you for taking that risk."

Though these sound like excellent phrases to use, we often forget to use them, especially when we are frustrated, angry, frightened, ashamed, or sad. Yet even if we are upset we can slow down,
avoid deliberately insulting behavior, allow ourselves to become
curious about why the other person is acting this way, and consider
what is taking place below the surface of what they are saying or
doing. We can ask ourselves what would make us speak and act this
way and respond from a place of caring rather than out of anger,
fear, shame, or apathy.

Listening for What We Do Not Know

Human beings are pattern-seeking creatures. When we receive ten
items of information, we are apt to notice only items one, five, and
ten and ignore the rest as unimportant or irrelevant—mostly
because these three fit into a pattern we recognize and accept, while
the others fall outside that pattern or contradict it. This tendency
allows us to reinforce previous learning, but it also keeps us from
recognizing patterns that are new or contradict those we have
already learned.

Listening is only as good as the information it allows us to hear.
When we listen for what we already know, we miss the turnaround
possibilities, the openings for transformational learning and tran-

scendence, the opportunities for waking up. Courage is required to seize these opportunities, to listen for what we do not know, for what is not spoken, for what doesn't fit, for what is odd or aberrant, and especially for what we do not want to hear.

How do we learn to listen for what we don't know, or doesn't fit, or we don't want to hear? To start with, we recognize that it is *exactly* these communications that have the ability to wake us up, set us free, allow us to learn something new, and release us from patterned thinking. Trivial, ordinary, acceptable conversations do not change us. We can listen forever to what we already know and accept, but it is the creative energy of what we resist, reject, refuse, and rebel against that opens us up and allows us to be and do something new.

Perhaps the most difficult pattern to overcome is the one created by the listeners' intentions regarding the people identified as having caused the problem we are trying to overcome. If you are a manager or a subordinate, a coach or mentor, a lover or ex-lover, a friend or enemy, a new or old acquaintance, the quality of your listening shifts as a result of your relationship, conforming to the pattern of your preconceived roles and intentions.

For example, we worked with an information systems organization in a large government agency that had proposed restructuring their reporting system and creating a new technology architecture for all departments. The chief information officer traveled to local branches throughout the United States, simply listening to employees talk about their ideas and attitudes about the change. Later, he held a two-day briefing on the plan for all employees that allowed him to answer their questions and respond to their concerns in an informal give-and-take atmosphere.

He discovered on his cross-country trip that important information about the changes had not been passed along by middle managers. Instead, it had been finessed, reinterpreted, misconstrued, and predigested, then given to employees to blindly accept. These miscommunications led to rumors, gossip, and resistance that threatened the new system's success. After listening carefully, he decided to give every employee a chance to hear firsthand about his intentions and plans without having the facts filtered and translated by their managers, and to ask difficult, painful questions about the decisions that had been made. The atmosphere he created was honest, open, and electric. Afterward, the change process continued to be bumpy and rocky in places, but it was embraced and implemented with enthusiasm because his communications had been completely open and honest, his listening had been active, empathetic, and responsive, and his direct responses to their questions had allowed the guesswork and speculation to be taken out of the process. In the end, he had been able to communicate directly with employees whose cooperation was essential for the change to succeed.

The Need for Self-Honesty

Herman Melville wrote: "Let us speak, though we show all our faults and weaknesses—for it is a sign of strength to be weak, to know it, and out with it." We are all reluctant, particularly at work or in public, to canvass our lives in detail, exposing our faults and weaknesses for everyone to see. Yet as Melville recognized, acknowledging our weaknesses makes us stronger because it leaves us with nothing to hide, while keeping our faults secret makes us reserved, wary, and false, and forces us to manipulate people into thinking we are someone we are not.

Hiding our faults also makes it more difficult to correct them using the turnaround processes surveyed in previous chapters. It is difficult to use transformational coaching or strategic mentoring or ask for turnaround feedback or participatory assessment if we cannot describe in detail what needs to improve. The chances are good that others see our faults in spite of our rigorous efforts to hide them, yet they feel unable or unwilling to discuss them openly because doing so would require them to be rude or acknowledge their own faults and weaknesses.

Organizations can end this dishonesty by creating cultures that reward courageous listening and encourage employees to speak more openly and transparently with each other about issues related to their personal and human development. They can create a context of values, ethics, and integrity in which people are supported in waking up and turning their lives around. Leaders can champion "courageous listening," by applying Melville's insight to themselves and openly acknowledging their weaknesses and mistakes. They can invite turnaround feedback and ask others to do the same.

Ask Courageous Questions

The best conversations are those that begin with a courageous question. Whether you are a leader, team member, coach, mentor, or assessor, waking people up starts with taking a risk and asking difficult, courageous questions and listening with equal courage to the answers. Here are some questions you can ask that may lead people to think more deeply about what they need to do to turn their work lives around, what holds them back, and how their roles may prevent them from being authentic:

- What is the crossroads you are standing on at this moment in your work life?

- What is preventing you from moving forward?

- What are the main challenges or problems you are experiencing at work? When was the first time you experienced that kind of challenge or problem?

- What are some things you have done that either contributed to or sustained the problems you are experiencing? Why did you do them? What are you afraid will happen if you stop doing them? Why is that unacceptable to you?

- What are some things you have *not* done that have contributed to or sustained these problems? Why did you not do them? What are you afraid will change if you do? Why is that unacceptable to you?

- What do you see as your main strengths and weaknesses? Where did you get the idea that those are your strengths and weaknesses? Did the person who gave you this idea have a reason for doing so? What was it?

- Do your strengths reveal weaknesses and your weaknesses strengths? How?

- How could you use your strengths and your weaknesses to solve your problems?

- What role are you currently playing at work? Who are you when you are not playing it? Which one is more authentically you?

- How would you respond differently if you were not playing that role?

- How might changing your role, attitude, behavior, or response change others? What would they do if you adopted a different attitude or redefined the role you are currently playing?

- What do you feel when you speak authentically, from your heart? How is that different from how you feel when you speak from a role? Which are you when no one is watching? Which do you prefer?

Attitude and Listening

You will be more effective in asking these questions if you adopt an attitude of curiosity rather than prying, of collaboration rather than manipulation. Fundamentally, prying and manipulation are exercises of ego that are based on a concern only for ourselves, while collaboration is relational and concerned with strengthening our partnership with others. While egoistic and relational forms of communication often appear similar, they are complementary opposites that produce widely differing effects. There are subtle differences, for example, between feedback and judgment, love and attachment, compassion and pity that are often confusing. Yet the first words are relational and interactive, while the second are oriented only to ego and self.

Of these, the relational forms are more balanced, stable, and satisfying than the ego forms, for both the speaker and the listener. Waking up means moving from egocentric concerns to genuine relationships with others. As we become more aware and authentic, we also become more available—both to ourselves and to others. We can find our differences fascinating as opposed to threatening, and learn from them. When we let go of ego approaches that cause us to see others only as extensions of ourselves, we are able to create more authentic, open relationships.

Listening, above all, is a relationship with someone that takes us *out* of ourselves, and thereby also takes us deeper *into* ourselves. Listening is waking up to the presence of an equal and recognizing that their ideas, emotions, and experiences are both similar to and intriguingly different from our own. When we are awake, we listen in a courageous way, become curious about who the other person is, and collaboratively negotiate how the space between us will be used.

Ken Dvoren, a social worker with the Department of Children and Family Services in Los Angeles County, whom we trained in mediation, wrote the following poignant explanation of the reasons real listening requires courage:

> When I'm conversing with someone, I find myself wanting to be listened *to* more than I want to listen. The person I'm talking with appears to want the same thing,

and so a subtle competition ensues. When I decide to listen to the other with interest and empathy, I move beyond myself and notice that rather than feeling neglected or diminished, I'm actually expanded. My identity, who I sense myself to be, now includes them, so that as I give to them, I am also receiving.

When I'm in conflict with someone, the stakes are even higher. I not only want to be heard but also to be agreed with and to be *right*. And it's even harder to listen to the other, because if I do I might understand them, and if I understand them I might agree with them, and if I agree with them I might think I have to give them what they want, and if I do then I won't get what *I* want. But if I take what feels to be the very real risk of truly listening, a remarkable event occurs. As my identity expands to include them, I start to appreciate their values and interests, and when I consider meeting their needs, I realize I will also be meeting my own. I have finally met my brother.

Listening and the Creation of Community

Courageous listening automatically creates common ground, a sense of community, and a feeling of collaboration and teamwork in solving problems. In teams, listeners participate in the creation of shared meaning regarding problems, which initiates a process of correcting them. *Committed* listening means being willing to act on the basis of what we hear. *Team* listening means being willing to act collaboratively in the interest of the group as a whole.

Teams can be defined by the quality of the communications that take place among their members. We interviewed several dozen team members about the importance of listening and communication. Here are some of their comments:

"First comes honest and open communication and the ability to resolve conflicts and be responsible for our work and redefine our process. It's not enough to come and do your job the old way any more."

"Learning to make decisions by consensus. We aren't born this way. We all want to shine and do things by ourselves, and we have to learn to listen and communicate to reach consensus."

"We have to work together, to share information, and not be intimidated, to open up to say what we think and feel. That's communication."

"We need to have good communication, to let our guard down and be totally honest and candid. We need to be advocates of what we believe in and totally honest about where we are coming from. We should be able to compromise and not be an island or a one-man band."

"On teams we give everyone a chance to speak and we listen and don't take it personally. We've had heated arguments and after having a conversation, everything is fine."

"As team members we are free to say things we disagree with and give positive feedback and receive criticism and feedback even though it can be a shock."

In the absence of equality, listening becomes distorted, and whatever relationships we establish become based not on consensus but on fear. Without equality, it is possible for those who are stronger to use their power over and against those who are weaker. For this reason, hierarchical organizations necessarily and inevitably distort listening. They make conflict chronic and unfixable, simply because the egalitarian relational qualities required for collaboration and teamwork are missing. Genuinely democratic organizations that are based on equality, on the other hand, generate feelings of community and environments that encourage respect, partnership, and curiosity about diversity, which, in turn, invites courageous listening.

Courageous listening is a form of shared responsibility. As such, it requires and encourages empowerment and ownership of results. It is an acknowledgment of equality and tangible evidence of respect and caring. Indeed, the highest form of listening is one in which we care enough to discover what is not working in someone else's life, and in exchange for their willingness to do the same for us, communicate our open, honest, caring, humble, respectful assessment of how they might become even better at doing what they want to do, and being more authentically who they already are.

9

Paradoxical Problem Solving

*The greatest and most important problems of life are
all in a certain sense insoluble. They must be so
because they express the necessary polarity inherent
in every self-regulating system. They can never be
solved, but only outgrown. . . . This "outgrowing"
. . . on further experience was seen to consist in a
new level of consciousness. Some higher or wider
interest arose on the person's horizon, and through
this widening of his view the insoluble problem lost its
urgency. It was not solved logically in its own terms,
but faded out when confronted with a new and
stronger life-tendency. It was not repressed and made
unconscious, but merely appeared in a different light,
and so, did indeed become different. What on a lower
level, had led to the wildest conflicts and to panicky
outbursts of emotion, viewed from the higher level of
personality, now seemed like a storm in the valley
seen from a high mountain-top. This does not rob the
thunderstorm of its reality, but instead of being in it,
one is now above it.*

Carl Jung

175

Part of what makes problems insoluble is our continued effort to think about and try to solve them using the same attitudes, assumptions, and problem-solving approaches that created them in the first place. Indeed, it is only through a transformation produced by an evolution in the nature of the problem, an innovation in problem solving techniques, or a transcendence in the mind of the problem solver that real solutions start to emerge. To solve problems in the workplace, we are therefore led to consider not only the nature of problems in general but why we get stuck, why we want to solve them, how to improve the techniques we use to identify solutions, and how to transcend and think about them in new ways.

Our deepest difficulty, however, lies in the way we approach and think about our problems. We commonly think of problems as requiring a solution, yet many of our problems are paradoxical and contain not one but multiple correct solutions, each of which defines an alternative future. Every problem therefore suggests a fresh possibility, a different direction, and a potential for learning and transcendence. Our fear of these new possibilities triggers resistance and stimulates an effort to reinforce the status quo by solving the problem in habitual ways. Each problem therefore defines a crossroads, a choice point, an instability that can be used to promote change, and an inertia that can prevent it from taking place.

For this reason, an important element in waking up consists of recognizing the paradoxical nature of our problems, finding better ways of solving them, and learning to transcend them by discovering their deeper meanings. By embracing paradox, we do not so much solve as move beyond our problems. In this way, we are able to attain the "new level of consciousness" and "outgrowing" to which Jung referred.

Learning to Love Our Problems

Every day in our personal and professional lives, we encounter a seemingly endless stream of problems. There are problems so petty we hardly take notice of them, problems so huge we can't begin to comprehend them, and problems that take us to the very edge of our skills, wake us up, and transform our thinking. In fact, all of work can be seen not just as the creation of products and services but as the solving of an endless succession of higher- and lower-order problems.

Problem solving, in this sense, consists of using human skills and intelligence to generate something new, something that did not exist before, something that existed only as a problem rather than as a new direction. Awareness, learning, growth, and change are all by-products of recognizing, exploring, wrestling with, and resolving problems. The most challenging aspect of the problems we face is not finding solutions for them, which in most cases we do relatively easily, but maximizing our opportunities to learn from and transcend them.

Learning from problems requires delicacy and fortitude, flexibility and perseverance, observation and commitment, artistry and scientific methodology. These qualities, in conscious, synergistic combination, arguably make problem solving the most subtle, precarious, and important skill of all. But to maximize these opportunities, we need to learn how to break the compulsion of solving problems and allow some problems simply to exist, frequently as paradoxes, riddles, contradictions, and enigmas.

When we do so, we overcome a major obstacle to problem solving, which is our tendency to see problems as negative, or as failures, rather than as opportunities for learning and improvement. In the process, we are able to take an additional step and learn to *love* our problems as sources of insight and growth. In this way, we increase our ability to solve them paradoxically—and thereby solving the first riddle of problem solving.

Breaking the Compulsion to Solve Problems

It is quite seductive to show others how to solve their problems or prescribe solutions they have to implement. It is easy to jump at the first answer, the quickest way out, the solution that costs the least. The more difficult, paradoxical approach is to resist this compulsion and learn to *live* with the problem, to analyze it in depth and consider it from all angles. Not only will the problem become clearer, the solution will be more elegant, multidimensional, and longer-lasting—and something more important may be learned in the process.

Turnaround feedback, coaching, mentoring, and assessment provide multiple opportunities for learning how to acknowledge, embrace, even love our problems and thereby avoid the natural managerial tendency to solve them, even when they belong to someone else. Growing up consists of learning to solve our problems ourselves and not relying on parents or managers to solve them for us.

A first principle of this approach is that people have a *right* to their problems. By stepping in and solving them, we cheat them out of owning important parts of their lives, of learning from their experiences, and of discovering that they are fully capable of finding solutions themselves. We are drawn to solve other people's problems, partly because it makes us feel powerful and helpful, partly because it is easier to solve their problems than our own, and partly because we do not have to live with the consequences.

We contribute far more to solving problems by stepping back for a moment and reflecting first not only on how but whether, why, and who should solve them. If you want to break this compulsion and recognize that problem solving is a choice rather than a necessity, here are five sets of questions to consider:

- You have solved thousands of problems and learned a great deal in your life. How open are you to the possibility that what you have learned is now irrelevant or wrong? How do you manage to stay in touch with your ignorance? How good are you at *un*learning? How able are you to live in the present without focusing on past problems or future solutions?

- You have learned countless ways to solve problems. Have you also learned how to *not* solve them? How willing are you to live with paradox, riddle, polarity, and enigma? Do you understand that by solving your problems too quickly, you could cheat yourself out of learning from them?

- You know how to make things happen. Do you know how to let them happen naturally and fluidly on their own? Do you know how to not intervene? Can you let things happen to you, or simply watch them as they happen? Are you addicted to controlling the outcome or the process?

- You understand a great deal about what is. Do you also understand what is *not*, and what could be? Do you see not only what but *who* is in front of you? Do you understand that what you understand includes the nature of your own understanding?

- You have developed a number of strengths and achieved successes. Do you recognize that for every strength, there is a corresponding weakness? Do you understand that continued success leads to complacency, while failure leads to learning and change? Are you certain which is the success and which the failure?

We all have the ability to check our reflexive habits periodically, resist the narcotic of problem solving, and put a brake on our tendency to help others. This allows us to avoid solving the wrong problem, or doing so in ways that eliminate or reduce opportunities for learning, growth, and change. As a member of Alcoholics Anonymous once told us, "If one more person had tried to solve my problems, I would have killed myself." Most employees appreciate receiving coaching, mentoring, leadership, listening and support in solving their problems, but dislike being micromanaged or having their problems solved for them.

It is tempting for providers of feedback, mentoring, coaching, and assessment to think they know how to solve other people's problems. Yet everyone solves problems differently and a solution for one person may not work for another. The universe offers an *infinite* number of paths to reach the other side of the room, and no two people will follow exactly the same path. The real danger lies in thinking we know the one correct answer and deciding to enlarge our egos at the cost of reduced skills in the person who has to live with the results.

By *not* offering quick solutions, we encourage others to discover their own. This does not mean abdicating or abandoning them. On the contrary, if we can provide just enough useful ideas, information, perspective, feedback, and support, we can encourage and assist them in finding solutions without solving the problem for them. The art of waking people up lies in knowing when to offer ideas and when to withhold them, how to support someone in grappling with difficult issues without taking charge, and how to help employees find their own unique way through the maze, transcend their problems, and feel they did it themselves.

Appreciating Paradox

Often, problems are expressions of underlying paradoxes, riddles, enigmas, contradictions, and polarities that, if understood, can lead to more profound and powerful solutions. Paradoxes and polarities are a part of nature. It is impossible to solve the problem, for example, of up versus down, light versus dark, or plus versus minus without at the same time abolishing both. The same can be said of life and death, pleasure and pain, good and evil, right and wrong, success and failure—and, of course, problems and solutions. It is impossible to eliminate one without eliminating the other. In today's workplace, problems are increasingly complex and paradoxical, yet the ways we solve them remain simple and one-sided. Everyone lives with paradoxes every day. By not oversimplifying the natural complexity of the problems we face but mining them for information about novel ways of improving the quality of solutions, we turn problems into sources of learning. Paradox means living simultaneously with two apparently contradictory realities, which is critical for people working in complex, team-based environments and for learning organizations.

Paradox, ambiguity, and enigma can be savored and plumbed for the rich array of alternatives they reveal without requiring a solution. There may come a time to select a solution and act, but before reaching closure, the complexity and paradox that actually exists in the problem should be completely explored. This requires us to hold two opposing thoughts at the same time. Ambiguity, paradox, and enigma do not reflect a lack of clarity about the problem, they express its deepest hidden, ubiquitous, dualistic truth. Umberto Eco described this idea well in *Foucault's Pendulum:* "[In the beginning] I believed that the source of enigma was stupidity. Then . . . I decided that the most terrible enigmas are those that mask themselves as madness. But now I have come to believe that the whole world is an enigma, a harmless enigma that is made terrible by our own mad attempt to interpret it as though it had a single underlying truth."

Finding a single solution for a multifaceted problem; or a fixed solution for a problem that is evolving; or a simple solution for a complex, compound, paradoxical problem often ends in making the problem worse and causing us to disrespect, dislike, and disempower our problems.

By respecting, loving, empowering, and learning to play with our problems and not trying to simplify their natural complexity, we are able to mine them for information and discover novel solutions. For example, a human resources organization with which we consulted many years ago sought to restructure its services. They had organized themselves into teams by specialization, including employee compensation and benefits, performance assessment and evaluation, training and development, and legal. The restructuring was motivated by negative feedback and complaints from internal customers who claimed they did not know where to go for consultation and had to seek resources from too many people to solve seemingly simple problems.

The human resources staff were confused themselves. Members of different teams who served the same client did not know who should tell what to whom, and often gave contradictory advice. They conducted a department-wide problem-solving process, analyzed the issues, and identified two ways they might restructure themselves. They could either remain in specialized areas of expertise and provide technical assistance to internal clients on demand, or organize as generalists assigned to individual clients and provide services on a decentralized, customer-oriented basis.

Instead of selecting one approach, they lived with both, debated them for months, and resisted making a choice for one or the other. Months later, in a planning session with their most important internal customers, a paradoxical solution emerged. The customers asked if human resources could live with both roles and structures and integrate them. This meant they would have to function as generalists with the customer to whom they were assigned, and specialists in solving particular problems when their expertise was requested by a colleague working with other customers.

The human services teams reorganized as customer-oriented generalists, with each specialist having a dotted-line relationship to colleagues with similar expertise. Through a paradoxical problem-solving process they created a new structure that has become a successful model in their profession. Turnaround feedback exposed these problems, while adopting a paradoxical approach to problem solving revealed a way of operating in a far more complex, nuanced, and multidimensional way.

Obstacles to Problem Solving

In addition to the compulsion of problem solving, there are other paradoxical, subtle, and challenging obstacles confronting those who want to assist others in waking up and solving their problems. Among these, the most counterproductive are seeing problems as negative, becom-

ing addicted to the problem or the solution, identifying the wrong problem, solving the problem unilaterally, and failing to learn from the problem. The sections that follow describe these obstacles in greater detail,
together with our reflections and strategies for overcoming them.

Seeing Problems as Negative

Most of us think of problems as unpleasant and experience intense
anxiety when we confront them. This reaction causes us to procrastinate, then solve them quickly and try to make them go away.
But when we adopt a positive attitude toward problems, we open
possibilities for resolution through imagination and creativity. Seeing problems as adventures frees us from seeing them as threats. As
the following account by reporter Michael Maccoby indicates, problems are merely opportunities for improvement:

> When I visited the Toyota assembly plant at Nagoya
> [Japan], I was told that there were an average of 47 ideas
> per worker per year of which 80 percent were adopted. I
> couldn't believe it; this meant almost an idea from each
> worker every week. The Toyota manager said, "I think
> you in the West have a different view of ideas. What you
> call complaints, we call ideas. You try to get people to
> stop complaining. We see each complaint as an oppor-
> tunity for improvement."

If we can see complaints, difficulties, glitches, and mishaps as
opportunities for improvement, gateways to the discovery of new ideas,
adventures, and sources of breakthrough in achieving better results,
we will embrace our problems and no longer see them as negative.

Becoming Addicted to the Problem or the Solution

There are times when we need our problems more than we need
their solutions, when their solutions are too close for us to recognize, or we want them too badly. Often, we know intuitively that

resolution will result in change, learning, and transformation, and tend to prefer the problems we know to the ones we don't. The possibility that we could create a better outcome can seem too wonderful to accept, or the specter of worse possibilities can cause us to get stuck in a rut with no idea of how to escape.

Yet, in each of these cases, the solution is already contained in the problem. Through introspection and analysis we can get closer to the source of our addiction by identifying what we think will happen if the problem is solved or not solved, and trying to solve that problem first. Through honest feedback, teamwork, and dialogue we can create enough personal distance from the problem to see it as though from above, understand the results of solving it more clearly, and use collaboration to reveal solutions that cannot be discovered by working alone.

Identifying the Wrong Problem

Sometimes we cannot solve our problems simply because we have identified the wrong problem, or defined it in ways that are vague or competing. What appears to be a single problem may actually be multiple problems tangled together, or involve unseen issues, with superficial problems hiding deeper problems beneath their surface. Often the real problem is that our goals are unclear or conflicting, or we are unable to communicate clearly about what is bothering us. Often we are afraid to rock the boat, or haven't considered all the options. Sometimes we are unsure how to evaluate our success, or lack the motivation to follow through and implement our choices. In these situations, our inability to solve the problem merely reflects the fact that there is another problem we have to solve first.

Solving the Problem Unilaterally

Problem solving should not be a lonely or solitary endeavor, but is most effective and enjoyable and works best when it is inclusive, participatory, and collaborative. Inviting others to join us in solving the problem enriches the solution pool. Being handed solutions to problems we have not participated in defining creates resistance, resentment, cynicism, and apathy, while searching for solutions together builds responsibility, improves the quality of solutions, and increases the opportunities for synergy and successful implementation.

Failing to Learn from the Problem

It is extremely difficult in organizations to overcome culturally ingrained, counterproductive methods of problem solving. Creating a learning-oriented culture means redefining problems as sources of growth, development, partnership, and self-esteem. Learning-oriented cultures are problem-friendly, as opposed to control-oriented cultures that regard problems as failures, or enemies to be annihilated. All turnaround feedback, coaching, mentoring, and assessment programs are based on the fundamental idea that problems are opportunities for skill building, personal growth, and organizational learning.

Empowering Curiosity and Imagination

The most important strategy in learning to love our problems is recognizing that every problem is not only an opportunity for learning and improvement but an object of curiosity, imagination, and play. When we adopt this attitude, we can let go of the problem and simply play with it, allowing our unconscious mind to search unaided for solutions. In a study at the University of California at Berkeley, several scientists who made breakthrough discoveries revealed that the solutions to their problems occurred when they were relaxed or at play or focused on something else. John Cleese wrote in response to these findings: "It's self-evident that if we can't take the risk of saying or doing something wrong, our creativity goes right out the window. . . . The essence of creativity is not the possession of some special talent, it is much more the ability to play."

If we view problems as objects of curiosity, imagination, and play, we do not hide from or deny their existence but actually *reward* people for finding them. When John Scully was selected as CEO of Apple Computer, he observed that there should be a premium on finding problems: "Defensiveness is the bane of all passion-filled creative work. We keep defenses down in several ways. One way is by thinking about problems differently—not as negatives, for example. We are thinking of giving people medals for problem finding, not just problem solving. Our world moves so fast that new problems are being created all the time. The people who find them have tremendous powers of creative observation."

Problems are the first sign that a new paradigm is emerging and waiting to be recognized. Every significant shift in our thinking began as an anomaly or problem connected to an old paradigm that could not be solved within its constraints. By using curiosity, imagination, and play, we escape these constraints and can discover creative new ways of understanding the problem.

Five Steps to Effective Problem Solving

When confronting a problem, we start by opening it up and identifying, analyzing, discussing, and debating as many different ways of solving it as possible. Afterward it is possible to close it down, clarify, and agree on a single problem-solving process that allows us not only to solve the problem but to improve our generic problem-solving skills. These boil down to five simple, practical, easy-to-use steps:

1. Recognize and accept the problem.
2. Define the problem and clarify the obstacles to solving it.
3. Analyze, categorize, and prioritize the elements of the problem.
4. Brainstorm options to satisfy everyone's interests.
5. Commit to action, evaluate, and celebrate successes.

Step 1. Recognize and Accept the Problem

Admit and accept that there *is* a problem. Name it with as much precision and complexity as it requires. Identify its causes and separate each one from the person who represents, expresses, or embodies it. Surface the underlying sources of the problem and commit whatever time and energy is needed to solving them. Assess the willingness of everyone to participate in defining the problem and discovering solutions. Ask what kept those involved from admitting or accepting that they had a problem. Then decide whether and how to go about solving it.

Step 2. Define the Problem and Clarify the Obstacles to Solving It

Gather information about the problem and restate it clearly and concisely based on what has been learned about it. Identify the issues, barriers, or difficulties that stand in the way of solving it, compare the problem with others, and notice its similarities and differences. Identify the questions that need to be answered in order to solve it, such as: What are the deeper causes of the problem? Do they include difficult behaviors, especially our own? Are they a result of unfair or unsuccessful organizational processes? Are adequate resources being directed at the problem? Are the organization's culture, structure, systems, communications, processes, techniques, or relationships contributing to the problem?

Step 3. Analyze, Categorize, and Prioritize the Elements of the Problem

Analyze, categorize, and prioritize the individual elements that make up the problem. Examine how it has been affected by the context and relationships that surround it. Explore its history and evolution over time. Identify a perfect state in which the problem no longer exists and then work backward from the future to trace its development. Check for factual inconsistencies, unstated assumptions, and expectations. Watch out for myths, stereotypes, and clichés and notice differences in underlying values, beliefs, and premises. Identify emotions that may have distorted the problem and search for their cultural, structural, and systemic causes. As this is done, analyze everyone's role and ask how each person might have contributed more to solving it.

Step 4. Brainstorm Options to Satisfy Everyone's Interests

Ask questions that reveal underlying interests in continuing or solving the problem. Explore paradoxes, contradictions, riddles, or polarities about the problem. Summarize unstated assumptions, expectations, myths, stereotypes, or clichés held by those connected with it. Brainstorm options, search for alternatives that satisfy everyone's interests, develop criteria for determining whether it has been completely solved, predict probable consequences of proposed actions, test conclusions in pilot projects, and develop strategies and action plans for implementation.

When organizational problems are solved collaboratively, the solutions are more readily accepted, implemented, and owned by everyone. At the same time, those who face the problem regularly should be empowered to design their own solutions. Collaborative *and* empowered problem solving does not mean excluding others, becoming silent, or rolling over and playing dead. It means investing the power to solve the problem in those who are most affected by it and inviting them to participate fully in collaboratively finding, implementing, and owning the solutions.

Step 5. Commit to Action, Evaluate, and Celebrate Successes

Commit to a course of action to solve the problem. Decide how to communicate solutions, how to deal with objections, how to evaluate successes, and who will review, monitor, and report on progress. Elicit feedback on what is working and what isn't, evaluate interim results, make midcourse corrections, summarize what was learned from the problem and how it was solved, identify ways of improving the process, celebrate successes, then pick a new problem and start all over again.

Multidimensional Problem Solving

Another way of approaching problem solving is to think of it as taking place in multiple physical dimensions, each adding a new degree of freedom. It is possible, for example, to think of problem solving in zero dimensions as simply being stuck, or at impasse. One-dimensional problem solving consists of sticking with one's own preferred solution. Two-dimensional problem solving represents median or compromise solutions, while three-dimensional problem solving adds depth and innovation to the process, allowing people to discover creative solutions by identifying and aligning interests, inventing options for mutual gain, and reaching consensus rather than compromise. We can also imagine a fourth dimension, which can be understood or interpreted in a three-dimensional world as synergy, collaboration, flow, or the flash of inspiration and insight that often emanates from play.

A single dimension of freedom is thus achieved simply by clarifying and defining the problem and identifying our position, or what we want as a solution. A second dimension is added when we listen to someone else's position and locate a compromise or middle ground between them. Every compromise is defined by a simple combination of these two variables. We move into a third dimension and add depth by identifying both sides' *interests*, or the reasons why they hold their positions. We can then invent options that align and satisfy them, even if neither side achieves its original position. This third dimension of thinking allows us to reach consensus on new, creative solutions, collaboratively implement them, and thereby improve our relationships, requiring a far more complex triangulation of three variables rather than two to describe. A fourth dimension is reached when insight and inspiration occur, when a problem is deeply understood and its paradoxical complexity is fully appreciated. This approach allows us to transcend or overcome the problem and become unstuck by changing our attitude toward it. In four-dimensional problem solving, we transcend narrow definitions of the problem and discover solutions that only appear when we move outside the range of lesser-dimensioned approaches. We can think of this fourth dimension as waking up to the true nature of the problem and playing with possible solutions. Nobel Prize–winning physicist Richard Feynman was well known for his genius as a creative, paradoxical, playful problem solver. In discussing his problem-solving methods, he gave the following advice:

- Don't respond to peer pressure.
- Keep track of what the problem really is; less wishful thinking.
- Have a lot of ways of representing things. If one way doesn't work, switch quickly to another one.

> The important thing is not to persist; I think the reason most people fail is that they are too determined to make something work only because they are attached to it.

Feynman's biographer, Marvin Minsky, wrote that when a problem appeared, Feynman would invariably say, "Well here's another way of looking at it," causing his colleagues to regard him as the least-stuck person they knew. We can all learn like Feynman to love our problems and, applying equal measures of scientific curiosity and artistic imagination, solve the paradox of problem solving.

10

Supportive Confrontation

We have been silent witnesses of evil deeds: We have been drenched by many storms: We have learnt the arts of equivocation and pretense: Experience has made us suspicious of others and kept us from being truthful and open: Intolerable conflicts have worn us down and even made us cynical. Are we still of any use? What we shall need is not the geniuses, or cynics, or misanthropes, or clever tacticians, but plain, honest, straightforward people. Will our inward power of resistance be strong enough and our honesty with ourselves remorseless enough, for us to find our way back to simplicity and straightforwardness?
                                            Dietrich Bonhoeffer

There are times, as German theologian Dietrich Bonhoeffer learned while living under fascism, when courage demands an end to equivocation and pretense, when honest simplicity and straightforwardness become essential, even though the message is painful to state and difficult to hear. What do we do when our efforts to listen courageously have failed; when we have engaged in paradoxical problem solving and nothing has changed; when turnaround feedback, transformational coaching, strategic mentoring, and participatory assessment have all proven unsuccessful? Before imposing discipline or terminating employment, it is possible to redefine the problem, raise difficult issues directly, and confront the employee in as supportive a way as possible with a clear, inescapable choice.

At first glance, there may seem to be no connection between confronting someone and supporting them, yet these approaches are closely intertwined. Confrontation can be communicated in an aggressive or supportive manner, just as support can be uncritical or confrontative. It is the combination of support and confrontation, honesty and empathy, kindness and precision, straightforwardness and heartfelt simplicity, that allows difficult messages to be heard, absorbed, and harnessed to personal development.

The reasons for initiating supportive confrontation are quite simple. First, there is a time for cutting through politeness, superficiality, pretence, conspiracies of silence, and formal niceties to deliver unfiltered truth as clearly and bluntly as needed for it to be heard. Second, it is important to support employees in waking up and directing their full attention to solving their problems, achieving their goals, and turning their lives around.

Supportive confrontation is distinguished from invasive personal attack by the constructive intention that drives it, the open, honest manner in which it is delivered, and the elevated level of personal and organizational support that accompanies it. Nevertheless, supportive confrontation can feel extremely aggressive and intrusive to the person who receives it. For this reason, it is not the first step in waking someone up and is usually initiated only when everything else has failed.

Carefully crafting a context that communicates affirmation, respect, and support can make a tremendous difference in how the confrontation is received. Even when it is supportive, confrontation should not be chosen with the intent of changing anyone into someone they are not. The process should not permit manipulation and coercion or be used solely to satisfy someone else's self-interests.

When the intention is negative, dishonest, manipulative, petty, hypocritical, judgmental, or disrespectful, the outcome will be useless at best and damaging at worst. On the other hand, if the deliverer clearly has the best interests of the receiver at heart; adopts an open, honest attitude; is willing to receive equally honest feedback in return; follows a collaborative, democratic process; and has a style that is deeply respectful, the confrontation is more likely to be understood as supportive and therefore be accepted and implemented.

Supportive confrontation is often used immediately before conflict resolution, in a last-ditch effort to avoid discipline and termination. It is likeliest to succeed if the organizational culture supports openness and honesty in communications; if the context is one that models awareness and authenticity; and if the support is backed up with congruence and commitment. It is also helpful if the environment for delivering the communication is private and confidential and the entire process is disconnected from any consideration of rewards and punishments.

Making the Case for Supportive Confrontation

Employees are encouraged by a broad range of hierarchical, bureaucratic, and autocratic structures, as well as by traditional managerial styles and organizational cultures, to play it safe, hedge their bets, get by with mediocre performance, and feel no responsibility for what happens at work. In these environments, employees are not only permitted to sleepwalk through their jobs, they are actively rewarded for doing the bare minimum.

In hierarchies, improved performance and behaviors are encouraged through positive motivational techniques such as rewards and incentives that are based on what employees *want* and appeal to their greed, or through negative motivational techniques such as punishments and disincentives that are based on what employees do *not* want and play on their fear. The former adopt the carrot as a motivational tool, while the latter select the stick. In each approach, something is left out. The positive approach often minimizes the depth, extent, and impact of the problem, while the negative approach often ignores the power of positive reinforcement and focuses on what has been done unsuccessfully to solve it. Each is effective with certain employees, while other employees remain untouched by one or the other, or by both.

Supportive confrontation focuses employee attention on the harsh truth that whatever has been done to solve the problem so far has not worked and most probably will not work. It also reveals the even harsher truth that the capacity to solve the problem already exists inside the employee, and requires only a willingness to admit being stuck, recognize the need for help, and ask for organizational support in solving it. These steps allow the employee to convert the problem into an opportunity for learning, development, and transformation.

This opportunity is often resisted by employees, who are afraid of the risks involved or have grown comfortable with their problems. They may not believe support will be available, or may think they can continue to duck responsibility for improving, or erroneously believe that their dysfunctional behaviors will not have adverse consequences. To justify their resistance they blame others, rationalize their actions, and try to escape responsibility for their behaviors. They divert attention to other issues, lie, duck and hide, make excuses, get angry, threaten retaliation, avoid work, fake compliance, and when these fail, fall back on injury, illness, and lawsuits.

Each of these excuses, rationalizations, and justifications simply sidetracks the communication, changes the subject, obscures the truth, or covers up an effort to get away with something even the employee knows is wrong. Each relies for its success on weakness, ineffective leadership, lack of determination, inadequate support, or fear of confrontation on the part of the managers, and a lack of motivation and responsibility on the part of employees, who can always find a thousand ways of avoiding what they do not want to do.

Managers who rely on hierarchical power, bureaucratic procedures, and autocratic decision making to enforce nominal compliance surrender the possibility of achieving anything better. This self-reinforcing system of resistance by employees and lack of leadership by managers makes supportive confrontation a critical tool in breaking the hold of apathy, peeling away the layers of rationalization, and finding alternatives to organizational systems that lock both sides into dysfunctional, frustrating, ultimately self-destructive behaviors.

Problems and Opportunities in Confrontation

Nearly all of us are frightened of confrontation. Our fear of being confrontative may flow from our perception that confrontation is unpredictable. Or we may feel that the situation is hopeless, or that others are perfectly aware of their behaviors and don't want to change. Or we may be frightened that they will retaliate or seek reprisal, or hope someone else will take responsibility for confronting the problem. In either case, our lack of skill in delivering confrontational feedback or fear that we will be accused of harassment or retaliation blocks us from saying what needs to be said and allows the problem to continue or get worse.

One of the greatest barriers to honest and direct confrontation is the silent back-scratching conspiracy that, while unspoken, is nonetheless understood by employees and managers alike: "I won't call you on your mistakes if you don't call me on mine." This tacit agreement allows employees to curb their critical input, maintain a code of silence, and suppress or surreptitiously spread disparaging information. Hungarian author Sandor Marai wrote pointedly about the suppression of communication that takes place even among friends in his novel, *Embers*: "We not only act, talk, think, dream, we also hold our silence about something. All our lives we are silent about who we are, which only we know, and about which we can speak to no one. Yet we know that who we are and what we cannot speak about constitutes the 'truth.' We are that about which we hold our silence."

Complicit in this conspiracy, we converse superficially with one another and limit our questions to topics that can be discussed politely and civilly without upsetting the other person. In so doing, we defend ourselves against integrity and them against honest feedback, transforming our politeness into a tacit acceptance of the status quo.

If we want to have an honest conversation with someone about a problem, we need to confront it. If we want to stimulate a significant personal, organizational, societal, or political change, we need to create a *minimal* level of impoliteness, discourtesy, and unpleasantness. Yet there is a discernable difference between minimal impoliteness and overt disrespect, duress, and harassment. Gandhi captured the quality of supportive confrontation perfectly when he wrote that in carrying out his doctrine of *satyagraha*, or "speaking truth to power," it is necessary to be simultaneously "gentle, truthful and fearless."

No one learns to confront someone else unless they are willing to make an effort and face the consequences. By not trying, we allow inappropriate behavior to negatively impact everyone within its reach. Our expectations regarding permission to engage in honest communications and supportive confrontations are established and modeled by our leaders. When employees see a leader back away from confronting negative behaviors, morale slips and motivation drops off precipitously. If the leader is the one whose behavior requires correction, failing to confront it simply increases everyone's isolation and ineffectiveness.

A contrary example of a leader who accepted the need for supportive confrontation occurred in an organization headed by a man with a strong, contentious personality. He held a meeting where he asked employees to push back and confront him with what he could do better, but everyone was afraid to speak. Finally, a courageous junior manager responded by communicating her perception that though he always told them his door was open, he rarely left his office, hardly ever walked around, and did not seem to want to discover the world around him. She assumed he wanted to protect himself from the feedback he would receive if he were more available. For her part, she said, she and her peers felt isolated from him. Their view was that he was withholding information from them and they felt blocked from access to the leadership and support they needed to produce the results he was demanding.

Her firm yet supportive confrontation allowed him to see that his door had not been as open as he thought and that he had been subconsciously defending himself from hearing anything critical regarding his performance. He publicly thanked the woman for her feedback and began to actively make himself more available, sending a message that he valued critical input.

When we confront others in skillful and supportive ways, performance, morale, and teamwork often improve dramatically as a result. When employees realize that problems and issues can be discussed openly and honestly and that their conflicts can be successfully resolved, they learn that they can be supported in admitting and correcting their mistakes, and that active, targeted, direct, supportive confrontation is better than silent judgment, veiled rejection, unresolved conflict, and discipline or termination.

Criticism Is Critical

To survive in a diverse, rapidly changing world, not only people but organizations need to continually self-correct. Self-correction means becoming aware of and capable of changing whatever is not working. But in many organizational cultures, identifying what is not working is seen as impoliteness, disloyalty, negativity, rocking the boat, not being a team player, complaining, whining, sabotage, or personal attack.

A communication is only as good as the questions it entertains or allows to be posed. In most conversations regarding poor performance, the most important questions are thought to be too risky or pointless and, as a result, are never posed at all. Instead, they are discussed unilaterally by each side, giving the other side little or no permission to challenge their underlying assumptions. They are conveyed hierarchically from top to bottom, making unbiased investigation appear unnecessary. They are communicated bureaucratically, focusing on narrowly interpreting the language of a rule or policy rather than addressing real problems. As a result, both sides adopt an unspoken assumption: that it is the responsibility of management to improve employee performance. In truth, that is the employee's job. The purpose of supportive confrontation is to ask the questions that reveal this truth.

Even though most organizations reward loyalty, what they actually *need* is criticism. Criticism is the highest form of compliment and the essence of loyalty. Posing the question "what is wrong" is the first step in a transition to "what could be." In organizational cultures that are based in democratic values, personal growth, organizational learning, and transformational change, supportive confrontation is a necessity rather than a choice.

To succeed, these organizations require employees who are capable of delivering turnaround processes and have been prepared and trained in delivering feedback at the level of honesty needed to solve the problem. They require team members who are capable of supportively confronting others, taking off the masks, breaking the conspiracies of silence, and directly, humanely, and powerfully communicating their observations regarding a team member's behavior or performance. Most important, they require leaders who are capable of actively modeling these skills and inviting supportive confrontation themselves.

Indeed, the best way to prepare for supportive confrontation is by starting with ourselves. This means critiquing the way we respond to criticisms directed at us, including feedback from the very employees we seek to confront. When we go out of our way to publicly and privately thank people for criticizing us, it sends a message that others can do the same, that criticism is not frightening, and that it is simply an opportunity for growth and improvement.

How to Prepare for Supportive Confrontation

To prepare for supportive confrontation, we start by surrendering our judgments regarding other people's personalities, motivations, characters, and intentions. We approach the session with a goal of mutual learning and improvement. Supportive confrontation is not something we are entitled to impose on someone by virtue of our hierarchical or moral superiority. It is an expression of our commitment to that person, to ourselves, and to our shared relationship. It is a demonstration of our willingness to jointly overcome and learn from our mutual problems.

In the beginning stages of feedback, coaching, mentoring, or assessment, and especially in supportive confrontation, agreeing on a set of ground rules for constructive dialogue can help us establish a positive context for the communication that will follow. These rules give express permission to be direct and honest with each other. They specify that whatever is said will be confidential and will follow an agreed-upon format. They express a commitment to speak respectfully and compassionately, and declare an intention to work toward constructive common goals.

When supportively confronting someone with unpleasant or uncomfortable information, it is always best to start by checking our perceptions with the other person to make sure our thinking is not isolated or skewed. We identify specific examples of problem behaviors using nonjudgmental language, share perceptions of the effects the behavior had on others, and ask why the employee chose to engage in it.

As they respond, we listen closely for thinking errors that may be distorting our understanding and ask questions to identify or clarify them as they occur. When appropriate, we reveal discrepancies between their *intent* and the *effects* their behavior is having on others. We discuss all options honestly, including their continuing to engage in the behavior. We ask them to identify their goals and suggest alternatives that may be more successful in achieving them. We cite examples of behaviors that produced positive effects in the past to reinforce their positive intentions and belief in the possibility of redemption.

For example, a senior manager we coached in leadership development faced a difficult problem regarding her second in command. She liked and respected this young man, but after six months on the job he was feeling overwhelmed, confused, and unable to handle the pressure. His team felt he was not responding quickly enough to developing crises and was not visible enough with important internal customers. He was too focused on strategic systems and processes and became paralyzed when faced with immediate short-term demands. This all took place in a fast-paced, competitive organizational culture with a pattern of shooting from the hip and cleaning up afterward.

She gave him gentle nudges, hints, and hopeful comments in her feedback every so often, but was too afraid to hurt his feelings to tell him plainly and directly what was wrong. She asked us to coach him because we stood outside the culture and might be able to get through to him. In our initial coaching session, it became clear to us that the feedback his manager thought she sent had not been received. He devoted most of our initial conversation to justifications, criticisms of the organization's culture, and defenses of his six-month record.

We took our observations back to the manager and supportively confronted *her* regarding her ineffective, indirect style of communicating with him. She accepted our observations and asked to rehearse with us the comments she wanted to make to him. We recommended they meet in his office so he would feel more comfortable and better able to absorb what she had to say.

They met for over three hours, as she presented him with detailed, specific examples of missteps, mistakes, and behaviors that fell short of what she had thought were agreed-upon expectations. Afterward, he thanked her for telling him the truth about what wasn't working. He felt he finally understood the mess he was in, which was better than being in the dark. They jointly developed a plan to support him in making specific improvements. As a result, they each understood what they needed to do to be successful and were able to commit to a mutually satisfying partnership. The team became more productive and both parties learned they could be supportive and confrontative at the same time.

The Method of Supportive Confrontation

Supportive confrontation works best when it takes place in a private, confidential environment that encourages open, honest, off-the-record conversations. If serious disciplinary issues are involved, it is better to conduct an informal, confidential supportive confrontation first. If that works, the matter is settled; if it doesn't, you can then schedule an entirely separate, unrelated disciplinary interview that is formal and on the record. The first effort is designed to spark dialogue and informal problem solving rather than create a record for discipline or termination.

After agreeing on whatever ground rules are needed for a frank and constructive dialogue to take place, the confrontation opens with both parties' stating their goals for the conversation, or what they value or appreciate in their relationship. They then agree on the applicable standards or criteria for judging the behavior or performance and write down in detail what is acceptable and what is not. They indicate what each of them may have contributed to the problem and express their intentions regarding improvement. The performer is asked to consider the effects the behavior or performance may have had on others, and agree on specific items that need to be corrected. The communication style of the confronter is direct and does not beat around the bush. At the same time, it is gentle, kind, and empathetic in tone and approach. Both speak as they would want to be spoken to if they were on the other side.

If the employee being confronted resists identifying the behavior or performance as an issue by asserting a positive intent, the confronter can ask whether that intent was actually achieved. If not, the confronter can cite the failure to achieve the intention as a problem that also needs to be solved. If so, the confronter can ask whether others agree with that judgment and cite evidence that they do not, or invite them into the conversation, or ask the employee to interview coworkers and colleagues and return with their answers.

Supportive Confrontation in Teams

Few performance or behavioral problems are created only by one person. Most are relational and co-created or at least tolerated by both sides. For example, instead of identifying a middle manager's problem as micromanagement, it may be more accurate to see it as resulting from a relational tension that develops between one who wants to know all the details and one who considers them unimportant; one who has to pay attention to multiple problems and one who focuses only on a single issue; one who is unable to give up control out of a fear of failure and one who likes to take risks. Indeed, there are dozens of possible ways of defining the problem other than as one person's micromanagement.

If the supportive confrontation takes place in the presence of the employee's team, it is best to use an outside facilitator with experience resolving group conflicts. In the team version of the process, each team member is given an opportunity to discuss the problem and its consequences, and identify what they and other team members did or did not do that encouraged or rewarded the behavior or failed to correct it.

Team members can then be assigned to work in random small groups to collectively explore issues, brainstorm options, identify more effective behaviors, and agree on specific actions they will take to solve the problem. These agreements on next steps can be written up and signed by those responsible as an expression of their commitment.

Handling Dodges and Evasions

When confrontations do not follow these steps, those on the receiving end often try to dodge, evade, and avoid telling the truth. We all
know thousands of ways of evading responsibility for our actions.
Some people build themselves up by putting others down. Others feed
their managers only what they want to hear or "need to know." Some
confuse themselves about their responsibility by minimizing the seriousness of the problem or the extent of their involvement with it. Or
they say yes without meaning it, or claim they are too busy, saying
there were more important things to do. Or they procrastinate and
put off doing anything about it, or deny they ever agreed to do it at
all, or retreat into apathy and cynicism, or counterattack with accu-
sations that divert attention from the task. In the process, they shut
down and become unreachable through conventional means.

Some employees simply say they can't do what is required for a
variety of excellent reasons. On hearing the words "I can't" in supportive confrontation, the challenge of the confronter is to reveal
the underlying source of the resistance and search for deeper understandings. "I can't" can be redefined to cover any of the following:

- I won't

- I'm scared of what will happen I do.

- I don't care about it.

- It's not my job.

- It'll never work.

- How dare you ask me to do that?

- I really couldn't do a thing like that.

- I don't know how.

- I want you to give me more resources.

- You never showed me how to do that.

- If I don't try, I can't be blamed when it doesn't work.

- Ask me really nicely.

- What makes you think I'll do something for you when you're always making life harder for me?

- What have you done for me lately?

In supportive confrontation we are unwilling to accept defensive reactions as the last word. To get beyond these protective barriers, we make certain that the ability to remedy the problem lies within the control of the person being confronted. We ascertain whether the task can actually be performed, whether the employee is the right one to perform it, and whether managers, coworkers, or the organizational culture are blocking or undermining their ability to succeed. We redirect attention back to the problem while bringing a high level of morale and self-confidence to solving it. We avoid "shaming and blaming," which reduce everyone's willingness to be open and honest about problems or to participate in giving and receiving feedback.

Shaming and blaming encourage employees to deny responsibility, blame others, feign ignorance, falsely comply, emphasize their true good intentions, or attack the person who delivered the feedback. None of these solve the problem They merely shift the blame onto someone else, preventing dialogue, responsibility, and a search for creative solutions.

In the face of these evasions and refusals to change, we have watched countless managers and team members throw in the towel and give up out of frustration. Yet defensive reactions are actually a positive sign, because they are active rather than passive and give us something we can retool to solve the problem. To defuse defensiveness and create an opening for supportive confrontation, we can ask:

- Why does it matter whose fault it is?

- Here's how I contributed to the problem. How do you feel you contributed to it?

- Regardless of what you intended, what impact did you have?

- If I wasn't clear that I wanted (or didn't want) you to do it, I apologize. What can I do to make sure this doesn't happen again? If I do that, what will you do in response?

- What effort did you make to find out what could be done or try to fix it?

- Do you see that there is a problem? How would you describe it? What would you recommend be done to solve it?

- Regardless of who did it, what can we do together to solve it?

- I would really appreciate it if you would work with me to solve the problem. What do you think I should do, and what should we do together?

For each defensive, aggressive, and avoidant response there is an equally effective supportive, collaborative, and engaging counter-response that bypasses shaming and blaming, returns attention to the performer, and focuses on solving the problem. For every dodge and escape, there are techniques for enabling the person with the problem to take responsibility for it. The effort to dodge or escape it can then join the list of problems that need solving.

Ways of Encouraging Responsibility

Fundamentally, responsibility is a question of proximity to the problem. The closer we are to the consequences of our actions, the more responsible we become. The best strategy for solving any problem without relying on supportive confrontation is to bring people into closer communication and more direct contact with the problem so they can understand the consequences of their actions and allow the distance to disappear.

The object of supportive confrontation is to increase an employee's willingness to accept responsibility for improving behavior or performance without feeling coerced into doing so. As we have indicated, supportive confrontation is a last-ditch technique to deploy when easier steps have been tried and failed to produce a result. Before resorting to supportive confrontation, it is useful to take a number of constructive preventive steps to encourage responsible behavior. Here are some ways of encouraging individual and team responsibility:

- Include everyone involved in planning a project in the decision-making process from the beginning.

- Build the capacity to be responsible slowly, moving from simple to more complex tasks.

- Jointly and collaboratively establish goals with clear timetables for progress reports, deliverables, and completion dates.

- Clarify roles and responsibilities and what is needed to meet them.

- Ask if each person is prepared to commit to what they agreed to.

- Post agreements, expectations, timetables, deliverables, and outcomes publicly.

- Make it clear that agreements are commitments.

- Meet periodically to review progress and ask early if anyone needs assistance in meeting their commitments.

- Jointly identify incentives for meeting commitments through acknowledgments, rewards, and other forms of support.

- If commitments are not likely to be met, clarify priorities and indicate what will happen if they are not.

- Ask those having trouble why they did not meet their commitments and what supports or assistance, rewards or punishments would help them do so.

- Use feedback, coaching, mentoring, and 360-degree evaluations to identify strategies that could result in improved responsibility.

- Implement a project tracking system to remind people of their commitments.

- Provide training to improve time and project management skills.

- Renegotiate commitments to make them more realistic.

- Say directly how you felt and what happened as a result of their failure.

- Ask coworkers to describe the impact of failing to meet their commitment.

- Ask coworkers to state what they think will happen if the commitment is not met.

- Evaluate the organization's responsibility processes and look for ways of improving them.

- Publicly chart progress in meeting commitments, including successes and failures.

- Examine your own expectations critically to see if they were realistic and were communicated effectively.

- Link pay to performance.

- Establish partnerships, teams, networks, and alliances to help people meet their commitments.

- Try to discover the real, underlying reasons why people could not meet their commitments and address those.

- Transfer those who can't meet their current commitments to positions they can perform without difficulty.

Supportive confrontation is based on a belief in the ability of the person confronted to grow and improve. It is a kind of "tough love" that strangers and enemies are not permitted to practice. Those confronted are presented with clear choices. They can choose to accept the information conveyed and do their best to change. They can convince the confronter that the information is wrong and renegotiate a new set of expectations. Or they can decide to reject the information and work somewhere else. It should be clearly communicated, however, that these are the limits to their options and that they cannot choose to act as they did before.

We recently worked with an employee at a help desk who played computer solitaire while his team members struggled to meet a high volume of customer requests. He had experienced a number of problems in the past, including an arrest for drug use and a bitter divorce. We assisted his manager in confronting him supportively and openly discussing these problems. The manager offered a variety of supports in exchange for his willingness to contribute to the team. In a private session, we used supportive confrontation to let him know that the stakes were high. We asked him if he wanted his job, and he said he did. We told him we thought he was about to lose it and if he wanted to keep it, he needed to own his problems and apologize to his fellow team members.

At a team meeting the following day, he apologized for his behavior without trying in the least to excuse it. He sincerely and tearfully promised to do better. Several team members told him they did not believe him because they had heard him apologize before. He said he understood and agreed, but this time would be different. The team agreed to support him by telling him immediately if they saw him slacking off. Six months later everyone agreed he had completely transformed himself and become a leader of the team.

The Varieties of Apology

In this example, an apology was used to signal an acceptance of responsibility and ownership of the problem. An apology does not necessarily mean someone thinks they were bad or wrong. It may simply mean they understand what others experienced and are sorry for whatever they did that added to their coworkers' discomfort. It may mean they have given up their anger and want to return to a more positive, normal relationship. It may mean they are willing to take responsibility for whatever they contributed to the problem. It may mean they value their relationship more than they value being right.

Apologies not only acknowledge responsibility for behavior, they encourage others to do the same. Every genuine acceptance of responsibility through apology melts away the anger that keeps people from hearing feedback and implementing it. An apology can be offered as an opening comment or be used as a way to model how to respond to criticism and allow others to save face. A manager or team member can say, for example: "I am sorry I haven't been successful in communicating with you about how to solve this problem," or "I apologize for not being clear enough with you about what I wanted you to do," and then ask: "Is there anything *you* would like to apologize for?" The ensuing conversation can be intense and transformational.

A sincere apology is unconditional, and does not depend on anything the other person says or does in response. It is inherently redeeming, because we know it is the right thing to do. In addition, the other person is far more likely to apologize and take responsibility for their behavior if we lead the way by apologizing first, without asking anything in return. In this way, every authentic apology opens with humility and closes with integrity. It transforms defeat into victory, and shame into self-confidence.

Clearly, supportive confrontation is difficult to carry out and does not always work. But for employees to lose their jobs or fail because no one had the courage to tell them the truth is far worse than anything that could be said in supportive confrontation. Anyone courageous enough to deliver supportive confrontation is automatically a caring, critical friend; anyone courageous enough to receive it is a promising, deserving learner.

11

Risky Conflict Resolution

*Our "opponents" are our co-creators, for they have
something to give which we have not. The basis of all
cooperative activity is integrated diversity. . . . What
people often mean by getting rid of conflict is getting
rid of diversity, and it is of the utmost importance that
these should not be considered the same. We may
wish to abolish conflict, but we cannot get rid of
diversity. We must face life as it is and understand
that diversity is its most essential feature. . . . Fear
of difference is dread of life itself. It is possible to conceive conflict as not necessarily a wasteful outbreak
of incompatibilities, but a normal process by which
socially valuable differences register themselves for
the enrichment of all concerned.*

Mary Parker Follett

Mary Parker Follett—who was one of the first to advocate conflict resolution and democratic principles in the workplace—
wrote this passage shortly after World War I, yet her observations
are, if anything, more valid today than when she wrote them.
Expanded personal mobility and enormous improvements in global
transportation and communication bring us into daily contact with
a diverse world. As globalization increases, we come to the growing

realization that diversity is rapidly disappearing, that it is a precious resource, and that it is a significant source—not merely of conflict but of learning, personal and organizational development, evolutionary adaptation, and life itself.

As the world each day becomes more interconnected and interdependent, we become less capable of tolerating the pointless damage and destruction that accompany fear of differences. At the same time, a rapid expansion in the power and effectiveness of risky conflict resolution techniques makes it increasingly unnecessary to return to antiquated, fearful, senseless, selfish, and domineering responses to diversity and the conflicts they engender.

Whether conflicts arise from cultural variations, personality differences, divergent belief systems, competing self-interests, or antagonistic demands for attention, wealth, and resources, we always have a choice about how to respond when it does arise. We can play it safe, retreat from dialogue, and move against our opponents based on fear of differences, a desire to suppress them, and a need to satisfy our own selfish interests. Or we can take a risk, engage in dialogue, and move toward our opponents based on a celebration of differences, a desire to learn from them, and a desire to collaboratively satisfy everyone's underlying interests.

Every conflict, without exception, creates an unparalleled opportunity to wake up. It increases our awareness of what is actually happening around us and teaches us how to become more skillful and successful in our communications and relationships. It allows us to understand, discuss, and learn from our differences, and to recognize that each of our conflicts offers us a unique opportunity to turn our lives around. Taking a risky approach to conflict resolution allows both sides to discover newer and deeper levels of understanding, improve their skills and relationships, and find better solutions than either side thought possible. For these reasons, conflict is a valuable personal and organizational resource and a powerful source of learning, development, and growth.

Two Kinds of Organizational Conflict

Conflicts regularly occur in every organization, workplace, and relationship. Most of these are interpersonal disputes that arise from simple miscommunications, misunderstandings, unrealistic expectations, unintended consequences, and exaggerated personal differences. Nearly all of these disputes can be prevented, abated, and successfully resolved if addressed at the right time by the right people in the right ways.

In addition to interpersonal disputes, every organization, workplace, and relationship generates chronic, *systemic* conflicts that go deeper and are far more difficult to resolve. These conflicts are often intractable because the issues they raise are more complex, and the solutions required are more profound and far-reaching. Whereas interpersonal disputes appear random and unnecessary, systemic conflicts are risky, stubborn, and essential to organizational learning, growth, and adaptation.

Conflicts allow individuals and organizations to periodically release accumulated stress and establish newer, higher levels of equilibrium. Just as earthquakes release accumulated tension between plates of the earth's crust, systemic conflicts expose the hidden fault lines in relationships. Systemic conflicts are early indicators of internal weakness and environmental instability. They signal a burgeoning need to change and an increasing resistance to doing so They are the *sound* made by the cracks in a system, the voice of new paradigms waiting to be born, the unconscious invitation to satisfy unimagined needs. They expose contradictory cultural messages, the absence of clear vision, and the need for shared values, committed leadership, collaboration, and teamwork. They mark the moment of discovery that something isn't working for someone and the unheralded arrival of a fresh opportunity to fix or transcend it.

Systemic conflicts are chronic in organizations that are separated into hierarchical layers and horizontal, bureaucratic departments, each of which competes with others for resources and recognition, and exists, to some extent, in opposition to all the others. As these conflicts and competitive strategies develop, a higher truth is lost—that they are all interdependent parts of a single organizational whole with multiple goals in common. Their momentary differences fluctuate with shifting events that highlight or overshadow them. Yet these same divisions and conflicts provide a basis for transcendence to higher levels of unity and effectiveness when employees engage in collaborative dialogue, negotiate their differences, and use risky conflict resolution to confront the chronic, systemic sources of their dysfunction.

Responsibility for Conflict

Feedback, coaching, mentoring, assessment, and supportive confrontation can all be used to help employees resolve their workplace conflicts. But to be successful, these methods require the person offering assistance to take a risk and ask both sides to accept responsibility for whatever they did or failed to do that may have resulted in, sustained, or escalated the conflict. Without their acceptance of some responsibility for the conflict, each will blame the other for what is actually within their control.

While we all recognize that "it takes two to tango," we often forget the corollary that it takes only *one* to stop the tango. We learn much more when, instead of accepting 50 percent of the responsibility for our conflicts, we take a risk and accept *100* percent. By doing so, we force ourselves to consider why we decided to join the dance, and why we seem unable to stop.

Taking responsibility for our conflicts extends not only to our acts and omissions but to those the other person executes in response. When we accept responsibility for what we have contributed to the conflict, they are encouraged to do the same. When both parties accept responsibility, impasse begins to disappear. Here are some risky questions that can assist conflicting parties in accepting responsibility for their actions:

- What did you contribute to making this conflict happen?

- With hindsight, how could you have handled it better?

- How would you evaluate your responses so far? What have you done that has been effective? What hasn't been effective?

- How have you suffered as a result of your own actions?

- How have others suffered?

- What does this conflict ask you to release or learn to accept?

- What is the most important lesson you can learn from this conflict?

- How would it be possible for your version of what happened and that of your opponent to *both* be correct?

- In what way could this conflict improve your life?

- Is there anything funny or ridiculous about your role in this conflict?

- What would it take for you to let go of it completely?

- What would happen if you did?

- Has your communication been effective in creating understanding in the other person? What could you do to improve it?

- What additional skills could you develop in handling the conflict? In responding to negative behavior?

By answering these questions, employees in conflict begin to confront themselves and wake up to the role they have played in aggravating or sustaining the impasse. Each person may then be willing to communicate more openly, agree to take actions leading to resolution, or apologize and make amends for their behavior. Together they may commit to correcting the underlying systemic sources of their conflict, transforming cultural attitudes that reinforce avoidance, or inventing new approaches to conflict resolution. By taking a risk, they may learn something important—not only about their conflict but about their opponent and their own capacity to make a difference.

Nonetheless, asking people to take responsibility for their conflicts is risky. Partly this is because everyone in conflict tells a story in which they are right and the other person is wrong. These accusatory, self-serving stories are designed to disguise and divert attention from the role they play in keeping the conflict going, and reinforce their defenses, justifications, countermeasures, and irreconcilable positions.

Yet beneath every accusation lies a *confession* both of desire and powerlessness, and beneath every confession lies an interest that can be framed as a simple *request*. If you would like to learn more about conflict stories and how to transform them into stories of resolution, see our book *Resolving Personal and Organizational Conflict: Stories of Transformation and Forgiveness*.

Roles in Conflict Resolution

Feedback, coaching, mentoring, and assessment can be used to mitigate unresolved conflicts and moderate conflict-encouraging behaviors. The feedback initiator, coach, mentor, or assessor can also become a mediator and assist in the search for collaborative solutions.

The role played by the mediator will vary based on the nature of the conflict, the depth of emotion, the contribution of organizational culture, and the needs of the participants. Providers of feedback, coaching, mentoring, and assessment need to make sure before performing these roles that they do not create confusion by contradicting or undermining their original roles. Here are some roles you can play to help conflicting parties wake up. Each role simultaneously expands and limits the attitudes, ideas, and actions of the person who plays it. It is therefore best to play it fully, yet realize that it is only part of a much larger role.

- *Educator.* Teach what the conflict means and how it produces distrust and answer any questions about the process you will use to resolve it.

- *Rule maker.* Establish ground rules that increase both sides' willingness to resolve their conflict.

- *Referee.* Ask them to articulate, agree on, and abide by ground rules, values, or organizational policies, monitor their compliance, and ask them to commit to implementing these agreements in their relationship going forward.

- *Power balancer.* Overcome perceived and actual power imbalances that interfere with genuine consensus so that each person can participate fully and collaboratively in negotiating solutions.

- *Role model.* Create increased commitment to congruent communication by listening, clarifying, summarizing, refocusing, and acknowledging both side's contributions.

- *Counselor.* Carefully surface underlying emotions that prevent them from discussing their conflicts with their opponent or reaching an agreement.

- *Chair.* Create an agenda and help them prioritize their issues as a way of reaching incremental agreements.

- *Facilitator.* Assist in conducting joint meetings, negotiating agreements, and easing future communication processes and relationships.

- *Adviser*. Assist them in identifying their long-term self-interests and clarifying their goals and objectives.

- *Option generator*. Stimulate a search for creative options for resolution that reflect both sides' self-interests.

- *Negotiator*. Support them in negotiating collaboratively with each other, perfecting their offers, reframing their objections, detaching the person from the problem, and separating their positions from their interests.

- *Resource*. Secure expert opinions or access to them, clarify factual disagreements, and search for criteria to resolve impasse.

- *Magician*. Use creative techniques including analysis of metaphors and stories, assignment of homework, brainstorming, and strategic silence to overcome impasse.

- *Consultant*. Consider for each person whether a particular proposal for resolution represents their best interests and recommend ways of adapting, modifying, or fitting it into their future plans.

- *Zen master*. Ask them to see the emptiness of their conflicts and the errors of dualistic thinking.

- *Lawyer*. Document their agreements in writing and encourage them to discuss what will happen if they experience future conflicts.

- *Historian*. Recall how the conflict felt before and after their discussion and what each person did that could have been done better.

- *Healer*. Encourage them to let the conflict go and move them toward forgiveness and reconciliation.

- *Celebrant*. Celebrate their commitment to improving their relationship by congratulating them on their willingness to approach their conflict honestly and bring it to resolution.

Some of these roles may come easier and more naturally than others. By adopting a range of strategies and mixture of roles, it is possible for those in conflict to reach a deeper understanding of the reasons they became stuck in the first place and move closer to resolution.

Preparing for Resolution

Conflicts often surface in the course of providing feedback, coaching, mentoring, and assessment. Offering assistance to those who feel trapped in these conflicts or have a pattern of attracting or triggering them may require meeting with the parties jointly or separately and working with them to find a solution. To prepare for a mediation, that is, a facilitated face-to-face informal problem-solving conversation between conflicted parties, we often ask each person to complete one or more of the following risky activities or exercises before our meeting:

- List your goals or objectives for resolving the conflict and all the points on which you would like to reach agreement.

- List what you think the other person in the conflict wants and their reasons for wanting it. Indicate where you disagree and why.

- Identify three things you would be willing to do to settle the dispute.

- Write the words you would use to describe the relationship you would like to have with the other person.

- List all the words that describe what you like or respect about the other person. If you are unable to do so, say why.

- List all the words that describe what you do not like or find wrong with the other person. Afterward, opposite those words, write the name of the person in your family who comes closest to exhibiting those characteristics.

- List your objections to the other person's behavior in the form: "I feel [fill in] when you [fill in], because [fill in]."

- List all the words that describe the positive qualities you display when you are in conflict with this person. Next, list all the negative qualities. Which person would you rather be? Why?

- Write down what you think will happen, both positive and negative, if you reach an agreement. Next write what will happen if you do not.

- List all the options for resolving the dispute without regard to whether they will work.

- Write down separately what you think each of you could have done that would have prevented the dispute from happening.

After both sides have thought about the conflict and completed one or more of these activities, ask them if they would be willing to exchange selected portions of what they wrote and respond to those raised by the other party. You may then be able to identify a number of areas of agreement and disagreement. These areas can then be explored, modified, and fine-tuned in a joint, informal problem-solving conversation.

In beginning a joint, mediated conversation to resolve a conflict, it is crucial to understand that the issue of who is right or wrong is, in principle, undecidable—both by you and by the parties. Workable solutions have to be discovered, modified, made acceptable to both sides, and affirmed by consensus. In our experience mediating disputes, it is clear that

- There can be more than one truthful "right answer" to experiential questions.

- Two different sets of facts can be honestly stated and accepted as true for the person who experienced them.

- Unilateral declarations of truth and falsehood are not particularly useful in resolving conflicts.

- The chances of convincing one party to accept the other party's version of why they are wrong are nearly nonexistent.

What is most effective in waking people up is for each side to take a risk, appreciate the other side's experience as a source of improved perspective and increased awareness, add their own, and try to find out what they have in common.

Eight Paths to Conflict Resolution

We believe every conflict creates multiple possibilities for waking people up and making them more aware, authentic, congruent, and committed. Every conflict requires hard-hitting turnaround feedback, transformational coaching, strategic mentoring, and participatory assessment.

In our book *Resolving Conflicts at Work: A Complete Guide for Everyone on the Job*, we provide detailed advice on mediating workplace disputes and describe eight paths to resolving conflicts, even among highly conflicted employees. These paths can be followed by peer mediators, feedback deliverers, coaches, mentors, and assessors, and used both to settle interpersonal disputes and resolve the underlying reasons for chronic, systemic conflicts.

These paths are

1. *Understand the context and culture of conflict.* Discovering the true meaning of the conflict for each party leads not simply to settlement but to expanded awareness, acceptance, and resolution of the underlying reasons for the conflict.

2. *Listen with your heart.* Listening actively, openly, empathetically, and with the heart takes the parties to the center of their conflict, the place where all paths to resolution and waking up converge.

3. *Embrace and acknowledge emotions.* When intense emotions are brought to the surface and not suppressed but communicated openly and directly to the person to whom they are connected, invisible barriers to resolution and transformation are lifted.

4. *Search below the surface for the hidden meaning of the conflict.* Beneath the issues in conflict lie hidden fears, desires, interests, emotions, histories, and intentions that tell us what is really wrong. When revealed they become a source of liberation and transformation.

5. *Separate what matters from what's in the way.* The road to resolution and turnaround lies not in debate over who is right but in dialogue, where the focus shifts from competition over positions to collaboration to satisfy mutual needs.

6. *Learn from difficult behaviors.* In every conflict we confront difficult behaviors that provide us with opportunities to improve our skills and develop our capacity for empathy, patience, and perseverance.

7. *Solve problems creatively and commit to action.* Creative problem solving helps resolve conflicts, but turnaround results require the energy, uncertainty, and duality of enigma, paradox, and contradiction, which are part of every conflict.

8. *Explore resistance and mediate before you litigate or file a griev-ance*. All resistance reflects an unmet need and is a request for authentic communication. Exploring resistance helps us unlock our conflicts and overcome impasse. Mediation encourages collaboration, dialogue, and solutions that meet mutual needs without the delay, pain, and expense of litiga-tion, grievances, and arbitration.

Each of these paths to resolution can create a breakthrough for any employee willing to risk taking them. Once the relentless lock-step of conflict is broken and dialogue begins, there is a natural unfolding of issues, emotions, and insights. This can lead to improved communication, collaborative negotiation, organizational learning, resolution, forgiveness, and reconciliation. For these rea-sons, every organization can benefit from training their employees in mediation and using peer mediators to resolve internal conflicts.

Lessons from Others

It is sometimes difficult to understand how conflict, which has so many negative side effects, can result in increased authenticity, awareness, congruence, and commitment. Here are some exam-ples drawn from our experiences with conflicts that were resolved using risky strategies.

1. Many conflicts emanate from a lack of leadership or clear direction at the top or from a failure to build buy-in from below. For example, after investing over $6 million in a failed reengi-neering effort, a Fortune 100 manufacturing company invited us to advise them in resolving conflicts that threatened to scuttle the entire change process. A number of sweeping changes had been recommended by upper management during a yearlong reengi-neering initiative that had been run into the ground with internal conflicts. Managers complained that line staff were stuck in old work processes, communication patterns, and narrow roles and

responsibilities. They claimed they wanted the changes, but felt unable to move their employees forward.

We began coaching the team that was leading the change effort and asked each person to indicate one meaning the changes had for them and one barrier they saw to successful implementation. We videotaped their answers and played them back. The tape was painful to watch, because it revealed that they were not even close to being a leadership team. Using supportive confrontation, we gave them hard evidence of their own lack of support for the change effort, their inability to convincingly articulate what the change meant, and the problems they had as a leadership team in supporting changes to which they were only superficially committed.

The videotape clearly revealed that the true source of resistance was themselves! In the ensuing feedback process, they spoke authentically and honestly to each other, and it gradually emerged that they were in conflict because they felt the whole idea had been forced on them by their boss, that it was likely to be a huge failure, and that they felt they would be blamed for his bad ideas! Rather than honestly discussing these issues or working together as a team, the tape showed them yelling at each other, retreating into their shells, being unable to reach key decisions, and not listening. After watching the tape in silent horror, each person took responsibility for what they observed in their own behavior and gave everyone else honest feedback about what they saw.

The tone, style, and success of the conversation that followed was in remarkable contrast to the one that preceded it. We asked them what they needed to do, have, or be to lead a successful change effort. They decided to begin by creating a vision for themselves as a leadership team. They identified a number of conflicts with their boss, brainstormed strategies for resolving them, and agreed to honestly inform him about the weaknesses in his plan. They next decided to invite all staff to a dialogue and strategy session to redesign the organization. They even decided to transform the change process by modeling the behaviors they wanted. They each agreed to work on becoming more successful communicators and better leaders, to work collaboratively as a team, and to actually shift the behaviors that were keeping the company stuck.

Throughout the entire process, everyone was completely awake, aware of the impact they were having on one another, engaged in authentic conversation, working in congruence with their values, and committed to their team vision. By exercising courageous leadership, they created an improved plan for personal and organizational improvement. We then conducted a risky conflict resolution session with their boss, who was angry and defensive at first but by the end of the session was able to compliment them on their excellent preparation and leadership. By the end of the second session, he agreed to implement their plan.

We then facilitated an open-ended dialogue and strategic planning session for over a hundred employees and reached consensus on an improved vision. They analyzed what was not working and needed changing in their structures, systems, processes, and culture. They identified what each person could contribute to creating a newer, better organization. At the end, we asked each employee to state how they felt about what they had done and what these changes meant to them. Emotions ran high, and their commitment to change was reflected in their action plans, which made it clear that they fully owned the reorganization plan. Their conflict had triggered a process that led to deep individual learning and organizational renewal.

2. In another example, we consulted with a highly conflicted technology organization that decided to restructure itself into self-managing teams. They came to consensus on creating a coordinating committee that would oversee the change process in the future and respond to any criticisms, conflicts, and glitches that might arise. Later, one employee—who was identified as having created a series of conflicts—drew criticism from many of her team members. Rather than dismiss her, the coordinating committee decided to hold an open feedback and conflict resolution session to discuss her

issues among all staff and reach the consensus they required for the change process to be successful.

The coordinating committee discovered in the ensuing risky dialogue that her real issues had nothing to do with the conflicts she had sparked, but stemmed from problems with her manager over how he was relating to her and her team over work assignments. Because she had been unsuccessful in raising or resolving these issues with her manager or her team, she felt she needed to bring them to the committee. It became clear when she presented her issues that many people, including her fellow team members, shared her concerns.

In exploring these issues, they realized that she had been using the change process to address her own issues with the team and had no real objection to the change. As a result, they were able to come up with a conflict resolution strategy with her manager and team members that allowed her to resolve the problems that were preventing her from supporting the change effort. New suggestions emerged to improve team and managerial communications. As a result of having her conflicts resolved, she became a leader in the organization and was able to make a vital contribution to the change process.

3. In another example, a company and its union jointly asked us to resolve a conflict with an employee who was accused of excessive absenteeism. She had worked for the company for more than sixteen years and been satisfactory in her work performance. She offered many reasons for her tardiness, including traffic jams, her car not working, and her windshield wipers not functioning on a day when it wasn't raining, none of which were convincing. Her manager had received complaints from other employees about her "foul mouth"; she had been suspended two times for tardiness in two successive months, had received a final warning, and had just been handed a letter of termination.

When we asked her in a joint session with her manager to respond, she indicated that her last evaluation gave her high marks in quality and a higher than acceptable rating in quantity of work. We took a risk and pressed her on her excuses. She admitted that she had become addicted to drugs but had not wanted to tell her manager. We took another risk and asked her to talk about her addiction and how it had affected her performance and relationships. She said she felt constantly out of control and that she was "going crazy." She said it felt like "going downhill without any brakes." She could not plan or be anywhere on time and often felt suicidal. She became obsessive about unimportant insults or slights at work and, as a result, felt herself falling apart. She then described her recovery through therapy, which was helping her immensely. She had recently returned to night school and graduated in the top of her class. She felt much better now and wanted to return to her work.

Her manager had been unaware of her drug addiction and personal efforts at recovery. While her answers were honest and personally moving, her manager was not convinced that she could perform according to company standards. We asked what he would need as a commitment from her in order to give her a second chance. After lengthy consideration, he said that he would consider reinstating her if she would agree to meet all her job requirements including work performance, attitude, language, attendance, and punctuality for a period of three months during which she would be on probation with a final warning in her file.

We met with her privately and asked her whether she wanted her job. She said she did. We asked her to take a big risk and tell her manager what she was willing to do to win back his trust. We invited the manager to rejoin us, and she told him she was willing to meet all the company's standards for the three months he required. But to prove she was serious, she said she was willing to extend her probationary time to *six* months, because she knew she had to earn his respect in order to recover.

Her manager was overwhelmed on hearing her answer. He said he now believed she would succeed and wanted to support her in being successful. We spoke to him a year later, and he told us she had not had a single complaint about her work. She had been on time every day, was getting along well with her coworkers, and had become a model employee.

The Importance of Attitude

The deciding factor in nearly every risky conflict resolution is the attitude of the parties, and the determination of at least one of them to resolve the conflict. Courageous listening, paradoxical problem solving, supportive confrontation, risky conflict resolution, and the entire process of waking up all fundamentally depend on attitude. Once there is a positive attitude, it becomes possible to shift traditional responses to mistakes, problems, and conflicts, and to develop higher levels of unity, more effective solutions, better communication, and improved relationships.

Constructive collaboration flows naturally from an attitude that regards conflicts as opportunities for learning and change. Once people decide they want to resolve their conflicts, the rest is easy. Conflicting employees discover they can easily let go of their resistance to dialogue and honest feedback and perceive they can gain more through collaboration than through unresolved antagonism. To them, the conflict suddenly seems unimportant, or a minor difficulty to overcome, or a challenge to address collaboratively.

By addressing chronic, systemic conflicts in this way, risky conflict resolution can also have an impact on a wide range of relationships and communications, even in hierarchical, bureaucratic, and authoritarian organizations. Waking people up and resolving their conflicts invites people to significantly alter their attitudes toward each other, change their relationships, and transform culture in democratic, value-driven ways. It does this by encouraging them to

- See their conflict as positive and an opportunity for growth and change rather than as a threat.

- Acknowledge subjectivity and emotions and use them to help resolve disputes, rather than denying them and relying exclusively on objectivity.

- Listen and engage in dialogue rather than dictate or argue.

- Respond to others' perceptions rather than flatly deny them or become defensive.

- Value diversity rather than homogeneity.

- Assume equality rather than superiority and inferiority.

- Search for mutual gain rather than unilateral victory and defeat.

- Work through problems rather than mandate solutions.

- Empower others rather than search for control or take advantage of powerlessness.

- Affirm multiple truths and diverse perspectives rather than single, unitary Truths, and avoid labeling disagreements as heresy.

- Continue striving for consensus rather than assume that zero-sum games are the only ones possible.

- Search for long-range solutions rather than temporary ones.

- Affirm cooperation as primary over competition.

- Work for closure and reconciliation rather than support continued hostility.

The true risk of conflict resolution lies not in searching for resolution but in surrendering to the fear of telling the truth, refusing to change our attitudes, and failing to seek common ground with our opponents. In the final analysis, conflict can be seen to consist of complementary yet mutually opposing attitudes toward issues that are shared and important to both sides. In this sense, conflict is simply a set of lessons waiting to be learned—not only by individuals but by organizations as well. Once employees wake up and change their attitudes, organizations will inevitably follow suit.

Waking up and resolving systemic conflicts finally requires organizations to transcend their hierarchical, bureaucratic, and autocratic systems and structures and adopt flattened, self-managing democratic alternatives in their stead. These new, participatory, collaborative forms of organization automatically wake people up and cultivate awareness, authenticity, congruence, and commitment at work.

Part IV

Relationships
Sustaining Organizational Awareness
and Authenticity

12

Waking Organizations Up

If you have built castles in the air, your work need not be lost; that is where they should be. Now put the foundations under them.

Henry David Thoreau

Waking people up is a bit like building castles in the air. The idea sounds wonderful, but if we fail to take Thoreau's advice and create solid foundations to buttress and sustain them, we may succeed from time to time but will fail in the long run. To achieve the transformational results outlined in earlier chapters, we need to integrate these processes and techniques fully into the day-to-day operations of organizations and radically alter the cultures, structures, systems, and organizational environments in which we work. In other words, if we are to consistently wake people up, turn their behaviors around, and create environments that support and inspire human values, we need to wake organizations up as well.

Most organizations evolve their cultures, structures, and systems through an unexamined process of accretion, jury-rigging them in response to immediate demands, conforming them to implicit assumptions, and copying them from others without much forethought, participation, or planning. This haphazard, confusing, unspoken approach to organizational development has resulted in the formation of hierarchical structures that diminish creativity and agility; bureaucratic cultures that undermine awareness, authenticity, congruence, and commitment; and autocratic systems that undermine participation and responsibility.

These conditions put people to sleep and make it difficult for organizational behavior to be intelligent, strategic, integrated, or collaborative. They also make it difficult to seize hidden opportunities, respond rapidly to environmental changes, root out systemic conflicts, embrace new paradigms, create customer partnerships, or solve complex problems.

Transforming Cultures, Structures, and Systems

A number of significant transformations in thinking, attitude, behavior, and communication are required to wake organizations up. These include shifts from judging people to supporting their growth, from solving problems to learning from them, from providing answers to asking questions, and from enforcing rules to encouraging values. They include shifts from passivity to participation, from individual to team responsibility, from managerial decision making to consensus, from competition to collaboration, and from management to self-management.

Each of these far-reaching transformations emerges as a natural and inevitable consequence of waking people up. Each allows organizations to apply creative learning principles to employee and customer relationships. Each undermines hierarchy, bureaucracy, and autocracy. Together, they create the preconditions for a larger transition to what we call *organizational democracy*.

As these transformations proceed, traditional organizational cultures, structures, systems, and processes frequently resist, or are used to hinder or prevent them from taking place. The most important of these problems, with their solutions, are

Problems	Solutions
1. Competitive, control-oriented, pronouncement-based cultures	1. Collaborative, learning-oriented, inquiry-based cultures
2. Hierarchical, management-based structures	2. Synergistic, team-based structures
3. Bureaucratic, rule-driven systems	3. Integrative, value-driven systems

Once these solutions have been implemented, democratic organizations are required to consolidate them into a single synergistic, strategically integrated whole. Each solution is elaborated and analyzed in greater detail below.

Collaborative, Learning-Oriented, Inquiry-Based Cultures

Culture, in the broadest sense, is a learned pattern of behaviors and beliefs that help us grow and adapt to a wide range of environmental demands. Cultures consist not only of explicit norms but implicit rules that people somehow learn and recognize without ever discussing them. Organizational cultures tell us how far we can go in criticizing the boss, what we need to do to get ahead, what to wear to work, how we should respond to feedback and performance assessment, how to be a coach or mentor, and what can and cannot be changed.

Over time, employees become habituated, unconscious, and unaware of the impact their culture has on their expectations, behaviors, attitudes, and performance. Hierarchical, bureaucratic, and autocratic organizational cultures result in divided loyalties, contradictory work styles, chronic miscommunications, isolated leadership, and resistance to change. This happens because anyone immersed in such a culture will find it difficult to practice or support democracy, diversity, collaboration, dissent, or genuine empowerment.

Organizations are created by people to mobilize their diverse resources, skills, and energies cooperatively so as to reach goals that cannot be achieved by any of them acting alone. In the process, they seek to maximize consistency by encouraging patterned responses that become encoded in their cultures. These are communicated formally through rules and procedures and informally through gossip and stories.

Qualities of Culture

Large organizations produce multiple cultures that differ for each level, department, function, and process. These gradually become more consistent over time and come to reflect the unique values, rules, processes, and systems of those who make up the organization's leadership and employee population. Here are some typical cultural qualities that differ even *within* organizations, some of which were identified by cultural anthropologist Edward T. Hall:

- Precision versus ambiguity in communications

- Open versus closed regarding personal information

- High versus low context required to establish the meaning of words

- Verbal versus written preference for sensitive communications

- Consensus versus individualistic in decision making

- Formal versus informal in process

- Direct versus indirect in delivering feedback

- Deferent versus rebellious in relation to authority

- Exclusive versus inclusive with outsiders

- Linear versus nonlinear in thinking

- Gestalt versus detail in orientation

- Fixed versus fluid in relation to time

- Open versus closed in relation to space

- Spontaneous versus restrained in humor and play

- Demonstrative versus private in emotional expression

- Permissive versus directive in managing others

In sum, organizational cultures can be competitive or collaborative, autocratic or democratic, oriented toward control or oriented toward learning, pronouncement-based or inquiry-based. Cultures that are collaborative, learning-oriented, and inquiry-based can bridge and unify antagonistic internal cultures. They can promote active participation and equality between employees, managers, and leaders on all levels. They can encourage teamwork, informal problem solving, conflict resolution, and open, honest communication. They can support internal dialogue, invite dissent, provide constant feedback, and orient their structures and systems to promote curiosity, learning, and play.

Cultural Change

Shifting from competitive to collaborative cultures involves changing a wide variety of organizational behaviors. The following chart, based partly on research by Stanford University professor Milbrae McLaughlin regarding change in public schools, contrasts the divergent behaviors that reinforce collaborative and competitive cultures:

Collaborative Cultures	Competitive Cultures
Norms of collegiality	Norms of privacy
Support for learning	Support for conformity to rules
Work is innovative	Work is routine
Work is shared	Work is proprietary
Work is challenging	Work is boring
Commitment to success of others	Low expectations of others
Dynamic interactions	Static interactions
Inquiry and curiosity	Acceptance of existing practices
Democratic decision making	Authoritarian decision making
Informal problem solving	Whining and complaining
Distributed expertise	Isolated expertise
Focus on process	Focus on blame or fault finding
Empathizing with others	Stereotyping others
Interconnected	Isolated
Conflict resolution	Conflict avoidance
Expectation of maturity	Infantilization
Personal professionalism	Deferral to management

One way of shifting from competitive to collaborative organizational cultures is through leadership. We worked, for example, with a facilities services organization in a large corporation whose leaders wanted to shift their culture from one of fragmentation, isolation, and competition to information sharing, cross-functional collaboration, and team-based, cross-departmental partnerships. The leadership team met to define the new culture, identify the elements they wanted to change, and communicate the new expectations, behaviors, and rules to their direct reports, the supervisors who were charged with carrying it out. One of the leaders sent us this e-mail following the meeting:

> After seeing the Leadership Team members interact and then the Supervisory Team discuss the proposed changes, I saw a clear difference. The Supervisors are far more driven and compassionate about what they are doing. I sense this has a lot to do with their commitment and desire to break out of the old mode of doing things. It is my perception that the Leadership Team, at this point, is not as developed and could have a hampering effect on the Supervisory Team's growth.

He had it right. Cultural transformation requires a leadership team with clear vision and a strong commitment to making their behaviors congruent with the values of the new culture. For cultural change to be sustainable, everyone in the organization needs to own the change and be willing to implement it with means that are consistent with the ends they want to create. In this organization, a strong sense of ownership was needed among hourly staff, craftsmen, custodial teams, engineers, and secretaries. If anyone had been left out of the process or failed to support the new behaviors, the leadership team's plans, no matter how brilliant, would have sunk without a trace.

Changing organizational culture requires changing personal attitudes and behaviors as well as organizational processes and relationships. A study of organizations that had initiated sweeping changes, reported in the *Harvard Business Review* by Richard Pascale, Mark Millemann, and Linda Gioja, found that organizational culture was the most critical element in defining their overall success or failure. Based on their research and our experience in hundreds of organizational change efforts, we believe the following questions regarding organizational culture need to be answered correctly if the change process is to succeed:

- *Power and vision.* Do people believe they have the power to make things happen and create change? Do they act as though they do? Is there a clear, compelling vision for the future? Is it shared by everyone on all levels? Is it a living vision?

- *Identity and relationships.* With whom or what do people identify in the organization? Do they identify and embrace the espoused values of the organization? Do they identify with their teams? Functional work units? Professions? The organization as a whole? Does the organization value relationships? How does it communicate this value? What messages sent by the culture support or undermine constructive relationships?

- *Communication, negotiation, and conflict.* What behaviors do people engage in when they have a conflict? How do others respond? Are conflicts swept under the rug or discussed openly? How do conflicts finally get resolved? How do people in the organization communicate? What rules govern the expression of emotions? What issues do people negotiate? What happens when there is impasse? What communication, conflict resolution, and negotiation styles are supported by the culture? How are they reinforced?

- *Learning and assessment.* How does the organization learn? How do people respond to new information that doesn't fit? How honest, open, and real are they in assessing problems? What style is adopted for self-assessment and assessment of others? What are the cultural norms regarding the performance assessment process?

Each of these cultural elements has a strong impact on the ability of an organization to wake people up and deliver turnaround processes and techniques. In addition, organizational cultures are like holograms in the sense that each small piece contains and reproduces the whole. As a result, changing a culture not only alters its isolated elements but potentially transforms the entire matrix of mutually reinforcing behaviors that create and reinforce it. This characteristic of culture makes it possible to alter the whole by strategically reconstructing even minor, seemingly unimportant parts.

Thus, collaborative, learning-oriented, inquiry-based cultures can be supported even in small ways. For example, in the facilities services organization we cited earlier, leadership team members realized that their culture was undermining the collaborative goals they had set for the organization. It was encouraging competitiveness, insularity, divisiveness, fear, and stress, which permeated the culture. They instituted a collaborative approach to the change process during which everyone agreed to shift the culture by implementing the following collaboratively designed changes:

- Work on eliminating the feeling of boundaries between people, departments, and teams.

- Break down preconceived notions of how to act and treat each other.

- Recognize the baggage from the past and eliminate it

- Work together, argue, and still go to lunch.

- Focus on specifics and not focus too wide.

- Have better communications among ourselves; eliminate mixed messages and competition.

- Build trust.

- Do not keep going around road blocks or ignoring them. Instead, stop and do something about them.

- Realize things can change and get rid of the negative.

- Know what each person brings and value it.

- Unify our division into one group.

- Have fun!!!!!

Creating Collaborative Cultures

A more collaborative, learning-oriented, inquiry-based culture starts with the use of processes that encourage teamwork, critical inquiry, and curiosity. This means creating a trusting environment in which employees openly and collaboratively address all issues, managers respect everyone's questions and comments, and each response is mined for useful information. Culture is powerful and lasting, and if every employee's commitment to changing it is not equally powerful and lasting, the culture will change them instead.

The first step in this process is to invite *all* employees to participate in the change process by asking them questions that allow them to identify the parts of their existing culture that weaken trust, participation, curiosity, and collaboration. Using the data from this analysis, employees can then reach consensus on a design that introduces new norms, values, expectations, policies, behaviors, and rewards to support the new culture. We call these questions a "culture audit," and add or alter questions based on unique conditions.

- What are the hidden rules in this culture regarding collaboration and competition or [fill in]?

- How are these rules learned, communicated, and changed?

- When are these behaviors considered appropriate or inappropriate?

- What behaviors are rewarded?

- What behaviors are punished?

- What topics can and cannot be discussed?

- When is it considered inappropriate to be curious?

- What do people do when there are problems or conflicts?

- Which problems or conflicts are swept under the rug?

- How do people finally resolve their conflicts?

- How are intense emotions expressed and responded to?

- How do people respond to difficulties and failures?

- What messages do leaders communicate through their behavior?

- What do people believe about their power to change conditions?

A second step in creating collaborative, learning-oriented, inquiry-based cultures is to reach agreement on shared cultural values. Employees may decide, for example, that their culture should encourage participation and play, or increase everyone's ability to be honest about what is happening within and around them, or be more open to receiving turnaround feedback, or do more to encourage trust.

A third step is to craft a long-term strategy for transforming the culture. This strategy should include creative ways of supporting those who have already begun waking up, and using turnaround processes and techniques to encourage others to do the same, including those outlined in earlier chapters.

A fourth step is to consistently implement and practice the new cultural behaviors, while regularly and publicly monitoring the change process to make certain it is congruent with shared values. It is important for those who consider themselves leaders or change agents to model the values they seek to instill in others, and practice humility, introspection, and equality throughout the change process.

A fifth step is to redesign the structures and systems, rewards and punishments, evaluations and assessments that encourage competitive, control-oriented, pronouncement-based behaviors and cause people to blindly defend themselves against collaboration, learning, and change.

A sixth step is to encourage organizational democracy and synergy and increase job satisfaction for everyone. The goal of collaborative, inquiry-based cultures is not to conform individual personalities to corporate requirements but to increase the capacity of all employees to learn and adapt, survive and grow, succeed and fail, based on who they are and who they want to become.

Synergistic, Team-Based Structures

Organizations have both formal and informal structures, which may or may not closely resemble or support one another. The formal structure of an organization is reflected in its organizational chart, while its informal structure is reflected in decision-making processes and patterns of deference in its relationships. These structures create a framework over which processes, communications, interactions, roles, and responsibilities are laid.

Synergistic, team-based structures create formal and informal links between staff at all levels and bring all roles together into a single integrated whole. These living, evolving, weblike structures generate shared responsibility, collaborative work styles, effective communication, and an efficient use of resources. They look and feel democratic. They wake people up and encourage awareness, authenticity, congruence, and commitment. Participants in these structures are naturally mindful of their responsibilities to one another and their responsibility to participate fully without having to be reminded by their managers to do so.

Not all structures possess this capacity for synergy. The fixed hierarchical structures that characterize most midsized to megasized organizations encourage those at the top to make decisions that affect those at the bottom without their participation or advice. Fixed hierarchical structures divide people, encumber the exchange of important information, block the give-and-take of opinions, impede the joint investigation of problems, and discourage the discovery of mutually satisfactory solutions. They lead those at the bottom to criticize those at the top and regard their decisions as impositions by people who do not understand what it is like in the trenches. And they lead those at the top to criticize those at the bottom for resisting change, being disloyal, and not understanding the big picture. For these reasons, they result in reduced motivation, morale, participation, and feelings of ownership, along with limited agility, creativity, and effectiveness.

Living Webs of Association

In *The End of Management and the Rise of Organizational Democracy*, we refer to the human-scale synergistic structures that overcome these effects as "webs of association," where relationships shape structures rather than structures shaping relationships, and where teams evolve to provide support when and where it is needed.

Webs of association are free-floating, living, evolving organisms that take whatever shape is needed to achieve their goals without being forced to conform to predetermined bureaucratic standards. When they expand and become large they require increased coordination and facilitation, rather than bureaucratic formality, hierarchical chains of command, or coerced uniformity.

Restructuring organizations nonhierarchically into teams and living, evolving webs of association encourages synergy by permitting diverse, loosely structured, self-managing teams to work in highly interactive ways. These structures reinforce collaborative, learning-oriented, inquiry-based cultures by creating open lines of authority in which everyone participates, decides, and is in charge. They reinforce integrative, value-driven systems by increasing consensus and democratic dialogue. They create environments in which turnaround feedback is accepted because it emanates from equals who can be trusted. They support transformational coaching, strategic mentoring, and participatory assessment because doing so eases everyone's burden. Awareness, authenticity, congruence, and commitment then become ways of life rather than isolated, individual struggles.

Self-Managing Teams

It is an ancient, biblical truth that anyone who seeks to remove an obstruction from someone else's eye first needs to remove the obstruction from their own. Synergistic, team-based structures are based on this truth. To bolster turnaround processes and the techniques that support them, these principles need to be thoroughly integrated into the organizational structures that must implement them. To create synergistic results, organizational structures need to communicate easily not only in a downward direction but upward and sideways as well. Collaborative, participatory, self-managing teams are thus essential to bridge divisions, departments, and domains of influence and to create the diversity and unity needed for people to wake up and work collaboratively.

For example, we assisted a large organization in restructuring from a hierarchy into self-managing teams. After their first year in this structure, team members identified the following advantages of the team-based approach:

> "Everyone is feeling more empowered. Individuals are taking on new responsibilities more willingly. People are not afraid to try problem solving. People who were stand-offish are more responsive to others' needs. I feel ready to ask for coaching anytime."

> "There is more participation, and we are giving everyone more of a voice in what is going on in the organization. It has given people a bigger sense of empowerment. People have more of an opportunity to interact with different levels in the organization and are taking initiative. If you are self-directed you become more assertive, where before you held back."

"Teams work when everyone is working toward one common goal and they put their all into the team to make it work. Another benefit is being able to learn what other people do and improve as a result of the feedback we give each other."

"We are very candid with one another. We take time to share disasters and then we clean them up. There is nobody with another agenda and there are no phony people."

"I see a lot of individual growth, better communication skills, people step up to the plate and are responsible for what they have to do."

"Some people are recognizing their new opportunities and using skills they did not realize they had. Everybody has a better idea of what everyone else is doing, what their successes are, how their own job fits into what everyone is doing, and how important it is to the organization."

"It has opened up a lot of communication with upper management, who are showing us more of the big picture. Also, they are keeping us in the loop on things a lot more than before. I had a great conversation when we did my performance review together and got a lot of new information."

Productivity figures supported these comments, and morale and skills rose to an all-time high. Although problems continued to exist, they were on a higher level and belonged to the teams rather than to management. Financial results improved dramatically, and customers who had been worried that teams would not be responsive or responsible found they received better service than before.

Centralization and Decentralization

Synergistic structures and organizational learning are also undermined by inappropriate centralization. The debate over centralization versus decentralization, of course, has no single correct answer. Difficulties arise in both directions. When feedback, coaching, mentoring, and assessment become overly centralized, they do not allow for adaptation or individual input; when they are insufficiently central-ized, the lessons learned through these processes are not communi-cated throughout the organization, depriving others of opportunities to grow and change.

The problem, therefore, is not *whether* but *what* to centralize and decentralize. For example, if we centralize the presentation of a ques-tion and decentralize the answers, the process will be productive. If we decentralize the question, the answers will be meaningless, and if we centralize the answers, we will lose the advantages of diversity and participation. For this reason, it is useful to centralize the ques-tion of organizational direction, vision, values, and goals while decentralizing the answers to allow for participation by all employ-ees in setting direction and ownership. Decentralization encourages diverse, individualized, unique practices to flourish and allows the process to be flexible, adaptive, and responsive, while centralization allows it to be coordinated and concentrated, and lets individuals, teams, and networks learn from one another's experiences.

It is always a mistake for organizations to overly regulate turn-around processes and techniques, which by their nature are personal and need to be negotiated each time they are initiated. It is equally a mistake not to have a centralized component at the beginning and end of the process, to encourage coordination and permit learning to spread throughout the organization.

For example, a Fortune 100 corporation asked us for help in addressing the centralization-decentralization problem. Through careful work process analysis, the leadership identified a number of core functions that could be generalized for all units, geographical locations, and work processes. As a cost-cutting strategy, they cen-tralized these core functions, which included organization-wide processes for feedback, coaching, mentoring, and assessment, as well as for strategic planning, information systems, financial services, and the leadership council. All other functions were decentralized into regions to allow for local control. Each region was headed by a cross-functional team that coordinated the decentralized functions and communicated their best practices to other regions.

Size Matters

Another obstacle to creating synergistic, team-based structures is the scale or size of the organization. When it comes to synergy, size clearly matters. It is important to prevent structures and systems from becoming so immense, complex, and disconnected that they lose the direct, personal connecting qualities that make them effective. It is easy for individuals, teams, and organizations to confuse growth with success and permit organizations to expand from being small, playful, and creative to being large, bureaucratic, and impersonal. Structures with a human scale allow everyone to see the results of their work, communicate openly and spontaneously, take personal and team responsibility for everyone's development, and make feedback, coaching, mentoring, and assessment a part of daily life.

For example, in one organization in which we worked, a division leader voluntarily surrendered a third of his budget and head count because he wanted to make his operational structure smaller and more effective, and felt part of his staff really belonged in a different division. In the past, promotion to higher levels in the organization had been based on size and budget, and his peers tried to convince him not to make what they regarded as a career-limiting move. He felt the organization as a whole would function better under his proposal and decided to take the risk. As a result, he was able to create a far more synergistic team-based structure in which employees worked more effectively, with higher morale and greater productivity.

Smaller does not mean fewer. In fact, if adaptability is any indication of success, a system that has fewer feedback loops is at a disadvantage compared to one that has many. The question is, how do we create "information rich" organizations with structures that are multifaceted and have multiple openings for learning and problem solving?

At a certain scale or size, in order to avoid breaking apart, structures automatically begin to transform themselves into bureaucracies. As a result, rules begin to trump values, minimum standards and external enforcement take precedence over maximum effort and internal responsibility. Everyone simultaneously follows the bureaucratic axiom "Don't Ask, Don't Tell" and blames others for not communicating or solving problems. In this way, bureaucracy becomes self-reinforcing, alienating, and dissatisfying for everyone.

Self-managing teams and webs of association are nonbureaucratic, human-scale structures that can operate synergistically—even in large organizations—to deepen relationships, encourage trust, and support the intimate personal communications necessary to wake people up and encourage turnaround processes and techniques. To succeed, they require integrative, value-driven systems that use a combination of centralization and decentralization to deepen relationships; encourage trust; support intimate, open, and honest personal communications; and help people wake up and become more aware, authentic, congruent, and committed.

Integrative, Value-Driven Systems

Organizational systems encompass complex, interdependent, interconnected, interacting elements that are shaped into a single, mutually reinforcing whole. They create coherence and a semblance of permanence in otherwise chaotic, changing organizations. Yet their boundaries are semipermeable, making them subject to environmental influences that they must constantly adapt to, learn from, and defend against. A balanced ecological relationship between a system and its environment is essential for survival, yet balance is not permanent and cannot be fixed because systems and their environments are always changing.

Because systems need to balance and integrate the conflicting forces that hold their disparate parts together, it is difficult for them to change. This makes the presence of conflict and opposition in a single unifying system beneficial, because it permits a magnification and accentuation of differences, thereby allowing adaptation to take place without destroying the system. In this way, diversity encourages expansion and integration by permitting a greater unity of divergent interests and synergies that allow the whole to become greater than the sum of its parts. Yet the presence of conflict and oppositional forces within the system also threatens its survival, because it introduces the possibility of chaos and change.

As feedback on a given topic accumulates, revealing a growing need to change, the organization can either use it as an opportunity for reintegration, learning, and adaptation, or it can block the information, isolate itself, punish those who delivered it, and resist innovation. The function of feedback is to encourage periodic releases that reestablish equilibrium so the system can steadily evolve in a continually changing environment.

Feedback Loops Stimulate Change

To survive and develop, organizational systems require thermostats or feedback loops to help them sense the direction of change and adjust without upsetting their internal balance. Hierarchical, bureaucratic, rule-driven systems find it difficult to do this. Instead, they create weak, restricted, rigid thermostats to regulate strong, complex, flexible systems, thus preventing the organization from learning and adapting to changing conditions. As internal inconsistencies, antagonisms, and conflicts multiply, the system becomes increasingly defensive and repressive and decreasingly able to learn.

Integrative, value-driven organizational systems are required to accurately synthesize and harmonize the contradictory feedback generated by their daily interactions. They orchestrate complex feedback from networks of processes and communications, and use it to improve the methods and techniques by which the business of the organization is conducted.

Value-driven systems exalt, in Douglas McGregor's phrase, "the human side of enterprise," making it preeminent. They dignify and prioritize employee needs for satisfaction, belonging, acknowledgment, respect, and identity. They reinforce collaborative, learning-oriented, inquiry-based cultures and support synergistic, team-based structures by providing opportunities for every employee to participate in the fundamental decisions that define the organization. They cultivate and encourage awareness, authenticity, congruence, and commitment. They make organizations more responsive to feedback, able to learn from mistakes, sensitive to new conditions, open to transformation, and oriented to human values.

Integrative, value-driven systems are more likely to use 360-degree participatory assessment processes that invite peers to evaluate each other. Participatory, peer-based assessment systems, in turn, multiply the capacity of organizations to learn, adapt, and evolve. They allow feedback to be integrated across diverse skills and departments, and they benefit from the improved performance, motivation, and morale that comes from letting employees run the process, increasing their capacity and responsibility for results.

Alternative Systems

Integrative, value-driven principles can be applied to redesigning a variety of alternative organizational systems. Consider, for example, wage, compensation, and reward systems. Wages and salaries are usually based on minimal performance standards that encourage employees to expend the least effort they can at work while reserving their excitement, creativity, and curiosity for what they do after work is over. Integrative, value-driven reward and compensation systems provide bonuses and salaries both to individuals and teams based not only on their output but on their attitudes, participation, teamwork, commitment, learning, and personal development, thereby encouraging continuous learning and change. Organizations that want to encourage employees to act like owners need to compensate them like owners, and reward them for contributing to financial success by allowing them to share in the profits.

Integrative, value-driven systems can also be applied to communications, process improvement, training programs, career planning, conflict resolution, decision-making, operations, and production systems. What distinguishes integrative, value-driven systems from their hierarchical, rule-driven antecedents are their openness to revision, reorientation, and renewal; their inclusion of all employees in their design and evaluation; their enhancement of human satisfaction, effectiveness, and productivity; and their ability to wake people up.

Collaborative, democratic learning organizations require integrative, value-driven systems that empower employees to think and act like organizational citizens. This means creating challenging, nonhierarchical career paths that do not force them to move into managerial positions in order to advance. Achieving status and rewards should not require abandoning one's expertise, skills, or competencies for entirely new ones, or pit one set of workers against another. Career systems can be redesigned to encourage the development of authentic job preferences and self-expression. They can allow employees to continue performing skills at which they excel without abandoning their expertise and passion.

A recent study of employees in over two hundred companies seeking to implement pay-for-performance systems reported that 58 percent of those interviewed would rather increase their pay by doing their current job better than by getting promoted. In line with this data, organizations are designing nonhierarchical career paths to flatten their managerial hierarchies, become more agile and responsive to changing conditions, shift to self-managing teams, compensate employees for doing jobs well, and cut unnecessary costs associated with managerial oversight.

In flattened, team-based organizations, integrative, value-driven systems allow promotion and advancement to be more creative, lateral, and based on skill and choice. These organizations design promotion systems that permit people with talent and technical skills to develop their expertise by learning, playing, coaching, mentoring, leading, and teaching others, while receiving compensation and status appropriate to management. This open attitude toward learning wakes people up, cultivates awareness and authenticity, and transforms work into a process of continuous learning.

We are under no illusions that the process will be easy. Yet we are clear that there is no alternative if we are to make work conform to human needs, and that doing so means waking up, cultivating awareness, authenticity, congruence, and commitment, and building democratic organizations that encourage and reward these behaviors.

Fundamentally, what matters most to us as human beings is less the products and services that organizations create than the relationships, processes, and opportunities for growth, learning, and self-actualization that flow from producing them. When we create collaborative, learning-oriented, inquiry-based cultures; synergistic, team-based structures; and integrative, value-driven systems, these cease being mere by-products of work and become consciously valued and encouraged—of, by, and for themselves.

13

Fostering Congruence and Commitment in Organizations

The highest reward for a man's toil is not what he gets
for it but what he becomes by it.

John Ruskin

If English critic John Ruskin is right that our reward for work is who we become by it, then the creation of democratic organizations that allow everyone to have a voice in who they will become ought to be our highest priority. Yet hierarchical, bureaucratic, authoritarian organizations not only put us to sleep, they encourage us to become incongruent and uncommitted to changing them. As we wake up, we become increasingly aware of incongruities or inconsistencies between our actions and our intentions. We begin to see where we lack focus and commitment, and what we are doing that is not working. Similarly, waking organizations up consists of noticing how their cultures, structures, systems, and processes encourage inauthentic, incongruent, uncommitted behaviors; how they put people to sleep; and how they can be transformed so as to foster congruence and commitment.

To live more aware, authentic, congruent, and committed work lives, we need to create organizational environments that connect ideals with behavior, values with policies, and intentions with effects. In congruent, committed organizations, values are aligned with processes and people act on their commitments without being coerced into doing so by their managers.

Because hierarchy, bureaucracy, and autocracy are inherently contradictory, it is difficult for these organizations to recognize, own, or eliminate incongruent behaviors. Insincere, dishonest, waffling, hypocritical organizational cultures cannot eliminate insincere, dishonest, waffling, hypocritical behaviors among their managers and employees.

In organizations that preach but fail to practice value-based behaviors, it is difficult for people to know or feel confident about who they are, and as a consequence, they tend to say one thing and do another. In their effort to avoid being blamed, they send mixed messages, respond defensively, and create outcomes and results they neither want nor desire. They experience a disconnect, an inconsistency, a lack of integration between who they think they are or pretend to be and who they actually are. A gap arises between their *intentions* and their *effects*, their self-images and the way others experience them, their visions and what they get.

Control Versus Learning Orientation

When individuals and organizations face rapid changes, severe crises, or chronic conflicts, they respond either by attempting to exercise control over their problems or by deciding to learn from them. Those who choose a control orientation try to master the problem by asking: "How can I assert sufficient control to ensure that problems as I define them are solved in ways I see fit?" The hidden assumptions underlying the control orientation are that problems are dangerous, that people can't learn or change, and that their problems will continue unless and until they are solved "my way."

Those who adopt a learning orientation, on the other hand, seek to investigate and learn from their problems. They see them as sources of information about how to avoid future difficulties. They ask: "How can I learn from this problem?" The assumptions underlying the learning orientation are that problems are opportunities, that people can learn and change, and that problems can be solved in multiple ways that satisfy diverse mutual interests.

Those who are frightened of surrendering control reject the learning approach, feeling it gives them little power over the problem or to ensure that the solution will meet their needs. Yet paradoxically, the control orientation, in the long run, results in *reduced* control because it fails to learn from the problem or discover the true reasons for its existence. If the only people committed to making the organization work are those who are in control, everyone else will take little or no responsibility for improving conditions or implementing solutions that do not meet their needs. With a learning orientation, everyone becomes involved in exploring, researching, questioning, analyzing, and discussing the problem, and is committed not just to solving it but to mutually resolving the underlying conditions that created it.

It is not easy to shift organizations from a control orientation based on assumptions of predictability and order to a recognition that control is less successful and in the long run unattainable. It is difficult to convince hierarchical managers that considerable damage can be done by trying to impose control, predictability, and order on complex, paradoxical, rapidly evolving human, social, and environmental systems that are inherently disordered and often chaotic.

If we consider the implications of these two divergent styles on organizations, we can see that each creates a self-reinforcing system that fulfills its own prophecy. The control orientation results in a kind of "groupthink" in which public image is separated from and contradicted by private reality; where intergroup dynamics are polarized, people protect their turf, and politicking and subterfuge hide problems and conflicts because it is too risky to raise them openly. As a result, problems continue to appear unsolvable, except by control.

The learning orientation, on the other hand, results in team creativity, in which public image and private reality are congruent, intergroup dynamics are based on consensus, people easily cross

organizational lines, and there is a premium on discovering problems because it is exciting to explore and learn from them. As a
result, problems are solved at a higher level, fueling not only individual but organizational learning and ensuring the same problems
do not return in a different guise.

Creating Learning Organizations and Relationships

Learning organizations are characterized by their clarity of vision,
their commitment to implementing their values, and their multi-
layered leadership. They are distinguishable from hierarchical,
bureaucratic, and autocratic organizations by their high levels of
interaction and teamwork, their focus on relationship building and
innovation, their support for risk taking, and their tolerance for criticism and failure. In learning organizations, there is a strong commitment to the success of others. People make decisions by
consensus, encourage honesty and openness, and organize themselves into self-managing teams with floating, ubiquitous leaders.

Employees in learning organizations eagerly accept challenges,
creatively solve problems, and continually reflect on how they
might improve without blaming each other for their mistakes. They
recognize that there is no one left to blame. They are willing to take
responsibility for the whole and increase performance standards for
themselves. They are frequently open and honest with each other
and, as a result, experience less conflict. They are aware of their
commonalities, value their differences, and spend time enjoying one
another's company. According to our colleague Peter Senge, who
first conceptualized learning organizations, they are defined by the
following elements:

- *Shared vision* articulates personal visions, communicates
  and asks for support, uses visioning as an ongoing
  process, blends extrinsic and intrinsic visions, and distinguishes positive from negative visions.

- *Mental models* encourage leaps of abstraction, balance inquiry and advocacy, distinguish espoused theory from theory in use, and recognize and defuse defensive routines.

- *Systems thinking* helps people value interrelationships rather than things, move beyond blame, distinguish detailed complexity from dynamic complexity, focus on areas of high leverage, and avoid symptomatic solutions.

In these ways, learning organizations detect, design, and nourish local learning practices and assist in the creation of shared meaning. They empower employees to analyze and transform their culture, reveal what prevents their learning, and eliminate it. They generate knowledge-enhancing systems that assess the impact of each new experience on results, processes, and relationships, and diffuse important lessons and innovative practices throughout the organization.

The complex process of creating learning organizations starts by fostering and supporting learning relationships, which are the core of all the processes and techniques we have reviewed. An example of the importance of learning relationships can be found in friendships, especially "best" friendships. Best friends are people we trust to give us turnaround feedback, coach us through difficulties, mentor us strategically, and assess our behavior honestly. Recent research suggests that having a best friend at work is not merely enjoyable but contributes to productivity as well.

In 2001 the Gallup Organization studied a random sample of U.S. workers aged eighteen and older. Of those who had a best friend at work, 51 percent felt engaged in their workplace, as opposed to only 10 percent who did not have such a relationship. A solid 60 percent of those with best friends said they would recommend the company's products or services, compared with 38 percent of those without; 75 percent of employees with best friends planned to be with the company in one year versus 51 percent of those without; and 50 percent reported they would spend their career with the company as opposed to only 25 percent without best friends at work. Finally, 65 percent with best friends reported that laughter or humor played a positive role in their productivity, as opposed to 31 percent without such friends at work.

In a different study, twenty-six groups of three friends and twenty-seven groups of three acquaintances were given detailed instructions on constructing models out of Tinkertoys. Those who were friends built an average of 9 models, compared to only 2.45 for acquaintances. Clearly, friendships are learning relationships that generate positive results not only for those involved but for their organizations as well. As a result of these studies, organizations can improve their operations, financial results, and job satisfaction simply by encouraging collaborative, democratic learning relationships and the friendships that form their base.

From Training to Development

To wake people up and build learning organizations and relationships, traditional hierarchical training programs need to be transformed into innovative, integrative developmental experiences. To create learning organizations and relationships that support people in becoming self-managing, responsible, aware, authentic, congruent, and committed, these qualities have to be built into the learning processes and methodologies by which these skills are mastered.

To understand the fundamental differences in outcomes that result from different learning processes and methodologies, we find it useful to distinguish

- *Lectures and rote memorization*, which grade students based on their recall of rules and facts and result in knowledge and information.

- *Education and classes*, which expose students to ideas and result in learning and understanding.

- *Training sessions and workshops*, which involve students in directed group discussions and result in technical competency and confidence.

- *Development and inquiry*, which encourage student self-awareness and facilitated dialogue and result in wisdom, integrity, and freedom.

Our friend leadership development expert Ken Anbender, who delineated these distinctions, points out that moving from lectures, classes, and training sessions to development and inquiry also highlights the difference between four critical competencies: knowing, doing, understanding, and being. Each of these competencies performs a valuable function, and each is needed to respond to different challenges. In addition, as organizations evolve, they require higher levels of competency and higher processes for producing them.

Development and inquiry, which focus on *being*, result in the deepest wisdom, the highest integrity, and the most committed leadership over the longest period of any of the practices described. Development and inquiry therefore become the primary learning processes of learning organizations. These distinctions are illustrated in Figure 13.1.

As employees participate in higher forms of learning, they cultivate the subtle skills needed to build collaborative, self-managing, democratic learning organizations and relationships. Each new level of learning calls for increased awareness, more authentic behavior, greater congruence between values and actions, and stronger commitment to personal and team development. This approach to learning makes it possible to shift organizational cultures, structures, and systems incrementally in a more democratic direction.

Organizational Congruence

When organizations lack congruence, their leaders and managers send contradictory messages, causing those they lead or manage to distrust them or question their motives. When managers do not feel

Figure 13.1. Core Learning Processes.

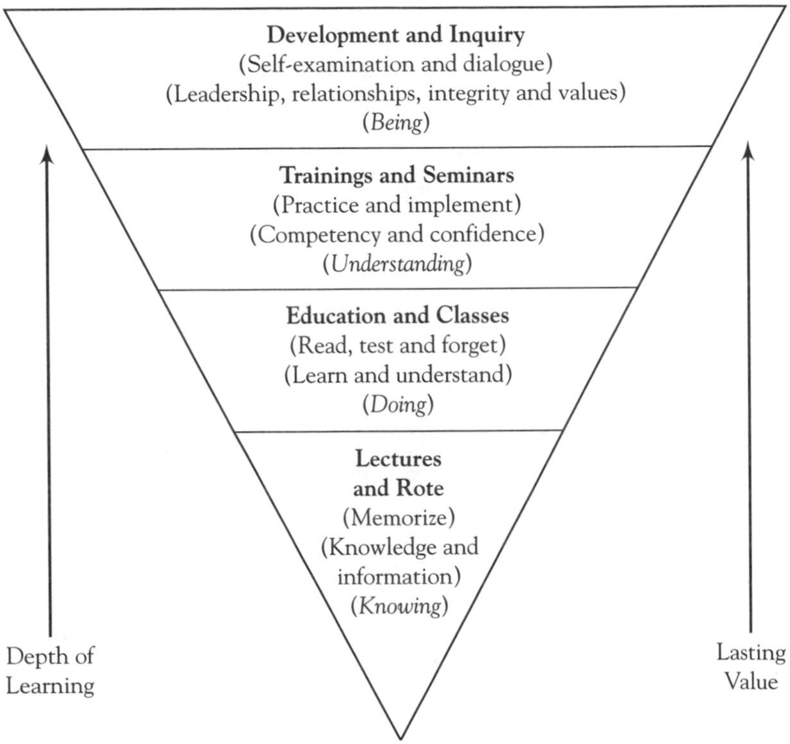

```
Development and Inquiry
(Self-examination and dialogue)
(Leadership, relationships, integrity and values)
(Being)

Trainings and Seminars
(Practice and implement)
(Competency and confidence)
(Understanding)

Education and Classes
(Read, test and forget)
(Learn and understand)
(Doing)

Lectures
and Rote
(Memorize)
(Knowledge and
information)
(Knowing)
```

Depth of
Learning

Lasting
Value

congruent within themselves, their relationships become a series of power plays, win-lose propositions, and zero-sum games with little opportunity for mutually satisfying interactions or results. To encourage congruence, leaders, managers, and employees have to increase their awareness, become more honest with themselves and others, and listen to feedback for indications that they are sending contradictory messages.

For example, we were asked to advise a company of asset managers and stock traders. The initial company began as a small, successful partnership where everyone did everything. They were highly innovative, grew informally, and distributed stock options equally. Suggestions and new ideas were accepted without regard to who proposed them. As each idea was tested in the market it succeeded or failed based on results. Everyone's behaviors were congruent with their values, organizational processes reflected their democratic vision, and everyone was fully committed to mutual development and collaboration.

As the firm grew, managerial layers were added, separate departments were created, and people became increasingly differentiated by office size, salary, stock options, travel budgets, and titles. Pressure grew to produce results, and in the process, staff who once worked shoulder to shoulder were now locked in competition with each other. Resentments ballooned over inequalities in office space, work assignments, and privileges. As a result they were bogged down in personal backstabbing and poor morale, litigation over sexual harassment, and bureaucratic procedures. Because no one felt safe giving the CEO feedback, he made uninformed, disastrous decisions. As a result, commitment lagged and profitability declined precipitously. The excitement and adventure of the early years were lost due to organizational incongruence, causing managers to take an increasingly rigid hierarchical approach to decision making.

Organizational congruence consists of making the walk match the talk, conforming process to content, and making values the centerpiece of organizational life. In the absence of organizational congruence, employees become reluctant to commit to improving either the organization or their own performance. Congruence is critically important to organizational success because without it employees are unwilling to trust that they can safely wake up, be authentic, congruent, and committed, and deliver honest turnaround feedback. To do that, they need leaders rather than bosses—that is, people in management positions who can foster authentic interactions, rather than those who use command and control and concentrate on mechanical rather than human systems. If congruence and commitment are desired qualities in employees, then bossing needs to give way to leadership, not only on the shop floor but in the conference room and classroom as well.

Democratic Values and Organizational Congruence

Developing shared values and reinforcing the behaviors that express them is fundamental to creating organizational congruence and committed action. This requires a shift from rule-driven values to value-driven rules. Reaching consensus on a set of shared values is a powerful way of waking organizations up and making everyone more aware, authentic, congruent, and committed. For example, the following sections present fourteen core values drawn from our book *Thank God It's Monday: 14 Values We Need to Humanize the Way We Work,* together with some suggestions for using them to encourage democracy, congruence, and committed action.

Inclusion

No one should be left out of the process of improvement—no function, faction, section, clique, group, department, role, team, or individual. Everyone has something to contribute, and can be heard without grinding work to a halt. Some ways of doing so include cross-team dialogues, debates, discussions, suggestion boxes, focus groups, secret ballots, facilitated retreats, team meetings, surveys, conflict audits, department-wide meetings, open houses, quality circles, employee-run forums, and social gatherings. Each of these provides access to discussion and decision making for every employee. Creating such opportunities empowers and encourages people to speak up and participate.

Collaboration

Work today is almost exclusively social and cannot be completed without collaboration, which may include negotiation, joint problem solving, consensus decision making, or conflict resolution. Collaboration is not compromise. It is building a partnership from the beginning without having to give up or give in. It is including everyone who has a stake in the outcome and creating solutions. Collaboration is an essential democratic skill that allows teams and networks to call forth the best in each individual while producing more than any collection of individuals could deliver.

Teams and Networks

Forcing decisions down through multiple levels in a hierarchy only creates traffic jams, communications silos, problem-solving bottlenecks, and a separation between those who know about the problem intimately and those who have the authority to decide how it will be solved. For these reasons, decision making from the top is becoming increasingly obsolete. Teams that are empowered, self-directed, and self-managed replace multiple layers of middle managers, and act both rapidly and responsibly. Networks of affiliated teams, organizations, suppliers, customers, and departments integrate design ideas to satisfy multiple sets of interests, increase the quality and quantity of communication flow, transact all aspects of business, buy and sell, hire and fire, and make virtually every kind of decision once thought to be the exclusive prerogative of management.

Vision

Envisioning is a natural, easy, democratic process that is a precursor to building consensus. Visions can be created on a large scale for three or five years, or the next six months of a team's work, or the lifetime of an individual. Visions are an excuse to talk about what matters. They can be recreated and revised whenever there is a need to return to basics and discover what everyone values individually and collectively.

Celebration of Diversity

Increasingly, and for the foreseeable future, organizations are a meeting ground for people from highly diverse backgrounds. The complexity and diversity of the workplace in terms of gender, race, ethnicity, nationality, physical capacity, age, language, sexual orientation, culture, and heritage not only reflects the marketplace and customer base, it increases the ability to respond to rapid change and alters decision-making styles, communication patterns, personal interactions, expectations, behaviors, and leadership skills. In a democratic work environment, diversity is an extraordinary source of richness, vitality, and strength. The challenge for every individual is to draw out the potential in each unique human being. Curiosity, trust, and celebrations of diversity are created by respecting each person's values and backgrounds and discouraging suspicion, distancing, and prejudice.

Process Awareness

A subtle knowledge of process, an awareness of how people interact with one another, an ability to work collaboratively, a knowledge of techniques for reaching consensus, and an understanding of group dynamics are essential democratic skills and requirements for success, particularly in collaborative learning organizations.

Open and Honest Communication

Information is a rich, useful source of democratic power. Whatever information we hoard or secrets we keep distort our relationships. Hierarchical organizations operate on the basis of secrecy and "need to know." Yet quality of results and satisfaction in producing them increase when they are built on solid information rather than on rumors, gossip, and misinformation. By starting with the value of complete openness and honesty and training those who receive information in how to use it skillfully, we increase the possibility of collaboration and synergy. Rather than assume a need for secrecy, if we assume a desire for openness and honesty and place the burden on those seeking to depart from it, we increase organizational democracy, agility, and adaptability.

Risk Taking

Without people who are willing to take risks, make leaps of faith, and experience failure, there can be little growth and learning. We do not find creative answers to problems by traveling familiar roads.

Mistakes, wrong turns, and failures are all a part of the process of learning and changing. As new ideas are explored and innovation is encouraged, risk taking and failure are not merely allowed but modeled, acknowledged, supported, rewarded, and celebrated.

Individual and Team Ownership of Results

It is only when we stop trying to shift responsibility to someone else and take personal ownership of whatever happens, including work that is someone else's primary responsibility, that we become committed to finding solutions. It is then that we realize we have an obligation to speak out and disagree if we don't think the job is being done right. As individuals speak out and take responsibility for the work of the team, team members support and become responsible for the work of their coworkers. Teams encourage their members to raise criticisms and problems, support them when they need it, encourage cross-training, and provide backup and honest feedback so they can achieve their highest potential.

Paradoxical Problem Solving

In complex organizations, problem solving is rarely linear. Employees confront paradoxes every day, and the natural complexity of their problems should not be overly simplified or solved too quickly. By living simultaneously with two apparently contradictory realities, people working in complex, living organizations are able to imagine newer, richer alternatives. If they do eventually need to choose a single solution and act, their solution will be stronger because it responds to a larger problem. By embracing paradox, we are able to benefit from complex solutions without fearing the contradictions that seem to arise from holding two opposite thoughts at the same time.

Everyone Is a Leader

Waking people up encourages employees to become leaders in their own work lives. Leadership belongs not only to those at the top of an organization, but is an obligation for everyone at every level. Leadership starts with employees' taking charge of their own lives and empowering others to do the same. It asks them to model the behaviors they advocate. It requires them to reach out to their coworkers wherever they are and supporting them, step by step, in becoming and achieving more than they thought they were capable of—and doing the same for themselves.

Leadership is not a thing, it is an *attitude* that is found in congruent, committed relationships. Leaders do not separate themselves from others or from responsibility, but seek to collaboratively define their relationship to both. They are willing to be different and risk opposing accepted opinion. They operate in a context of values and work to bring them into existence. They are open to giving and receiving turnaround feedback, transformational coaching, strategic mentoring, and participatory assessments. Leadership does not mean occupying one of the few available executive positions. It is a matter of treating the organization as though it *belongs* to you— not exclusively, but collaboratively with others.

Personal Growth and Satisfaction

Our lives are designed and shaped creatively by and through our work. Cross-training enhances our skills, while flexible schedules and collaboration support our growth and personal enjoyment. Teams provide us with ways to feel satisfied and useful on the job, have fun with one another, and fulfill our responsibilities. Leadership in teams affords us opportunities to grow and expand into roles we never thought we could play. We can then see ourselves as whole people on the job rather than cogs in a grinding machine. Democracy ultimately means it is acceptable for us to be ourselves at work and to feel that we are entitled to satisfy our needs and desires.

Seeing Conflict as an Opportunity

When we encourage democracy and self-direction, increase personal interaction between teams and networks, open up communication and problem solving, negotiate boundaries, make decisions based on consensus, and substitute collaborative for autocratic styles of management, conflicts that once were swept under the rug naturally rise to the surface. Every conflict reveals opportunities for learning, growth, change, improvement, better and more intimate relationships, and deeper understanding of ourselves.

Conflict resolution allows problems to be admitted, aired, resolved constructively, prevented, channeled, and defused before they result in serious damage. Many organizations use informal problem solving, peer mediation, executive advisers, internal review boards, ombudsmen, peer counseling, dialogue groups, arbitration, and other alternative dispute resolution processes to reduce unresolved conflict, encourage prevention, and improve collaborative democratic relationships.

Embracing Change

Jobs that once existed for life have become temporary in a rapidly changing, increasingly globalized workplace. Communications that once took days or weeks now happen instantaneously. Structures that were accepted as the norm are being redesigned from scratch. There are no blueprints, no charts, no tales from travelers who have been there before. There is only experimentation, risk taking, and change, which focuses on discovering what works, what produces results, and what is most satisfying. The best strategy for surviving in this environment is to embrace change and continually strive for learning and improvement.

These values and others like them create a context of awareness, integrity, congruence, and commitment that can direct and guide organizational behavior. They are particularly effective when they are adopted through a participatory consensus-building process that allows each value to be fully discussed, debated, and owned. Through democratic participation, organizations can bring their cultures, structures, and systems into congruence with their shared values and encourage everyone to commit to doing the same.

Congruence in Organizational Processes

Congruence means that there is consistency and interconnection between the meaning or content of *what* is done and the method or form of *how* it is done. Congruence in communications, for example, is established by agreement among words, tone of voice, feelings, body language, facial expressions, gestures, and follow-up behaviors. Organizations with congruent processes are seen as credible, trustworthy, and easily understood. Their employees feel listened and responded to, and are therefore more open, honest, fearless, and connected with each other. When organizations lack congruence in their processes, commitment fails, distrust mushrooms, people retreat into cliques, and conflicts remain at impasse.

Every process encodes and recreates a particular kind of content. Processes define organizations and shape the relationships and attitudes of those within them. For example, during new employee orientations, many organizations focus on introducing their rules, policies, and procedures but spend little time finding out who their employees are or addressing the fears and anxieties that every new employee brings to a new place of work. A more congruent approach to orientation would encourage open conversation, dialogue, and disagreement and elicit feedback regarding ways the orientation process might be improved.

Meetings are often used as opportunities to report on what people are doing, or by managers to pass information on to their subordinates. In congruent organizations, they are also used as opportunities to wake people up, define strategies, clarify goals and values, build relationships and teams, encourage individual and organizational learning, and promote dialogue over issues that matter. Congruent organizations make their explicit and implicit messages match, and their ideals are used to shape their reality.

To create a sense of congruence in organizations, we need to become more congruent within ourselves, to devote time and energy to waking up and discovering who we are. As we increase our awareness of what is taking place within and around us, we become more honest with ourselves and others. We monitor our words and deeds to make certain they conform to our values and correct them when they do not. And we take a risk and give our coworkers honest turn-around feedback when they act incongruently.

Consensus Decision Making and Commitment

Every democratic organization requires that foundational choices and critical issues be decided by consensus. As a process, consensus encourages people to wake up, engage in congruent behavior, and commit to implementing the ideas that are agreed on. Not only do individuals benefit by being included and having a significant voice, teams and organizations are also strengthened by consensus deci-sion making. As people are empowered to learn and act responsi-bly, they are able to contribute to the common good. There is a direct connection between power and participation, as philosopher Hannah Arendt notes: "While strength is the natural quality of an individual seen in isolation, power springs up between men when they act together and vanishes the moment they disperse. And whoever isolates himself and does not participate in such being together, forfeits power and becomes impotent, no matter how great his strength and how valid his reasons."

Consensus decision making occurs when everyone has a stake in the outcome, and for that reason has both a right and a respon-sibility to participate in making decisions that affect it. The possi-bility that employees will decide incorrectly is not and has never been a convincing justification for excluding them from responsi-bility for participating in the decision. If a wrong decision is made, it is possible to learn from experience and do better next time.

Consensus is not the same as unanimity. In consensus decision making, everyone affected by the problem is involved in discussing and agreeing on the solution. They agree that they are willing to live with the decision and do not feel a strong need to object to it, even if they prefer something different. If all the employees who do

not agree 100 percent still feel their voices were heard, a full discussion was held, and they are willing to live with the choice, support the decision, and implement it in good faith, consensus has
been reached.

Consensus takes the power of participation several steps further
by allowing all voices to be heard, turning dissent into dialogue, and
encouraging all factions to recognize the need for common action.
The primary limits on making decisions by consensus are the willingness of those involved to surrender their right to make the decision unilaterally, the willingness of those with power to share it, and
the willingness of those who make the decision to act responsibly
and implement it. It is possible for organizations to apply full
employee participation and consensus decision making to nearly
every major issue they face, including such foundational issues as

- *Selection*. Who makes hiring, transfer, and firing decisions, and how?

- *Size*. How many employees are in each work group, and
  how do they interact and combine?

- *Scale*. What level tasks are assigned to each subgroup,
  and by whom?

- *Roles and responsibilities*. Who assigns, defines, and clarifies who does what?

- *Training*. Who has a chance to develop skills and in
  what areas?

- *Pay*. How is compensation determined and how are
  profits and losses distributed?

- *Coaching and mentoring*. Who decides who receives coaching and mentoring and who coaches and mentors?

- *Leadership*. Who selects and removes leaders and how is
  leadership exercised?

- *Assessment.* Who decides on the standards for performance and the methods by which people will be evaluated?

- *Promotion.* How are people advanced and by what criteria?

- *Motivation.* How are people encouraged and empowered?

- *Relationship building.* How are communications and interactions nurtured, and how are rules made and enforced?

- *Conflict resolution.* How are conflicts surfaced and resolved, and how do emotional healing and reconciliation take place?

- *Feedback and evaluation.* Who gives feedback to whom, and what gets evaluated and by what criteria?

For each of these decision points, employees are able to make successful decisions using consensus processes that encourage the development of value-based parameters, congruent behaviors, collaborative relationships, democratic leadership, and committed action.

From Waking Up to Committed Action

The main organizational reason for waking people up is to improve the ability of individuals, teams, and organizations to make better decisions, act responsibly, and achieve turnaround results. As we increase employee motivation, responsibility, and participation, we bring the entire process to its highest and final level in the form of committed action.

We engage in committed action only when we are awake and therefore able to bring awareness, authenticity, and congruence to what we do. By engaging in committed action, we not only agree to take risks and challenge the status quo, we begin to act as owners and responsible organizational citizens. We commit to participate in essential decisions the same as any other citizens in a democracy.

There are many ways of taking action, which can be expressed in a variety of settings, using a broad range of roles and serving multiple purposes. Committed action means acting as though your life depended on what you do and taking responsibility for whatever consequences your action produces.

The first step in promoting committed action is engaging those who will be asked to act and encouraging their participation in making all the decisions requiring action. The second step is *action planning*, which defines the action to be taken, identifies the people who will take it, fixes a date when it will be done, and lists the resources required for completion. Here are some questions that can be used to facilitate action planning:

- Is the action clear?

- Is the description of what needs to be done detailed enough?

- Who is going to do it?

- Who will help?

- Are everyone's roles and responsibilities clear?

- Whose permission or agreement is needed for the action to be successful?

- When will it be done by?

- What will happen if it isn't done on time?

- Are the resources and support adequate?

- What follow-up actions may be needed?

- How will results be evaluated?

- How will successes be acknowledged and celebrated?

Action plans are concrete descriptions of what is going to happen. They are practical and specific in focus. They are immediate and clearly related to vision, values, and goals. They are detailed ways of implementing strategies and overcoming barriers. They are integrated and interconnected, resource-based, team-oriented, time-sequenced, adaptable, and contingent. As they create plans, people wake up and adopt a framework that encourages their committed action.

There is a magic to committed action that can be seen not only in the extraordinary results it produces but in the enhanced self-esteem, empowered capacity, and orientation to learning it stimulates. When teams of people commit to a course of action and focus their intention on achieving a particular goal, everything in their environment begins to align itself and become a resource to support their success. Congruence and commitment allow intention to merge with the energy of democratic collaboration to produce results that cannot be achieved without them.

Committed action requires courage and clarity about who we are and what is important to us. It calls forth shared values, consensus decision making, and responsibility. We understand that we cannot create the organizations we need using top-down, linear methods. Worse, to do so would violate the very ideas and values we seek to establish. Instead, we recognize that this work must be done in congruence with our values, forcing us to take a further step and recognize that individuals and organizations will only *fully* wake up when their cultures, structures, and systems are strategically integrated into a single democratic whole.

14

Ubiquitous Leadership and Organizational Democracy

Finding the leader within, our heroic self, does more than unshackle us from the external leaders to whom we so desperately have held fast. It also frees up much more leadership talent for the entire society, in every organization, at every level. This new breed of leaders will be more self-reliant and thoughtful. These will be leaders who can handle the magnificent uncertitude of our times, the anxiety it augments, and the opportunities for learning and change that both uncertainty and anxiety generate.

Jean Lipman-Blumen

We began this exploration of the art of waking people up by creating a context in which we described the need for awareness, authenticity, congruence, and commitment at work. We explored the core processes of turnaround feedback, transformational coaching, strategic mentoring, and participatory assessment. We examined the techniques of courageous listening, paradoxical problem solving, supportive confrontation, and risky conflict resolution. We considered ways of waking organizations up by creating collaborative, learning-oriented, inquiry-based cultures; synergistic, team-based structures; and integrative, value-driven systems. We examined ways of fostering congruence and commitment at work.

We now need to ask: What kind of leadership is needed to nurture and sustain these efforts? What kind of organizations result from combining these elements and integrating them into a single strategic whole? What are the organizational, social, and political consequences of waking people up? What kind of organizations keep them awake? What put them to sleep in the first place?

As the German philosopher Nietzsche wrote in 1880 regarding the implications of our capacity for conscious thought, "Individuals and generations can now fix their eyes on tasks of a vastness that would to earlier ages have seemed madness and a trifling with Heaven and Hell. We may experiment on ourselves!"

We must therefore ask: What are the implications of these experiments on ourselves for our overall development as human beings?

New Forms of Organizational Leadership

Organizational democracy, like its political counterparts, is premised on the idea that every employee is capable of exercising leadership— and must do so for the spirit of democracy to remain alive. In the opening to this chapter, distinguished professor and author Jean Lipman-Blumen suggests that by supporting leadership development ubiquitously among rank-and-file employees at every level, we not only protect democracy but increase our capacity to deal with uncertainty and change.

The democratic process asks *everyone* to enhance their leadership skills in the service of societal, organizational, team, relational, and personal improvement. Democratic leadership is based on the premise that we cannot help others unless we help ourselves, and that we cannot help ourselves unless we help others. Trying to do one without the other leaves half the task undone.

Leadership, in this context, does not always require genius, charisma, momentous achievements, or great works to prove itself. As political commentator Hendrik Hertzberg wrote in reflection on Robert Kennedy's leadership, "Robert Kennedy, on his own, left no great legislative legacy, founded no great institution, led no great movement. His most extraordinary accomplishment—and it was extraordinary—was to embody in himself, and create in others, a kind of transcendent yearning for the possibility of redemptive change."

This observation about Kennedy, written years after his assassination, points to his ability to inspire and motivate others to strive for a better world. This idea of leadership is well within the capacity of every employee at every level in every organization. In this view leadership is a creative relationship in which something new is brought into existence, both in ourselves and in others. From the point of view of waking people up, democratic leaders model and inspire people to be honest with themselves and with others; search for ways of assisting others to improve their skills and deepen their understanding; and support them in moving to a place where these new skills and understandings can benefit the entire organization.

The idea of ubiquitous nonhierarchical leadership is vastly different from the practice of management as it occurs in most organizations. Douglas McGregor explained the difference: "People don't want to be managed. They want to be led. Whoever heard of a world manager: World leader, yes. Educational leader. Political leader. Religious leader. Scout leader. They lead. They don't manage. The carrot always wins over the stick. Ask your horse. You can lead your horse to water, but you can't manage him to drink. If you want to manage somebody, manage yourself. Do that well and you'll be ready to stop managing. And start leading."

Turnaround feedback, coaching, mentoring, and assessment turn leaders into lifelong learners and solicit the information they need to be successful from those they lead. As an illustration, we worked recently with a large government agency and asked every staff member to identify areas in which they could improve. The boss said she needed to request feedback more readily from her staff. In response, a staff member mentioned that in her experience anger always cropped up in her voice when she received feedback. With an embarrassed laugh, she acknowledged her tense style, made fun of it, and agreed to do her best to curb it. She asked her staff to promise that they would remind her to do so. In this way, a staff member provided leadership for the entire organization by giving honest feedback to her boss. The boss demonstrated leadership by making herself vulnerable and setting an expectation that others would do the same. And by doing so, she became the leader everybody wanted.

As leaders receive transformational coaching from the people they ordinarily coach, they are given opportunities for continued growth. As an illustration, we assisted a junior employee in coaching a senior vice president from a different department in technology skills in an effort to bring her kicking and screaming into the twenty-first century. This vice president of an entrepreneurial manufacturing company worked only with paper and pencil. Computer technology, the Internet, and videoconferencing were frightening to her. Although her direct reports were organized in a decentralized structure and scattered all over the country, she refused to communicate with them by e-mail or videoconferencing.

Her coach was a young man who responded to her fear and defensiveness and clearly but gently helped her learn to go online and use new communication technologies. Both of them emerged from the coaching process as better leaders. She learned to use all the tools available to her, and he learned he could provide transformational coaching to his boss and not be intimidated by her superior status and power.

If leaders are able to receive strategic mentoring from those beneath them in the hierarchy, they can continue to develop their strategic capabilities. For example, we worked with a large urban art museum that attracted a new president who had a great deal of experience in analyzing and addressing urban problems but lacked experience as an art curator or manager of a commercial institution. He needed turnaround feedback, coaching, and mentoring from his subordinate staff.

Many employees were uncertain about his expectations and priorities, but he was committed to a democratic style of leadership and offered an open invitation to reciprocally coach and mentor all staff who were interested in developing their career goals and working to reach them. By extending himself in this way, he sent a signal that he was available to everyone in the organization. He saw mentoring as a strategic process and made it clear that advancement and career development were organizational priorities, both for himself and every staff member, regardless of their position.

Participatory assessment is equally critical to leaders in democratic organizations, not only because it offers improvement opportunities for everyone, but because it allows them to model how one can learn from mistakes without judgments, punishments, or retribution.

For example, a community college decided to institute a 360-degree assessment process, and the president of the college asked everyone to evaluate him as the first step. He reported back to everyone publicly on the feedback he received, made immediate improvements, and was universally respected for his courageous leadership in doing so.

In another example, a team-based financial services division of a large corporation instituted a participatory 360-degree assessment process. The leader of the division made it clear at the beginning that since there was an open position for team leader on the accounts payable team, he would use the assessment process to let the team and its internal customers select the person who would fill the position. In effect, he made the assessment process an opportunity for team members to *elect* their new leader. As a result, a new, democratically selected leadership was able to emerge and thrive.

Waking Up and Democracy

Hierarchical, bureaucratic, autocratic organizational practices clearly put people to sleep and undermine their awareness, authenticity, congruence, and commitment. This is partly because hierarchical organizations demand so much of employees, while requesting so little. The little requested is that they obey hierarchical authority, comply with bureaucratic rules and policies, and satisfy managerially imposed performance standards. The much that is demanded is that they waste their work lives by living them in an apathetic trance.

As a result, employees surrender their right to participate in making important decisions that directly affect their work lives, violating the first principle of every democracy—that governing requires the consent of the governed. When top managers make strategic decisions without input from employees, democracy is diminished and hierarchy is enhanced. When managers make top-down decisions without employee involvement, democracy is blocked and autocracy is advanced. When abstract rules, policies, and procedures are applied to people who are unable to participate in defining or enforcing them, democracy is discouraged and bureaucracy is encouraged.

As we have shown, these systems actively distort communications, increase distrust, and exacerbate chronic unresolved conflicts. They block the flow of meaning across organizations, obstruct teamwork and collaboration, and undermine relationships that sensitively depend on awareness, authenticity, congruence, and commitment.

In *The End of Management and the Rise of Organizational Democracy*, we consider these questions in depth and will not revisit those arguments here. It is appropriate, however, to indicate our belief that democracy is a superior means of making decisions in organizations. What is more important here is that it is not only the best environment for waking people up but an *inevitable* consequence of doing so. By democracy, we do not mean putting every decision to a majority vote. We mean that the inalienable rights of life, liberty, and the pursuit of happiness deserve recognition in the workplace. We mean that even private organizations need to acknowledge the value and importance of freedom of speech, assembly, and religion, of due process of law and equal protection guarantees that were written into the U.S. Constitution for reasons that have equal validity in the workplace. Ultimately, it means no less than eliminating the separation between governing from being governed. As Abraham Lincoln wrote: "As I would not be a slave, so I would not be a master. This expresses my idea of democracy. Whatever differs from this, to the extent of the difference, is no democracy."

Unfortunately, the relationship of master to slave has not completely disappeared. It is alive and unwell today in the workplace, albeit in a far more civilized form. Yet it continues wherever hierarchy, bureaucracy, and autocracy dominate the relationship between managers and employees. By waking either the slave or the master up to the truth of their human equality and their potential for expressing it in the workplace, we undermine industrial slavery and make organizational democracy inevitable.

The same can be said for waking organizations up to the importance of participation and collaborative leadership at work. Every increase in democratic approaches to leadership creates an expanded sense of ownership, empowerment, and competency on the part of employees and a diminished sense that autocratic managerial elites are required to run organizations. In an awake environment, it becomes clear that democracy is fundamentally an act of *ownership*, whether over government or organizations, and that ownership builds responsibility and fuels learning and improvement.

This conflict between the rise of organizational democracy and the decline of hierarchical organizational power is occurring inside many organizations today. Yet there are hundreds of efforts to convince people to remain asleep; forgo participation in the difficult, time-consuming, unpleasant obligations of organizational citizenship; and leave the task of ruling to "superiors" who are represented as being more qualified and experienced.

This battle has gone on for centuries. It first established, through the American Revolution, Civil War, and extension of the franchise to women, that all adult citizens have a right to elect their leaders and agree on the principles by which they will be governed. Only now is it beginning to be recognized that there is an equal, commensurate right on the part of employees to select *their* leaders and agree on the principles by which *they* will be governed. Although governments and workplace organizations are fundamentally different, there is no reason why democratic principles should not be implemented in both.

To further the development of organizational democracy, a number of significant hurdles must be overcome, most of which stem from the numbing, soporific effects of hierarchy, bureaucracy, and autocracy. These include

- Conditioned passivity and reactiveness

- Narrow definitions of responsibility

- Personal blame for poor results

- Rewards for competition and the pursuit of self-interest

- Stories of victimization and demonization

- Reliance on external leaders, outside assistance, and orders from above

- Isolation, separation, and fragmentation

- Uniformity, amalgamation, and inseparability

- Conflict avoidance and denial of problems

- Resignation, resistance, covert behavior, and unresolved systemic conflicts

Whenever individuals are not given feedback on their behaviors, or are marginalized for disagreeing with their bosses, or are allowed to suffer through years of unresolved systemic conflicts, subtle encouragement is given to hierarchical relationships, bureaucratic processes, and autocratic forms of decision making.

Organizations will only succeed in getting employees to act responsibly if they trust them and treat them as first-class citizens.

Power and responsibility go together, and responsibility means being willing to risk censure by actively criticizing and transforming organizational practices that damage the human spirit.

Strategic Integration

For organizational democracy to overcome these obstacles and fully develop in the workplace, it is necessary to bring all the separate and distinct processes and techniques we have described, together with the cultures, structures, and systems that support them, and the ubiquitous democratic leaders who inspire and lead them, into a single, cohesive, strategically integrated, democratic whole. Strategic integration connects diversity with the unity that underlies it, drawing people together across organizational lines.

The effort to build organizational democracy can also be seen as an effort to increase the number of organizational dimensions, or degrees of organizational freedom. Each additional dimension represents a new freedom of movement across organizational lines and a new possibility for strategic, integrated, democratic action.

Zero degrees of organizational freedom corresponds to organizational dictatorships, such as occur under slavery. One degree of freedom is created by hierarchies that allow people to interact and decisions to be made vertically. A second degree of organizational freedom appears with cross-functional, self-directed teams that are empowered to collaborate and make decisions horizontally across hierarchical lines. A third dimension or degree of organizational freedom, *depth*, arises when employees develop shared values and visionary leadership. We believe there is a fourth dimension, which occurs when strategic integration merges the other three dimensions *synergistically* into a single democratic whole that becomes greater than the sum of its parts. Figure 14.1 diagrams a physical representation of these four dimensions.

Strategic integration produces organizational synergy by crossing the boundaries that separate people. These include *vertical*

Figure 14.1. Organizational Dimensions.

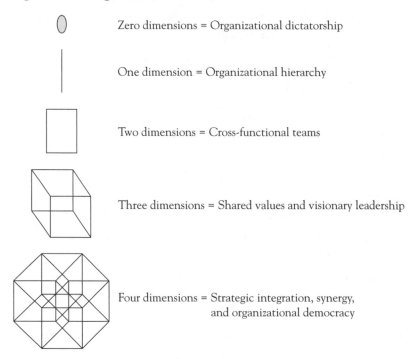

Zero dimensions = Organizational dictatorship

One dimension = Organizational hierarchy

Two dimensions = Cross-functional teams

Three dimensions = Shared values and visionary leadership

Four dimensions = Strategic integration, synergy,
and organizational democracy

boundaries created by hierarchy, power, and privilege; *horizontal* boundaries created by bureaucracy, turf wars, siloed departments, and isolated individuals; *depth* boundaries created by lack of shared values and visionary leadership; *external* boundaries created by competitors, vendors, suppliers, customers, clients, and citizens; and *internal* boundaries created by organizational cultures, resistance to change, competition over power and status, unresolved conflicts, and dysfunctional relationships that block integration.

By creating an integrated, synergistic strategic approach to waking people up, leaders at all levels combine and coordinate the organizational learning processes we have described and use them to expand organizational democracy. Organizational democracy ultimately results from the integration of turnaround feedback, transformational coaching, strategic mentoring, and participatory assessment;

the strategic application of courageous listening, paradoxical problem solving, supportive confrontation, and risky conflict resolution; the promotion of collaborative, learning-oriented, inquiry-based cultures; synergistic, team-based structures and integrative, value-driven systems; the cultivation of awareness, authenticity, congruence, and commitment; and the rise of ubiquitous democratic leadership. In Figure 14.2 we diagram these integrated strategies to illustrate their mutually supportive, holistic character.

As Figure 14.2 reveals, these roles, values, processes, and techniques are interconnected, indivisible experiences. Any one of the elements displayed can trigger or support the others, and in democratic organizations they can be combined and reshaped into a single holistic approach. There is no prescribed sequential order or

Figure 14.2. An Integrated Strategy for Waking Organizations Up.

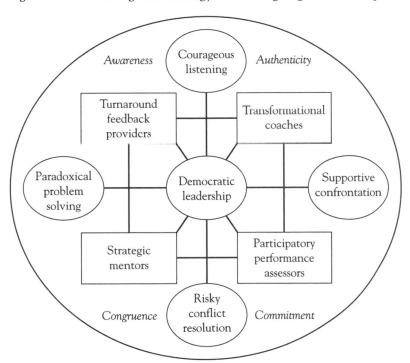

hierarchy of importance to any single element. Waking people up is a fluid, responsive, organic process requiring unique forms of integration and strategy to meet the changing needs of each person and the organization as a whole.

Fundamentally, the role of ubiquitous leaders in an organizational democracy is to expand the number of degrees of organizational freedom and orchestrate these elements to create synergistic learning relationships that link people across artificial boundaries. Organizational separations and divisions that are not integrated produce role confusions, feelings of irresponsibility, misunderstandings, stereotypes, systemic conflicts, and internal dissension that can be used to justify and rationalize bureaucratic division, hierarchical control, and autocratic command. Every organizational division is simply a different way of understanding, processing, and solving common problems. The task of democratic leaders is to reveal the whole to each of its parts and integrate the concerns of all into a single synergistic, strategically integrated whole.

Cultivating Love at Work

The full implications of waking up and building democratic organizations include not merely increasing efficiency and profits but expanding our capacity for love at work—love for ourselves, for others, for life, and for meaningful creative work—work that allows us to express and develop who we are. In democratic organizations, it is possible for rank-and-file leaders to release and channel the immense emotional energy and creative capacity that is connected with love. Nobel prize–winning novelist and chemist Primo Levi described the beauty that awaits us when we are able to love our work:

> If we except those miraculous and isolated moments fate can bestow on a man, loving your work (unfortunately the privilege of a few) represents the best, most concrete approximation of happiness on earth. But this is a truth

not many know. It is sadly true that many jobs are not lovable, but it is harmful to come on to the field charged with preconceived hatred. He who does this sentences himself, for life, to hating not only work, but also himself and the world. We can and must fight to see that the fruit of labor remains in the hands of those who work, and that work does not turn into punishment, but love.

The joy, pleasure, and fulfillment that come from doing work we love fuels extraordinary performances and brilliant, satisfying results. While autocracies lull employees into apathy and hypnotize them into subservience, democracies demand their personal and collaborative participation, responsibility, and leadership. Joy and pleasure are encouraged by participating in the leadership of democratic organizations and harnessing the power of collective creativity and commitment. In democratic organizations where everyone is a leader and decisions are made by consensus, it is easier to be oneself, and therefore to love. Our love of work, when voluntarily given, is the greatest motivator of all.

Our ultimate goal, therefore, is to create organizations that support people in waking up and living richer, more loving work lives. Waking up is like planting a seed. We can count the number of seeds contained in an orange, but who can count the number of oranges contained in a seed? Who can foresee the consequences of even a single person waking up and bringing their capacity for love to work? The possibilities are unimaginable. So, with poet Mary Oliver, we pose a parting question: "Tell me, what is it that you plan to do/with your one wild and precious [work] life?"

As authors, our commitment has been to communicate our ideas and experiences in the difficult art of waking ourselves and others up, and cultivating awareness and authenticity at work. We now pass the baton to you. We invite *you* to become a leader—not just in creating democratic organizations, but in bringing as much love as you possibly can to your one wild and precious work life.

Index

Also from Kenneth Cloke and Joan Goldsmith:

The End of Management and the Rise of Organizational Democracy

The Book That Redefines Management

There is a search in process for a new context and paradigm for the organization of the future—an organization that must be capable of producing high-quality, competitive products that satisfy customers without destroying the planet or degrading human life. *The End of Management and the Rise of Organizational Democracy* calls for a radical set of organizational development initiatives that will combat the destructive forces of globalization, put an end to authoritarian, paternalistic management, and move organizations toward a new "organizational democracy." Kenneth Cloke and Joan Goldsmith detail the practical opportunities, alternatives, and models for these new organizations and challenge leaders to transform their workplace environment into one shaped by a context of values, ethics, and integrity. They reveal how a combination of collaboration, self-management, and organizational democracy can break down long-standing boundaries and foster the far-reaching, sustainable changes critical to success in the twenty-first century.

Hardcover, ISBN: 0-7879-5912-X; US$26.95

FAX	CALL	MAIL	WEB
Toll Free	Toll Free	Jossey-Bass Publishers	Secure
24 hours	8am–	10475 Crosspoint Blvd.	Ordering at:
a day:	8pm EST	Indianapolis, IN 46256	www.josseybass.com
800-605-2665	800-956-7739